D1154997

My Just War

My Just War

THE MEMOIR OF A JEWISH RED ARMY SOLDIER IN WORLD WAR II

Gabriel Temkin

PRESIDIO

Copyright © 1998 by Gabriel Temkin

Published by Presidio Press
505 B San Marin Drive, Suite 300
Novato, CA 94945-1340

Library of Congress Cataloging-in-Publication Data

Temkin, Gabriel.
  My just war : the memoir of a Jewish Red Army soldier in World
War II / Gabriel Temkin.
      p.   cm.
  ISBN 0-89141-645-5 (hardcover)
  1. Temkin, Gabriel. 2. World War, 1939–1945—Participation, Jew-
ish. 3. Jewish soldiers—Soviet Union—Biography. 4. Jews—Soviet
Union—Biography. 5. Soviet Union. Raboche-Krestianskaia Kras-
naia Armiia—Biography. 6. World War, 1939–1945—Campaigns—
Eastern Front—Personal narratives, Jewish. I. Title.
D810.J4T43   1998
940.54'217'092—dc21
  [B]   97-36778
                                          CIP

Printed in the United States of America

To Hanna

Contents

Preface

Is it right to call a war "just"—any war, which by its very nature is so inhumane? Like many other wars, the war in which I became personally entrapped was a bloody hell, frightening, stinking, and dirty—literally, and sometimes also in a moral sense. Yet this was a "just" war, as it was for the democratic Allies of the Soviet Union fighting in a common cause. Never perhaps have the "just" and the "cause" been so closely intertwined as they were in the war against Nazi Germany.

On 1 September 1939 Hitler, having a week earlier concluded a "nonaggression pact" with Stalin, attacked Poland and quickly overran it. This was my homeland, where I was born and where I lived with my family in the city of Lodz until I was eighteen. In mid-September the Soviet Union occupied eastern Poland, and my native country ceased to exist as an independent state. A few months later, fleeing Nazi persecution like thousands of other Jews, I left Lodz for Bialystok, taken by the Soviet Union. My immediate family—mother, father, sister, two younger brothers—perished in the Holocaust; the same was the fate of most of my other relatives. During the years of Nazi occupation Poland lost six million people, half of them Jews.

On 22 June 1941 Germany invaded the Soviet Union. I was drafted into the Red Army after the outbreak of that war. The devastation and death toll due to Hitler's invasion of the Soviet Union was staggering. The current estimate for military losses is 8.7 million, but the majority of Soviet war deaths were nonmilitary—most who died in the war were civilians. The total figure of Soviet war losses are currently estimated as 26 to 27 million dead.

According to recent Russian estimates, the Germans took a total of 5.7 million Soviet soldiers as prisoners of war, of which about 3.3 million died in captivity. I was one of those lucky POWs who escaped from a German camp, still in Russia, where prisoners were being "silently" liquidated by mass starvation and disease. I rejoined the ranks of the Red Army after its spectacular victory at Stalingrad, and remained with it until the end of the war.

I have been carrying these memoirs within myself for a very long time. Why have I finally made up my mind to write them down? Wisława Szymborska, the Polish Nobel Laureate in Literature, says in one of her wonderful poems: "The joy of writing. The power of preserving. The revenge of a mortal hand." No one could have better explained why people write memoirs.

I am not so conceited to think that I have written "for posterity." Historians have already thousands of books and memoirs, in addition to archive documents, available for writing their books on World War II and the Holocaust. But indifference toward stories about World War II and the Holocaust will probably grow as soon as the last survivors are gone. All memoirs notwithstanding, the Nazi crimes in World War II and the Holocaust will gradually fade away in historical memory and will perhaps appear no more important than the Spanish Inquisition is considered today.

In one of my daytime nightmares, Hitler had won the war and the Nazis imposed their new order on the totally *Judenrein* world. A few generations later, heil-Hitlering Germany was de-Hitlerized and ordinary Germans, guided by noble feelings, apologized for what their ancestors had done to the Jews. This cleared the ground for historians to undertake impartial and objective—as becoming of true scientists—comparative studies: "The Inquisition and the Holocaust."

In short, these memoirs have not been written because, fearing that people would forget, I had presumptuously assumed that I could somehow prevent this from happening. I wrote mainly because it was I who could not forget.

Most names in my memoir are real. I hope nobody's feelings will be unduly hurt by this.

Acknowledgments

Several friends read the draft manuscript of this book and offered valuable comments. I express sincere thanks to them and especially to Dr. Hanna Strawczynski. I am also thankful to Dr. Paul B. Miller, editor of the U.S. Holocaust Memorial Museum's publication *Holocaust and Genocide Studies,* who read chapters six and seven of the manuscript and provided encouragement when I most needed it.

I benefited from the thoughtful comments and advice of E. J. McCarthy, Executive Editor of Presidio Press, for which I am most grateful.

My gratitude is due to my children, my son, Henryk, and my daughter, Helena, who encouraged me to write these memoirs and were supportive in many other ways; and to granddaughter, Avital, who helped in reproducing some of the old photos.

I owe a great debt to my wife, Hanna, who, as always, assisted me in my writing. I had her constant wise counsel; she was the manuscript's keenest critic.

Leaving Home

1. World War II Begins

It was 6 September 1939, five days following Hitler's invasion of Poland and the beginning of World War II, when for the first time in my life I left my family home in Lodz. The radio transmitted the authorities' appeal to the male population, eighteen years of age and older, to leave the city and go to Warsaw and the Vistula, where new lines of defense were being organized. I was eighteen and so, together with thousands of men, I went on foot eastward. The roads were crowded with retreating soldiers as well as civilians. Very few civilians were in automobiles, some rode motorcycles, more were on bicycles or horseback, many in horse-drawn carts, but most walked, like myself. Some were carrying big bundles on their backs. From time to time the movement of the crowds would come to a halt in order to let some organized military unit pass. More often, it was just slowed down by traffic—peasant carts piled high, some with children on top, sleeping or dangling their legs, and cattle on long ropes— entering the main road or leaving it. Crossing small towns, I saw for the first time in my life rows of houses, right and left, burnt out or still in flames. People became an easy, completely defenseless target of the German Luftwaffe, which was throwing bombs by the bunches indiscriminately. Stukas, flying low or diving toward the crowd, had their sirens turned on to frighten people running in a panic for cover. I saw German aircraft hunting with their machine guns for groups or even individual Polish cavalry soldiers, who were forced off the road in a desperate gallop.

The distance between Lodz and Warsaw was only about ninety miles, but I failed to reach the capital. I was in a small crowd when on the third day after leaving Lodz we were overrun by a German forward unit on motorcycles. It was just after an air strike. A dead civilian, cross-legged, was lying in a ditch close to a destroyed horse-drawn wagon, its belongings scattered on the road. The German motorcycle unit was followed by soldiers and officers in several cars. They stopped, and most got out of their vehicles. Another car full of officers sped by, then quickly returned, and came to a halt, and its officers also got out. All wore steel-gray uniforms that were unfamiliar to me. The officers—their hands in black gloves, their arms stretched out at an obtuse angle—greeted each other with a happy *Heil Hitler!* So this is what conquerors look like, I thought to myself, watching their stern, arrogant faces.

An *Unteroffizier* was yelling at our small crowd sitting at the edge of the road. He lined us all up and, after a while, yelling once again, ordered all those sixteen years and younger to come forward. Expecting that youngsters would be released, I too stepped out into the tiny row of those under sixteen. I heard him barking, *"Weg mit dir!"* (Out of my sight!)

On my way back to Lodz I spent a night under a roof in a farmer's barn. Early in the morning the farmer woke me up, handed me a chunk of bread with a cup of milk, and said: *"No, Zydek, zjedz sobie, pomodl sie, iz Bogiem!"* (Well, little Jew, have your breakfast, say your prayers, and God speed you!) Taken by the farmer's kindness, I was at the same time also depressed: how come people used to say that I didn't look like a Jew, but he at once recognized me as a Jew.

Coming closer to Lodz, on its outskirts, I asked some Polish women how the Germans treat people. They were quick to reassure me: *"Niech sie Pan nic nie boi, oni tylko Zydkvow lapia"* (Don't worry at all, they are only after Jews). This came, indeed, as a great consolation to me.

I was back in Lodz. Only a few days passed since I had left it, but the city was not the same, and I wasn't the same person. I had seen war, death, and destruction, a mighty army that came to kill and to enslave my native country. I looked in the faces of soldiers who were mistreating people and above all Jews, only because they were Jews.

My mother stood in the door of our apartment on 18 Pilsudskiego Street. She embraced me and checked my body all over to make sure I had, indeed, as I told her, not been wounded, and finally made me promise that I would never leave home again. I made that promise.

2. "Bist Du Jude? Warum Da?"

In 1939 the total population of the city of Lodz was nearly 700,000, of whom about 233,000 were Jews. As soon as they occupied Lodz, the Germans unleashed a reign of terror on its Jewish population.

Jews were being seized, beaten, kicked, robbed, forced to do all kinds of jobs, and mistreated while working. Soldiers of the Wehrmacht and *Volksdeutsche*—local civilian Germans—were freely indulging their whims.

I remember the destruction of the temples. The oldest and biggest, known as the Old Town Synagogue on Wolborska Street, was built of stone. The construction was carried out by Italian master craftsmen and laborers who were brought to Lodz specifically for this purpose. It was very tall and beautiful. When I was a young boy, until the age of thirteen, I loved to go there on Sabbath and holidays, not to pray, just to listen to the cantor performing solo chants during services and—what I enjoyed most—the accompanying boys choir. Their songs were enchanting. Now the Germans put lots of dynamite into this synagogue and blew it up.

Jews were afraid to show up in the streets. German soldiers liked to amuse themselves grabbing religious Jews and cutting off their beards and sidelocks, at times together with the skin. Hunted on streets, in stores, removed from bread lines, taken from their small businesses or homes, Jews were put to all kinds of dirty, hard work, abused, and often mercilessly beaten—anything to inflict as much physical and mental pain as possible. For the slightest offense, real, or, as in most cases, alleged, or invented by the tormentors, Jewish hostages were being taken and sometimes shot or hanged in public places. And all this was just a prelude to the Holocaust.

Lodz was soon to be incorporated into the Great Reich, and the name of the city was changed to Litzmannstadt. The Polish population had itself been turned into second-class citizens. Some, alas, collaborated with the Nazis in various ways and, encouraged by their horrible treatment of Jews, were taking advantage of the precarious situation of their neighbors. Throwing out Jews from bread lines became a common occurrence. One heard quite often of cases of Poles refusing to pay debts or even grabbing personal belongings of their Jewish neighbors. I knew of a poor Jewish tailor who had just finished the job of fixing a pair of pants for his equally poor Polish neighbor. The latter came, took the pants, and said: "Now, Jew, the time has come that I don't have to pay you." A new word had entered the Polish vocabulary—*szaber*—which meant looting, stealing, or pillaging.

Poland between World War I and World War II had been a fertile ground for anti-Semitism. The country was poor and, since the Great Depression, had been in an almost permanent state of economic crisis. This condition provided the background for growing anti-Semitism, which permeated all spheres of life. There was cultural anti-Semitism, most conspicuously practiced at the universities, where *numerus clausus* rules were established—strictly limited quotas for admitting Jews. Those admitted were segregated into so-called bench ghettos, special places for Jews to sit at lectures, seminars, in laboratories, and other places. The most pervasive and painful for Jews in general, however, was economic anti-Semitism.

As the economic conditions of a great many Poles deteriorated, people were looking for scapegoats. Boycotting Jewish businesses became a widespread phenomenon, especially since Slavoy Skladovski, Poland's prime minister, while denouncing acts of physical violence, declared publicly in June 1936: "Economic boycott of Jews—yes, I shall say so."

A wave of pogroms was rolling over the country in the second half of the 1930s; in 1935, 1936, and 1937 there were several pogroms. Of course the worst was yet to come with Hitler's invasion of Poland.

Like the instability of the country's economic situation, my family's fortunes were also on shaky ground. My father, who in my early childhood had been an owner of a small but prosperous hosiery factory, later lost his business and had great difficulty finding a steady job. My education reflected these fickle conditions. In my early childhood I attended a private school. It was my good fortune that I received a good primary education; I owe much to Mr. Hammer, the principal of that school, and to its dedicated instructors, especially those in literature and German. I could not continue, however, with my formal secondary education, though as an A student I was admitted to a gymnasium free of tuition. In 1935, at the age of fourteen, I was deemed to be lucky to have gotten a full-time steady job as a delivery boy in a warehouse of Fabrykant and Rozenblat, Jewish owners of a medium-sized textile mill in Lodz.

After that I had to educate myself. However, I had a strong urge, a passion, for reading, which from 1937 I shared with my girlfriend, Hanna. We were swallowing books, and many of them we read systematically together, sometimes joined by our common friend, Mala Makowska. We read books on economics and other social sciences. We were studying Kautsky, Bogdanov, Kropotkin, Engels, Lenin, Plekhanov, and, as we became a little more sophisticated, Karl Marx. Already as teenagers, both I and Hanna, especially she, had been lucky to develop a true taste for good literature, so that the belles lettres that we read were chosen by us for both artistic value and social content. Aside from Polish writers, these were translations of foreign authors: Russian, English, American, French, German.

Almost every penny in tips I got as a delivery boy was spent on library fees and on buying books. By the time the war began I had already been a proud owner of a small home library, with the *Origin of Christianity* by Karl Kautsky as its prize possession.

It was those books, kept in our apartment, that worried my poor mother when the Germans entered Lodz. After my return home, she told me, tears in her eyes, and visibly afraid of my reaction, that she had destroyed the books, all of them, tearing them piece by piece. I was calm, however, and rather surprised, as the job she had undertaken was not an easy one—destroying those hardcover books. True, I had been very fond of them, but I had by now other, more serious concerns than the loss of my books.

But what had my mother been up to in getting rid of books she knew were so dear to me; why were the books a worry to her as the Nazis were entering Lodz? It had something to do with my leftist sympathies; my mother probably saw evidence of that in those books. Of course, the Nazis had no need for excuses to persecute Jews. Besides, my involvement with the communist youth movement had not been that serious and, therefore, I thought there should be no files incriminating me as a communist sympathizer. But my loving mother continued to worry about her Gavrylek even after she got rid of his suspicious books.

I had been a member of the illegal KZMP (Communist Youth League of Poland) for about a year, from mid-1937 until the summer of 1938, when it was dissolved together with the KPP (Communist Party of Poland) formally by the Comintern, de facto by Stalin. What were we doing—young, mostly Jewish boys and girls of our cell? In the main we were educating ourselves—Hanna and I quite seriously—in the basics of Marxism-Leninism in anticipation of a new socioeconomic system in which there would be no exploitation, anti-Semitism would be eradicated, everybody would have the right to a job and to an education, there would be equality and happiness for all. Overall I remember this short period of my membership in the KZMP as the time of great expectations.

Trying to hasten the forthcoming revolution, we were also involved in more down-to-earth activities, like collecting money to support the republicans fighting in the Spanish Civil War against Franco, or distributing leaflets protesting Poland's part in Hitler's dismantling of Czechoslovakia. It was for distributing "Hands Off Czechoslovakia" leaflets that Hanna had been arrested and kept at a police station overnight.

Soviet socialism was not the best model of those great things to come. But I, like others, was making all kinds of allowances: for difficulties of the transition, for the old resisting the new, and for imperialist plots and capitalist hostility toward the USSR. I became skeptical, however, when I read the1937–38 press reports from Moscow of the trials of prominent political and military leaders—more and more of them—being accused of and admitting their guilt in having committed all those terrible crimes. How could this be possible? I got confused even more when the KPP and KZMP were disbanded, accused of having been widely infiltrated by the Polish police. That accusation was incredible; by and large I trusted my comrades and leaders, and I just could not believe in the possibility of degeneration and treacherous behavior spreading all over.

The next shock, this time it was like a bolt from the blue, came in 1939. On 21 August 1939, Ribbentrop and Molotov announced that Germany and the Soviet Union had signed a "non aggression pact." Within ten days Hitler invaded Poland. Seventeen days later the Soviet Union occupied the eastern part of my native country. As it turned out, much more than "nonaggression" was involved. In accordance with a secret Soviet-German understanding, Stalin and Hitler had in advance divided up the lands of Poland, which was to be liquidated as an independent state. To side with Hitler, and to stick a knife into its neighbor's back was in my eyes an unforgivable breach of trust and, as a communist sympathizer, I felt ashamed for the Soviet Union's deeds. Where were the high, noble principles I believed a socialist state would always adhere to? When these historical events caught up with me my expectations were shattered, my faith in Soviet Socialism undermined.

When I returned to Lodz, I went back to my job in the warehouse. My Polish coworkers—Antoni Balcerzak, Jan Baran, and Ludwik Stepien—were there, but the Landaus, the Jewish brothers holding responsible positions with the firm, did not return and nobody knew what happened to them. The old customers, mostly Jewish, were out of business. The new ones, German officers, were ordering textiles in large quantities, pretending to be haggling about prices and "paying" with *Bescheinigungen*—worthless certificates of receipt. David Fabrykant, the old owner of the firm, was indignant with the German "new ways of doing business." It was difficult for him to accept that the decent Germans he knew in the past were gone; his son, Henryk, often had to intervene.

It was late October or the beginning of November when we were told to prepare for the imminent takeover—a German *Treuhander* (trustee) would become the manager of both the factory and the warehouse. Soon afterward, Henryk Fabrykant left Poland on a visa to Norway, his wife having been a citizen of that country. After the war I found the old Fabrykant's name in a Lodz ghetto document titled *Aufstellung* (balance sheet), enumerating valuables taken by the Germans from Jews. The things taken from him on 3 December

1942, labeled *verschied Schmucksachen* (various jewelry), had been assigned a value of about 750 reichsmarks.

The warehouse where I worked was in a building on 6-go Sierpnia Street, No. 2, at the corner of the former Piotrkowska Street, the city's main street, now renamed Adolf Hitlerstrasse. Since it was renamed after the Führer, it became off limits to Jews. A Jew walking along or just crossing it would be putting himself in great danger, perhaps even risking his life. And it was easy enough to make the Hitlerstrasse *Judenrein* (free of Jews), since its Jewish inhabitants had been dislodged, and all the Jews of Lodz, regardless of age, were ordered in mid-November to wear yellow armbands. Some Jews—like myself, working in that warehouse—were provided with temporary *Passierscheine* (passes) to walk or cross the Führer's street.

The German authorities were very specific about the marking of Jews. We had to wear a ten-centimeter-wide armband of "Jewish yellow" color on the right arm, directly below the armpit. A month later, after I left Lodz, Jews were ordered to wear—instead of the armbands—yellow Stars of David on the right side of the chest and on the right side of the back.

Providing a semicomic footnote to the tragic days that lay ahead was my encounter with a German soldier patrol on Adolf Hitlerstrasse. One afternoon in the second half of November, I was walking down that forbidden street not far from the Grand Hotel, where German officers had been headquartered. With a permit in my pocket and wearing the required yellow armband, I came across two young soldiers, perhaps my own age. They too were wearing armbands, but adorned with swastikas. They looked at me surprised. I presented my *Passierschein*, and was asked *"Bist du Jude?"* (Are you a Jew?) I nodded. *"Du siehst doch aus wie Deutsche"* (You look German), they shouted at me. *"Aber ich bin Jude."* (But I am a Jew.) I gave the only answer I could, and one of them yelled at me even louder: *"Warum da?!"* (Why that?!) Indeed, why had I been a Jew, and what was wrong with that? The two soldiers were surprised, confused by my blue eyes and blond hair—I did not fit the image of a Jew as depicted by the Nazi propaganda. I remember all the details of that incident well, perhaps because it seemed to sum up our whole tragedy.

As many had already lost their means of existence and were being terrorized day by day, some Jews began pondering the problem

of leaving Lodz for the eastern part of Poland, occupied by the Soviets. But it was not an easy decision to make. In spite of what the
Germans were already doing to them, the Jews could not imagine in
their wildest dreams that extermination was in store for those who
would not escape. While terrified of the Nazis, many had qualms
about the Soviets also. Above all, most people were fearful of leaving home, all possessions, sources of income—however precarious—and becoming refugees in the face of an oncoming winter.
Only the young, mostly single could undertake such an adventure.

While I was deliberating, Hanna, who was urged by her family, had
already made up her mind to go. My mother, whom I had promised
two months earlier that I would never leave home again, was sensing
my desire to leave with Hanna and, worried for my safety, was ready
to let me go. I still was uneasy and apprehensive about leaving my parents but, on the other hand, I could not let Hanna go away without
me. Finally my family had made a decision which in retrospect appears outlandish, though at that time it did not seem irrational.

The decision was that I should go together with my father, who
would take care of me, while my mother and my two younger brothers would remain in Lodz until they could legally emigrate on visas
sent by my father as the head of the family. This was how things used
to be done in normal times, when people were trying to emigrate; it
was difficult to accept that normal times were gone. Jakub, ten years
older than I, made a similar fateful decision. He left his wife and baby
daughter behind in Lodz, and he was never to see them again. Many
people behaved likewise; families were splitting in the belief that it
was just for a short while, and that it was a way to secure legal emigration papers for those left behind.

At the end of November 1939 we left Lodz—I with my father,
Hanna with her brother, Mayer, and his wife, Dora. We all went on
the same train. I can still see my mother and my two younger brothers waving farewell. Less than three month later, in February 1940,
they were herded into the Lodz ghetto. I did not know if I would ever
see them again.

After a night's stay in Warsaw, we arrived at Malkinia, the railroad
station on the new border between Germany and the Soviet Union.
This is where my next direct encounter with the Germans took place.
German soldiers yelling and cursing at the top of their lungs rushed

us—a couple of hundred people—to a courtyard adjacent to a building they turned into a kind of customs clearinghouse for Jews. They were taking small groups of people into that building, while the crowd held in the yard was forced to sing Jewish songs. Germans are known to be music lovers, and they were obviously enjoying themselves listening to those strange melodies, but perhaps the basic idea of forcing us to sing was to muffle the screams of people beaten as they were going through those customs checks invented for us. I have never forgotten the feeling of humiliation as we were singing those Yiddish folk songs. To this day I shudder whenever I hear the sad tune *"Belz, my shtetele Belz."* Finally, we too were pushed into the building, where the Germans dug into our miserable possessions—a loaf of bread and some spare underwear. They took away my father's twenty-zloty bill, the only one he had, but we were spared a beating. Pushed outside through a back door, we were met there by a group of young Polish boys, armed with sticks, who enjoyed themselves giving us a farewell beating. My father's head was bleeding and Hanna put some iodine that she somehow acquired on his wound. Several hundred yards ahead was the last German outpost. The sentry looked at my twenty-zloty bill, the only one I had, and jovially declared: "*Mensch, zwanzig zloty! Es ist doch zu viel* (Man, twenty zloty, that is much too much). He took my twenty zlotys away, giving me back six two-zloty coins—either he wanted to assuage his conscience, or his pockets of too heavy a load, or both.

Finally, we entered the no-man's land, a neutral zone between the Germans and the Russians. In the darkness loomed a large field covered with snow and a crowd of people, some of whom had been waiting there several days for the Russians to let them in. In this no-man's land, to my astonishment, we met my brother Jakub, who had left Lodz a couple of days earlier. People had been waiting in that no-man's land for days or even weeks, I was told. But we were lucky; it took only a couple of hours before the Russians let us in. We were treated as human beings again, and this was the greatest joy of our border crossing.

3. A Refugee in the USSR

The next couple of weeks we spent in Bialystok as *bezhentsy* (refugees), often nicknamed *zapadniki* (Westerners). We were housed in summer cottages on the outskirts of the city in a suburb called Zwierzyniec. It was a crowded place; men and women slept in the same room on the floor, on whatever bedding they had. Apart from myself, my father, and Jakub, we shared our room with Hanna, her brother, Mayer, and his wife, Dora, and some other people. But Hanna and I did not mind these little hardships. The cottages at Zwierzyniec provided accommodation for hundreds of refugees like ourselves. We were getting a free hot meal from a soup kitchen and a bread ration daily. To warm up, read a newspaper or a book, have a chat with other refugees or with Red Army soldiers, we could make use of the *Krasnyy Ugolok* (red corner), which was opened for us in Zwierzyniec.

Red Army soldiers were friendly, and mutual curiosity led to long talks in a Polish-Russian sort of Volapük, helped by sign language and a lot of guessing. They were our first instructors both in the Russian language and in ways of Russian-Soviet life. We were impressed hearing what was true and half true, what we wanted to hear, and what we thought we knew perfectly well from reading about the USSR: There was no such thing as unemployment, it was easy to get a job, education was free, including colleges, where every student received a monthly stipend—and there was, of course, no anti-Semitism, it had been eradicated once and for all. Both Hanna and I were elated. Disappointments—small and large—were still ahead of us.

The signs over the stores and the slogans all over in the streets of Bialystok exposed us to the new language which we, especially Hanna, were quickly learning. Walking for many hours along these unfamiliar streets, we were inhaling the air of regained freedom in a way that only those deprived of it can really appreciate. Some Poles had reproached Jews for greeting the Red Army with open arms although that army came to eastern Poland as an invading force. Well, it was an invading force, but the Jews were also correct in their perception of the Red Army as the only force shielding them from Nazi life-threatening persecution.

A happy surprise awaited me on the streets of Bialystok. I met my sister, Pola, with her husband, Moniek Hostik. They were staying in a rented room in the city. We embraced, told each other about the border crossing, and worried together about those left behind. Could we hope to be joined soon by other members of our families? Pola took an immediate liking to Hanna. "Children," she told us, "get married."

Under rules established by Soviet authorities, refugees could not count on getting any employment in Bialystok or elsewhere in eastern Poland, now called Western Belorussia and Western Ukraine. The only way out of this predicament was to move to the Soviet territories proper, and this only via a system of organized recruitment. Jobs were available usually in remote places, mainly in the Ural Mountains or beyond, where new heavy and war industries rapidly developed.

In the third week of December we were told that a recruitment team from coal mines in the Urals had some jobs for the Bialystok refugees. We had to face reality and respond to an offer that would change our lives once again. Hanna, Jakub, and I were willing to go. In our naïveté, we still believed that this would also help in arranging for legal emigration of our relatives. Jakub, who had left his wife and child in Lodz, really thought that by securing a job and becoming a permanent resident of any part of the USSR, he would speed up the process of getting those dream visas for them. The three of us made up our minds about going to the coal mines of Kizel, in the Urals. Mayer and Dora wanted to wait for a better chance, and thus for another recruitment team. They, too, would go somewhat later to the Urals, to Kamensk Uralski. Families were getting divided still further. Late in December the three of us boarded the train, while my father, Pola, and Moniek bid us farewell.

The separation from my father was painful for Jakub and even more so for me. My father could not bring himself to go so far away from those he left behind. In addition, my poor father, who left his wife with two young boys in Lodz, and was to take care of me, needed to be taken care of himself. Under the circumstances, the best he could do was to remain with Pola and Moniek, who in turn had some ideas other than to go to Russia. Moniek wanted to go to Wilno, but his plans were frustrated by events beyond his control.

The Soviet Union occupied Wilno along with the eastern part of Poland in September 1939. A month later, Lithuania was forced to grant military bases to the USSR, while Wilno was given to that country. Apart from the partition of Poland, the Ribbentrop-Molotov pact provided for a demarcation of "spheres of interest," and in 1939 the USSR secured for itself military bases also in the other Baltic states of Latvia and Estonia. In 1940, after Hitler's overwhelming victory over France, all three Baltic states were occupied and made constituent parts of the USSR. Finland, however, refused to grant territorial concessions in the vicinity of Leningrad, and on November 30, 1939, the Soviet Union went to war with that country.

Wilno became off limits for refugees from Poland. Likewise, the authorities in Bialystok were trying to get rid of all whom they called Westerners as soon as possible. Under these circumstances, with Pola pregnant and Moniek uneasy about leaving for Russia, they made a fateful decision. In February 1940 they crossed the border back to Nazi-occupied Poland. Half a year later I would learn from my mother's letter that my father, unable to return to Lodz, went to Komarow. This was a small shtetl in the Lublin district, where his mother, my grandmother, Lea, was still living with some of her ten children. The circumstances of my father's and my grandmother's death remain unknown to me. I also have never been able to find out anything specific about the fate of Pola and Moniek Hostik.

The train to the Urals was made up of many freight cars, adjusted for people traveling in large groups for many days or even weeks. Our *echelon* was a kind of special train, used in the Soviet Union as means of transporting army units and larger groups of prisoners, especially those sent to Siberia, the Far East, or the North. We belonged, of course, to neither of these categories, and were treated rather well. Each boxcar had a small upper window and was roomy, housing about twenty people, sleeping or resting on two rows of covered wooden bunks. In the middle of each car stood a *burzhuyka*—a small iron stove, heated with coal, which we were getting from depots at railroad stations or were stealing from flatcars carrying coal. Inside the boxcar, colloquially named *teplushka* (heated van), one felt hot when close to the *burzhuyka* and pretty cold away from it. The train was moving very slowly, yielding the right of way to every passenger train and stopping often for many long hours. At the frequent stops, everybody disembarked to stretch, buy something to eat, and take a look around at what was going on . Each person had been given a generous one hundred–ruble advance payment against future earnings, which we could spend in the freight car shop, which carried limited foodstuffs and cigarettes, or at a buffet or a restaurant at railroad stations. These stops also provided us with boiling water for tea, to be found under big signs *KIPIATOK*—boiling water—which I initially took for names of places and, only after seeing one "boiling water" sign after the other, realized my mistake. As free people, we were not guarded, and, in any case, there was really no need for that, since escape was not on our minds. Even if it were, we would not have been able to get very far away, because we had no domestic passports, which every Soviet citizen was required to carry on him at all times.

Hanna and I soon found some more comfortable ways of traveling to the Ural Mountains. We had to go to the railroad stations for meals and, as it was warm and interesting at the stops, we once missed our *echelon*, which had already left. Soon we began "missing" our train on purpose. Stopping for a bite at a railroad station and delaying our exit, we would afterward board a passenger train, any passenger train going eastward—of course without tickets—and travel that way until the train conductor told the two young Westerners when and where to get off in order to catch their *echelon*. It was during that time we spent in the passenger trains catching up with the *echelon* that I got my first taste of life in the Soviet Union.

Close to the railroad station in Minsk, the capital of Belorussia, I was impressed with wide streets and new, large buildings, much taller than those I saw in Lodz, Warsaw, or Bialystok. Mostly office buildings, but also some apartment buildings, they all had similar shapes and ornaments, were all of the same beige color, and looked monotonous and a bit unreal, as if a reproduction of some architectural drawing. On one of those streets we saw a large dairy store with blocks of cheeses, butter, eggs, and other food prominently displayed in its window, and we went inside. There, by the almost empty shelves stood a small crowd as if waiting for new deliveries. "I would like to buy some butter," I said to the salesgirl. She had a glance at the two Westerners and her face turned into a smile as she announced: "*Grazhdanin, u nas vsye yest no seyczas nyetu*" (Citizen, we have everything, it's just presently not available). I was somewhat surprised both by the solemnity of the salesgirl's declaration and by the sight of the empty shelves. When we left Bialystok, the stores had still a relatively good supply of food. And so, outside, I took a closer look at the window display. Only now I noticed that all the cheeses, butter, and other food were made of wax.

In Smolensk, thinking stupidly that butter would be available there, I went into a store exactly like the one in Minsk and I got exactly the same response to my request: "Citizen, we have everything, but not right now." This time, however, I did notice that the smile on the salesgirl's face disappeared the moment she turned to the other customers. She sounded worn out and angry as she shouted at somebody: "*Nadyen ty moy khalat, a ya poydu gulyat*" (Put on my frock, I'll go dancing). It finally dawned on me that exactly the same answer was staged in advance for the benefit of the thousands of Westerners expected to pass cities in *echelons* to the East. Even the smiles were not the usual way of greeting a customer. What I still could not understand was why the bureaucrats in the Ministry of Commerce, or somewhere else, would go through all the trouble of staging such silly shows. Had they nothing better to do? Did they not know that the Westerners would find out about the true state of affairs anyway? And what were they ashamed of? Could they not just tell us about supply difficulties due to the war with Finland? Again, what I did not know at that time was that the supply difficulties were not temporary, that the Soviet economy, also in peacetime, was a shortage economy. Besides, had I been somewhat less naïve, I would have known already that no official could mention any difficulties related to the war with Finland to us. Such things were just not done in the USSR. While the whole world was watching it, the coverage in the Soviet press of that war became very thin after the initial exultant boasting. Indeed, that war was far from being the bragged-about instantaneous success. The misfortunes of the war against tiny Finland revealed the weakness and the vulnerability of the Red Army due, to a great extent, to the purges of 1937–38.

It is necessary to draw attention to this if my Red Army story is to be fully understood. The purges of the Red Army had cost the lives of three out of five marshals of the Soviet Union. Recently published figures show that from May 1937 to September 1938 about thirty-six thousand men were purged in the army and more than three thousand in the navy. As a result of the repressions, all military district commanders were removed, ninety percent of district chiefs of staff and deputies, eighty percent of corps and divisional commanders, ninety percent of staff officers and chiefs of staff (see D. Volkogonov, *Stalin: Triumph and Tragedy*, Rocklin, Cal.: Prima Publishing, 1992, p. 368). The blow to the Soviet armed forces was immense. If the purges had any logical sense, their aim was probably to eradicate potential resistance to Stalin's rule. This was achieved, but at a terribly high price. The Red Army lost most of its competent officers.

I was still a young and naïve man, and much too talkative, particularly for the conditions and the mood of the people there and at that time. In Bialystok I had learned how to put a Russian sentence together, and one day, practicing the new language, I wanted to get into a good conversation with the people in the passenger train in which Hanna and I were catching up with our *echelon*. The co-passengers were friendly and asking questions about life in *panskaya Polska* (the country of Polish lords). In turn, I was curious about life in the Soviet Union and, at this particular moment, I happened to be interested in the fate of its old marshals.

Showing off as only a silly young man can, I mentioned I knew all their names and the whereabouts of almost all of them. Two marshals, I said—the greatest—Voroshilov and Budienny—were, of course, still in charge of the Red Army; two other marshals—Tukhachevsky and Egorov—had been executed, but what about

Marshal Blyukher, what was going on with him? There was no answer to my question. Instead, dead silence, and my audience moved away from me as if I were a leper. They obviously thought I was either crazy or an agent provocateur. Whatever the case, taking up a topic like that with a stranger, in public—a topic which, if they talked about it at all, it was only in whispers with family members and closest friends—was dangerous in the extreme. I myself had not the faintest idea how dangerous it was for me. I still had a lot to learn. Had I been less biased against Poland's "bourgeois press" and what it had written about the purges of the military in the USSR, I would not have asked about the whereabouts of Marshal Blyukher. He had been shot and thus his name, like thousands of others, was already unmentionable. A year earlier in Lodz, I read and talked about those purges, but I had no inkling how widespread they were; I could not imagine that millions of people were involved. It was quite possible that among my interlocutors, who turned away from me in horror, were some whose family members had been victims of the purges. Be that as it may, the reaction to my question gave me a lot to think about; it taught me more than any answer they could have given me. I suppose I remember the details of that and similar incidents so well because these were my first real contacts with ordinary Russian people, my first opportunity to learn about their real life.

Except the Marshal Blyukher question incident, we were often being met with sincerely friendly smiles. Recognizing the refugee in Hanna and me, people in the passenger trains would greet us with motherly or fatherly expressions. It was likewise outside the trains. In Ufa, at the foothills of the Ural Mountains, I went to a store close to the railroad station to buy some candies for Hanna. It was a cold winter day for which I was not prepared at all. People, mostly women, wearing *valenki* (felt boots), warm kerchiefs covering their heads, had been patiently standing in line outside the store on the snow-covered sidewalk for a long time. As soon as they recognized that I was a refugee, I heard several voices calling out: "Go ahead, young man, lest you freeze to death." In front of a bread store, also in Ufa, women waiting in a long line for white bread informed me: "Deliveries are being delayed, come back later and we'll let you in, watch out not to freeze till then."

There were shortages of everything, including train tickets. As we were passing and entering railroad stations, we could always see people waiting for their trains, often for days, on benches, but mostly on floors in waiting rooms. Those who could afford it were crowding the restaurants, which were much better supplied than in the cities, though also much more expensive. These restaurants often ran out of food, but rarely had shortages of alcoholic beverages. Most railroad stations we had seen on the way to the Urals were new, huge, impressive architectural structures. Indeed, I thought they must have been built with the idea of impressing the traveler. The tradition of the Potemkin villages was apparently still alive. Initially, I was also impressed by the outside of those imposing buildings until I saw the crowds inside.

One scene, which I can still visualize easily, was particularly depressing. In a huge waiting room the size of a king's ballroom, with tall marble columns reaching its high ceilings, hundreds of people were down on the marble floor, while a magnificent main wall was covered from floor to ceiling with an enormous portrait of Stalin. The giant Stalin was pictured in a soldier's greatcoat and in military boots. Most of the people lying at his feet asleep were poorly clad, many in tatters. I still see it all like a painting before my eyes. But I think that even the greatest Russian artists, famous for their paintings of everyday Russian life, would not have been able to depict the scene inside that railroad station. And for the simple reason that this scene, like the old silent movies, had a musical accompaniment. All the radio loudspeakers were going full blast as the Red Army chorus was singing songs glorifying the great, wise Stalin.

Our tortoise *echelon* labored for many days before approaching the Ural Mountains. In Smolensk it turned south and, bypassing Moscow, was crawling eastward to the Volga, which it passed at Syzran, moved on to Ufa, where it made a sharp northern turn into the Urals, toward Molotov (Perm) and, finally, Kizel. An enormous country with so much space! The scenery, almost all the way, was magnificent, though flat till Ufa. The huge plain was covered with large unbroken carpets of snow, miles and miles of deep, sparkling white snow, rarely dotted with towns or small villages; forests of all colors, from light green to dark blue and black, were sitting close to the railway or spread all over the horizon.

In the Ural Mountains the weather was cold, forty degrees below freezing, fortunately with no winds. At that temperature, work on the outside should officially stop, except for removing snow so that trains could run, even if very slowly. We got into a heavy snowstorm and our train came to a standstill until after the storm was over. Then I saw the work of snow removal. It was done exclusively by women, many women laboring hard with shovels and crowbars; the few men rarely appearing among them were supervisors giving instructions. Hanna glanced at me, we both recalled the book we read before the war by an American writer about the liberated women of Soviet Russia. Myth and reality. During the two weeks of travel to the Urals I learned some very good lessons on liberty and equality, on real life that my books had not taught me.

As we disembarked from our train at the small wooden railroad station in Kizel, the temperature on the thermometer showed minus fifty-two degrees centigrade. It was difficult to breathe; the air when inhaled caused pain in the nostrils, the steam exhaled from the mouth turned instantly into frost. Before disembarking, we were warned to cover ears and noses, and, if possible, not to expose any skin at all, even on the short walk from the train to the station, so as to avoid frostbite. All I could see when I opened the heavy doors into the station was a dense fog in the entrance, which resembled a tunnel made of ice. Inside, at a buffet, young men and women were eating ice cream.

A couple of days later, after we had rested in a warm barracks turned into a dormitory, we were given job assignments. Hanna, who back in Poland had taken a typing and bookkeeping course and, in the short time since in the USSR, had managed to pick up enough Russian to pass a test, got a clerical job as typist-and-assistant-secretary. Jakub and I, like most other men, were assigned to the coal mine. Back in Poland I had read about coal miners in the USSR using the most modern equipment, and I hoped for a pneumatic hammer to work with. Instead, I was given a shovel and told to forget about any other tools; there was a shortage of pneumatic hammers even for experienced coal miners.

Despite the harsh weather, in the coal mine it was not cold at all. Moreover, I was literally sweating at my work. I tried hard but I was not strong enough and could not physically adapt to shoveling coal and fulfilling a high daily quota. The job turned out to be beyond my capacity. I had to give up after a couple of weeks. It was most distressing. To my shame and frustration, I could not come even close to imitating the famous Donets coal miner, Stakhanov.

"You have no prospects in Kizel," I was told by the Blumins, a Soviet Jewish couple, college graduates about ten years older than I was. They both came to the Ural Mountains from the city of Gomel in southeast Belorussia, where their relatives were still living. In Kizel they worked as professionals, he as a mining engineer, she as a pharmacist. They befriended us, often had us for dinner in their cozy, warm apartment, where we conversed freely on many issues as they were open-minded, well-read, and evidently fond of Hanna and me. I continued to ask many stupid questions. For instance, I was curious about the price of Blumin's new boots. When he told me that he paid four hundred rubles, the figure shocked me, it was beyond my comprehension, and I exclaimed: "But that is twice a decent monthly salary of an average guy!" "Well," he said, "the problem is to get a pair of such boots, not the price." That simple comment put everything I knew about supply and demand in a new light.

"Go to Gomel," the Blumins advised us. I could show off with some information about that city. Gomel (in Polish, Homel) was an old medium-sized city that was incorporated into Russia during the first partition of Poland in 1772. I could also recall that the roots of my family on my father's side were in Gomel, though I knew nothing of having any relatives there. But most of my information about Gomel really came from a book by Ilya Ehrenburg, which I read before the war in a Polish translation. "Do you know the *Stormy Life of Lazik Roytshwants* by Ehrenburg?" I asked them. They knew other books by that popular author, but not this one, first published in Paris in 1928. In the USSR it was considered anti-Soviet and it was thus taboo. I did not think of it as anti-Soviet. Let me add here that Lazik had been said by some literary critics in the West to be a twin brother of Hashek's good soldier Schweik. I saw Lazik differently. He had been depicted by Ehrenburg with the bittersweet humor of Yiddish literature. To me it was a novel about the semicomic and rather tragic life of a poor little Jew—a Chaplinesque character who happened to be caught in the "cogwheel of history."

The Blumins were a kindly and courageous couple trying to help us, Westerners, willing to take risks in a place where most others were in a permanent state of fear. Hanna and I had at that time no idea that the Molotovski (Perm) district we were living in was packed with prisons and forced labor camps, that it was an essential part of the gulag archipelago, as Solzhenitsyn later called it. But the Blumins probably knew all this. Still, Blumin gave us the address of his relatives in Gomel. His wife provided Hanna with a Soviet-made red beret so that while purchasing train tickets to that city she would not look like a Westerner. By stretching out a helping hand, these compassionate, good people took a tremendous risk—it could hurt much more than their careers.

Jakub contributed to the cost of our tickets and bid us farewell; he remained in Kizel till the spring of 1941.

Our journey to Gomel in passenger trains lasted only several days, of which the most exciting had been the stopover in Moscow. We left the rail station and took the metro going in the direction of Red Square, but the subway was so gorgeous that we spent several hours there, traveling from one station to another just to visit those magnificent palaces full of marble columns, sculptures, and embellishments abundantly covered with semiprecious stones. Then we went to Red Square. Lenin's mausoleum was closed that day and so, instead, we visited the Museum of the Revolution at the entrance to Red Square. Afterward we enjoyed the sight of the Kremlin walls, and the bell tower with an enormous clock and the Red Star at the top. We stood in amazement in front of the imposing onion-shaped, colorful cupolas of the sixteenth-century Cathedral of St. Basil. It was also closed, so we watched it while standing at the *Lobnoye Mesto*— the spot where the tsars' executioners once chopped off the heads of rebels, heretics, dissidents.

It was early spring 1940 when we arrived in Gomel without domestic passports, no place to stay, and no money. Fortunately, the relatives of the Blumins recommended us to their neighbors, an older Jewish couple living in a small house, who had agreed to rent out a tiny seven- by twelve-foot room for eighty rubles a month, and were also willing to wait for the first payment till we got jobs. We lived in that room, on 20 Sadovaya Street, till July 1941. As we had no money, we had to sell something, and the only thing we could possibly sell was Hanna's jacket. I went to the kolkhoz market and got eighty rubles for it, which kept us going until our first payday.

There were some refugees living in the city. I met Salek Epstein, my friend from Lodz, and I got to know Josek Sharfartz, with whom we became very close. He was working as a weaver in a small factory and offered to teach me his trade. "Don't worry," he told me, "here you'll get a job easily, and if you want, you'll be a weaver in a matter of days." Indeed, he was helpful in finding a job for me at Gomtextil, a technologically outdated and therefore "cooperative" factory producing textiles. A little later Hanna got a job there too, in the office of the same cooperative. With jobs secured, we obtained residency permits.

After a while Hanna got a better job at OBLONO, the district's educational board, as a typist. I soon became a weaver, and worked at Gomtextil until I was drafted into the army in July 1941.

The cooperative was busy working three shifts and producing essentially three kinds of textiles: (1) belts, (2) linen and tarpaulin, and (3) carpet runners. The belts were produced for the army. Work on these weaving machines required strict attention, but was comparatively the easiest one because the yarn used for belt production was very strong. I and several other weavers, all men, were doing that job. The machine production of linen and tarpaulin—again done by men only, some two dozen of them—required skill, experience, and patience, mainly because the yarn was of very low quality, discarded by state factories and sent to cooperatives. Carpet runners for civilian use was the main output of Gomtextil. The yarn used for production, a mixture mainly of hemp and dust, could not possibly be handled by any machine. Thus, the weaving of the runners was done on old-fashioned looms, foot-powered, with the weaver moving the shuttle manually backward and forward between the threads. It was the hardest and dirtiest kind of work, and was the exclusive domain of women. About a hundred young women, many just out of kolkhozes on off-season jobs in the factory, worked on three shifts, tramping their bare feet on the treadles to drive the looms. They were cheerful most of the time, visibly satisfied with their jobs, which provided them with money wages normally not available to members of collective farms. Gomtextil had only one big factory hall, and the dust from the weaving, especially those carpet runners, was overwhelming. "Who would buy floor covering like that?" I asked. It was, of course, a rhetorical question. I had already come to realize that under the all-permeating shortages, almost everything supplied would find customers.

As elsewhere in the Soviet Union, life was difficult in Gomel, particularly in the beginning for us refugees. The Soviet Union—I already knew this—was an authoritarian state; the secret police, or NKVD (People's Commissariat of Internal Affairs), was looking for and persecuting so-called "enemies of the people." People like us—Westerners—were, of course, prime suspects, though we had not been bothered, at least not yet. It does not follow, however, that we were in a bleak mood. Far from that!

We appreciated the bright sides of our new life. It was the USSR where we had found refuge from the Nazis, and this was not something we could easily forget. We, strangers, got jobs here, and people were generally friendly to us. There were other good things to be said about our new country. Most important was that, as Jews, we were treated by the authorities like everybody else; that was, at least, how I felt for the more than a year of living in Gomel. If there was anti-Semitism among the population—and it surely existed—it remained hidden, which was probably due to the fact that before the war it was a punishable offense. Another and perhaps simpler reason why I had not noticed any local anti-Semitism was that in Gomel we associated mostly with Jews. Fifty thousand Jews were living in the city, a third of the total population. Our friends were Jewish, almost exclusively refugees like ourselves. The men-weavers and most of the Gomtextil managers were Jewish. There was even a Temkin among them, commonly disliked by everyone, including me.

My books had not deceived me on another important point—the opportunity for education in the USSR. And we were determined to avail ourselves of that opportunity. No sooner had we somehow settled in the new place than both Hanna and I enrolled in high school evening courses. Minding my two weaving machines, I was often doing my homework, talking and repeating something to myself. Nobody could hear me because of the noise in the factory hall, but my coworkers, seeing my lips moving, were making gestures: crackpot.

Never mind, I felt great being able to combine work with preparing for my classes.

During the entire period of our stay in Gomel, both Hanna and I were able to occasionally communicate with our families in the Lodz ghetto. Their letters were very sad, depressing, though they obviously tried not to reveal their despondency.

There was no comfort to be taken from what was going on in the rest of Europe either. In April 1940 the Germans occupied Denmark; shortly afterward it was the turn for Holland, and Belgium, where Hanna's older sister lived with her family. In June Hitler's armies and he himself entered Paris. And in late summer the Luftwaffe began dropping bombs all over England. Were Hitler's armies invincible? Who could stop him if not the Red Army? Such were the conversations we shared with friends in Gomel as the year 1940 was coming to an end.

Located eastward of the Prypet Marshes, Gomel, in my recollection, was a sleepy provincial town with small wooden houses along mostly unpaved, tree-lined streets, with little traffic except on its two main streets, Sovietskaya and Komsomolskaya, where buses were running. The city had a nice park on the banks of the Sozh River. I would go there sometimes with Hanna, and sitting at the river, we would recall *The Stormy Life of Lazik Roytshwants*. Poor Lazik! He, too, used to sit at the Sozh, maybe at that very place we were sitting now, under the burden of heavy thoughts, pondering his main question that was, in a sense, also our problem: Where could a poor rabbit hide himself when history is marching along the roads?

Though history in the making could not be forgotten and was permanently on our minds, we had a good life in Gomel. We were young, in love, hopeful about the future. Together we were earning enough—about four hundred rubles monthly—to buy a pair of boots like Blumin's . . . "if one could get them." Bread was rationed, but available and enough for the two of us. We were satisfied with bare necessities. Some luxuries, like butter and sour cream, we could buy on the kolkhoz market. One day Hanna returned from that market in the company of a woman from a Gomel-area kolkhoz, who was carrying a heavy milk can all the way, about three miles. She came to fetch some spare bread Hanna promised her. On another day off I was lucky to buy in that market a fairly old but much-needed cooking pot for thirty rubles. Our tiny room was "an open house" for friends. Many refugee-Westerners were passing through it, some coming to Gomel, others leaving it.

In the spring of 1941 we welcomed Mayer, Dora, and her two brothers, Berek and Abram Bilander—all returning from the Ural Mountains. Except for Berek, they all moved to Retchitsa, a small town not far from Gomel. The only way of reaching it was by a boat on the Sozh River.

Jakub left Kizel for Bialystok in early spring 1941. He wanted to go back to his wife and baby daughter in Lodz. Many other refugees had similar desires. The news about this must have reached our families in the Lodz ghetto, because Hanna received a strongly worded letter from her father, who advised her not to try to come back. Unlike Jakub, we had no such intention. He went to Bialystok, where Soviet authorities had announced that they reached an accord with the Germans about an exchange of refugees. It was presented as a humanitarian gesture undertaken in order to lessen the plight of refugees on both sides of the border. No sooner had Jakub signed up than he was arrested by the NKVD and deported to a forced labor camp, like the others who applied. He ended up in a forest camp in the Komi district, in the far north. Only after Hitler's invasion, when the Soviet Union signed agreements with Sikorski's Polish government in London, was my brother—along with thousands of other former Polish citizens—released from the camps. He then spent the rest of the war in Siberian towns as a free Westerner.

I should add that Jakub, like others who wanted to return to their families, had reasons to believe that with the Soviet-German "honeymoon," an exchange of refugees would actually take place. Thanks to that honeymoon, we were allowed to send parcels of food in limited quantities and kind to the Lodz ghetto. We managed to send such food parcels twice, I to my family and Hanna to hers. Letters from them acknowledged receiving the first parcels. We did not know if the second ones reached them; the end of that honeymoon was approaching fast.

In the book *The Chronicle of the Lodz Ghetto 1941–1944* (ed. by Lucjan Dobroszycki, New Haven: Yale University Press, 1984, p. 25), I found the following entry, dated 1 March 1941: "Today a proclamation of the Eldest of the Jews was posted calling on the inhabitants of the ghetto immediately to inform family and friends in writing that they are no longer to mail any parcels of food to the ghetto since the Chairman 'must confiscate' parcels on orders from the German authorities."

Hitler Invades the Soviet Union

4. Drafted into the Army

In the early spring of 1941 strange things began to happen in Gomel. At night we heard the sounds of heavy armored vehicles moving west. In daytime we could see Red Army troops on trucks moving in the same direction. It was quite clear that a redeployment of significant military forces in border areas was taking place. The city was full of rumors and whisperings about an impending war with Germany. What I witnessed at that time made me doubtful about the often-repeated claim that Hitler had surprised the Soviet Union with his invasion.

The loudspeaker in our tiny room was blaring martial music all day long. "*Yesli zavtra voyna, yesli zavtra v pokhod, bud' sevodnya k pokhodu gotov*" (If tomorrow there is war, if tomorrow we are to march, be for the march ready today). At the same time, the top authorities tried to calm the tempest by hiding their heads in the sand. On 15 June 1941 Soviet newspapers published a government declaration: "According to the information of the USSR, Germany is observing the terms of the Soviet-German pact as strictly as the USSR. Therefore, in the opinion of Soviet circles, rumors about Germany's plan to break the pact and to undertake an attack on the USSR are quite unfounded."

I will never forget that early Sunday morning of 22 June 1941. The morning was sunny, Hanna went to the market to buy some food, while I stayed at home resting after my Saturday night shift at Gomtextil. Suddenly the military marches and songs on our loudspeaker were interrupted and a gloomy voice made an announcement about Hitler's "treacherous attack by surprise." Soon Molotov spoke to the population of the USSR. Some parts of his speech seemed strange to me because they sounded as if he was pleading with Hitler: What have we done wrong, we tried our best to be true to the agreements we made with you—Molotov was saying. But I liked the end of his address: "Our cáuse is just. The enemy will be smashed. Victory will be ours." These words did not sound hollow to me. This is how it was going to be, and I would be participating in that just war. But I thought of other things too. What will happen to us so close to the German-Russian borders? What is already happening to our families in the Lodz ghetto? I had to set to work to occupy my mind.

And what did I do after I somehow absorbed the shocking news and came to my senses? I went about tearing into pieces my "Nansen" passport which I had preserved until that day, though in 1940 we were issued Soviet citizens' passports with a special paragraph restricting our movements as residents. Perhaps it was also an unknown-to-us code for some other limitations of our rights. When Hanna, back from shopping, noticed what I was doing, she wondered: "For heaven's sake, why are you doing this?" Indeed, why?

My father, whose family roots were in Gomel, was for reasons un-known to me denied Polish citizenship when the country gained in-dependence in 1918, though he himself was born and was living as a resident in Poland proper. Stateless, he and his children, after they reached the age of eighteen, were each given a "Nansen" passport. I had no idea, and I still do not know, to what privileges, if any, we were entitled as holders of those non-Polish passports, and likewise what their relation to the Nansen International Office for Refugees, an arm of the League of Nations later superseded by the Interna-tional Refugee Organization, was. Still, I was busy destroying my old "Nansen" passport in these first hours of the war, because I feared that it could make me suspect if the NKVD came across it. And that fear was well-founded. We had been living in the USSR for almost a year and a half, enough time even for young, naïve people, as we were, to notice the suspicious glances with which we were often met by officials. And it was not just glances. We came dangerously close to learning, fortunately not the hard way, about the pervasive lack of trust and fear that permeated all walks of life in the USSR. Our small community of refugee-Westerners became particularly vulnerable. A few days after the war began there were arrests in Gomel, and among those arrested was someone we knew, a refugee like ourselves, innocent as a lamb.

It was the beginning of July. The weather was good—warm and dry—ideal conditions for the German Blitzkrieg. Hitler had planned his "eastern campaign" to end with total victory in five months. If he expected any tough resistance, it was only at the beginning stage of Barbarossa, because—as he put it in a conversation with Goering— "we shall be fighting an *ideological* enemy, and an ideological enemy of fanatical persistence at that." Reality turned out to be different, no doubt to Hitler's delight at least initially. Having destroyed thousands of aircraft, tanks, and field guns, and inflicted terrible bloodshed on the Red Army, the Wehrmacht was, within two weeks, deep inside the Soviet Union. There was anything but the fanatical ideological resistance Hitler had expected. True, after a while the Red Army began to resist and put up a dogged fight, but again, it was not because of ideological fanaticism.

It is hard to believe that Stalin, at any time—on the eve of the war or later—shared Hitler's view about that ideological fanaticism. Communist ideology, if it ever inspired the Red Army, was a spent force, in great part because of the blow Stalin himself dealt to its officer corps in the purges of 1937–38. The ordinary Russian soldier was known for his legendary endurance. This had, of course, little to do with ideological indoctrination as a factor conditioning the army's morale. The huge conscript Red Army was still a peasant army with fresh memories of forced collectivization and dekulakization (the word "kulak," literally a "fist," was used to label a well-off peasant, while "dekulakization" in Soviet terms meant "liquidation of the kulaks as a class"). Several years had just passed since hundreds of thousands of peasants were expelled from their native villages; many were executed and millions starved to death in famines.

Winston Churchill, in his memoirs (*The Hinge of Fate,* Boston: Houghton Mifflin Co., 1950, pp. 498–99), describes a night conversation he had with Stalin in Moscow, 15 August 1942: "Tell me," I asked, "have the stresses of this war been as bad to you personally as carrying through the policy of the Collective Farms?" This subject immediately aroused the marshal. "Oh, no," he said, "the Collective Farm policy was a terrible struggle." "I thought you would have found it bad," said I, "because you were not dealing with a few score thousands of aristocrats or big landowners, but with millions of small men." "Ten million," he said, holding up his hands. "It was fearful. Four years it lasted . . ." "These were what you call Kulaks?" "Yes," he said, but he did not repeat the word. After a pause, "It was all very bad and difficult—but necessary." "What happened?" I asked. "Oh, well," he said, "many of them agreed to come in with us. Some were given land of their own to cultivate in the province of Tomsk or the province of Irkutsk or farther north, but the great bulk were very unpopular and were wiped out by their laborers."

Despite all the heavy indoctrination, communist ideology could not have erased this kind of fresh memory in the minds of the peasant army, and Stalin must have known that. He must have also been well aware of at least some of the consequences of what he had done to the Red Army's officer corps; it was on his orders that four thousand officers were released from gulag camps in 1941. All evidence goes to show that Stalin believed in a universal method, other than ideological indoctrination, of emotionally conditioning his subjects and getting things done—fear. It was the opposite of the Russian saying: *Nye za strakh, a za sovyest* (Not for fear but because of conscience). But could fear alone have inspired the Red Army to stand ground and fight back? The morale of an army depends, of course, on many factors, including fear. However, if fear was to become a predominant factor, it would have to be fear of a different kind and dimension—profound, primordial fear for the very physical survival of one's children, family, homeland. And it was Hitler's horrible deeds, not Stalin's, that had done the trick of creating that kind of fear: his *Untermensch* "philosophy," which underlay the German attitude toward the Russian masses, his mad treatment of millions of Soviet POWs, and his war of total destruction and pillage. This war was a war of extermination, and the Germans never made a secret of that. It stirred up hatred, the thirst for revenge, finally ripening into the cause, which would inspire the Red Army in furious battles over a four-year period. The cause was named "patriotism."

This was not Stalin's original idea of inspiring an army, but he was quick to recognize its spiritual power and began to exploit it in many skillful ways. On 3 July 1941 I was glued to the loudspeaker when Stalin, in his dramatic first broadcast since Hitler's invasion, addressed the Soviet people as "brothers and sisters." In his Georgian-accented Russian he spoke of the "Great Patriotic War."

I was still in Gomel in the first week of July, listening to more and more bad news about the Red Army retreating everywhere, including the central front to the near west of our city. The Germans were not in a hurry, however, to take Gomel in a frontal attack, and no wonder. The city, as I mentioned, was located to the east of the Prypet Marshes. The main thrust of Hitler's armies on the central front was a two-pronged wedge: one to the northeast directed toward Moscow, the other to the southeast aiming at Kiev. Gomel was in a kind of corridor to be cleared up later. We feared that the city might be encircled and it would be too late for us to get out. But while deliberating how and where to escape, we had to wait for evacuation instructions. Big factories were already being evacuated while we both continued to work—Hanna in OBLONO, I in Gomtextil.

After Stalin's speech, the *Narodnoye Opolchenye* (home guard) was formed. As eligible for military service, I, too, was enrolled in one of its units and provided with an old rifle—model 1899—to be taken home. But I was not given any ammunition or military training; Hanna put the rifle under our bed. Quite soon afterward, we were horror-stricken by the spreading rumors about the Red Army's defeat in the vicinity of Minsk, though we did not know exactly the dimensions of that disaster. The double battle of Bialystok and Minsk ended on 9 July with the collapse of the Soviet West Front under Marshal Semen Timoshenko. According to German records, they took more than 240,000 prisoners of war. On the same day, the Wehrmacht captured Zhitomir and Vitebsk, and on 11 July German tanks crossed the Dnieper River at Mogilev. The Nazis were coming ever closer. Gomel was already half encircled.

On 11 July I got a mobilization card with summons to appear immediately at the city's military authority. There I was given a *putevka* (traveling instructions), an *attestat* (travel certificate with provisions for military food rations), and ordered to present myself on a given date (I think it was in about two weeks) at a military training camp in the vicinity of the city of Orel, more than two hundred miles away.

Transportation was not provided, and there was no time to say good-bye to friends. I had to leave almost immediately.

The next day, early on 12 July 1941, Hanna saw me off to the eastern outskirts of Gomel. Imprinted in my memory is her slight figure as she was standing in her pink print cotton dress, silently smiling at me. She was to remain in Gomel, waiting for one of the trains that were being formed at the railroad station to evacuate women, children, and the old—whoever was willing to take advantage of it. What would happen to her? Would she be evacuated in time? She was very bright but physically not very strong. Left to herself, I wondered if she had the strength—and luck—to endure the wartime deprivations living somewhere deep in Russia? Would we ever see each other again?

When I left Gomel, I was in a group of mostly local inhabitants, all unknown to me. Since the group was unorganized, it quickly dispersed, everybody by himself, mixing with other groups heading in the same eastern direction. From time to time I would catch a train, but mostly I was going to the training camp on foot. The railroad stations were destroyed or in flames. The trains and the roads were frequently, day and night, under air bombardment. I had not seen a single Soviet plane in the air. Because there were very few anti-aircraft machine guns, let alone antiaircraft artillery batteries, the Luftwaffe reigned in the skies. Stukas were not only dropping bombs at targets of their choosing, but were often diving at and machine-gunning people after having scared them with their dreadful sirens. I saw people killed, some of the bodies twisted together. The wounded, especially the lightly wounded, were often crying for help, which was rarely available.

Still, the work of the military railroad men both at the stations and on the trains continued. As soon as a raid was over, the debris was cleaned up, some rudimentary repairs were made, and trains were moving again, slowly, stopping quite often, but moving. I was surprised to notice a big difference in this respect between Poland in September 1939 and the Soviet Union in July 1941. In Poland the Luftwaffe had managed in the first days, if not hours, of the war to disorganize the railroad transportation system completely. This was not the case in Russia, fortunately. Because of the distances here and the lack of an alternative transportation system—there was little movement of supplies by trucks—having a functioning rail was a sine qua non for the Red Army to retain its fighting ability. Moreover, what I saw and what impressed me most was the evacuation of industry to the east. In spite of bottlenecks and loss of life and equipment, the railroad had managed to accomplish a fantastic migration of industrial and military factories, together with many of their workers, to the east of Russia. This ultimately was to enable the Soviet Union to carry on the war.

But on my way to Orel there were fewer and fewer trains going in the desired direction, and the going was very slow and often interrupted. The main reason was, of course, the rapid advance of German troops moving northeastward in the direction of Moscow. On 16 July German troops captured Smolensk and, two days later, Yelnya, southeast of Smolensk. I feared that they might take Orel before I "presented myself" at the military training camp there.

The roads I was now walking, even dirt roads, were crowded with people like myself and with factory workers being evacuated on trucks to the east. There were also Red Army troops moving in all directions, but mostly westward. The Luftwaffe would spare neither the military nor civilians; the planes, having dropped their bombs, were flying low, shooting their machine guns indiscriminately. They must have unlimited supplies of bombs, I thought frequently as I was passing towns hardly having any military significance, where many houses were bombed and turned into rubble, or, being wooden, were burned out so that only chimneystacks and piles of ashes were left of them.

Not yet a good walker, I would quickly get tired and sleepy. I remember an air strike—the Stuka dive-bombers were using their deafening and scary sirens to paralyze the will of the soldiers to fire back with their rifles. It was a hell of a noise but, hiding in an open ditch along the road, I fell asleep. It was, I am sure, a very short nap. What woke me was the dead silence that enveloped me when the air strike came suddenly to an end.

The Luftwaffe's favorite places for dropping bombs, especially incendiary ones, were forested areas close to main roads. Not seeing, but expecting, and rightly so, that the woods were providing resting places for army units and their horses, German planes were bomb-

ing them, particularly at nightfall. I can still see the beautiful birch
forest, pure birch, a rarity, no other trees but birch—I never before
or after saw a forest like that—where I was resting one night while
incendiary bombs were igniting fires. The burning grayish-white
trees were turning reddish, as if blushing and ashamed of what was
going on. It was in that beautiful birch forest that for the first time I
smelled burned flesh. I still could not distinguish the smell of burning horseflesh from that of human.

As I mentioned, on my way to Orel I saw Red Army troops moving in the opposite direction—westward. Some in trucks, many on
foot, their outdated rifles hanging loosely over their shoulders.
Their uniforms worn out, covered with dust, not a smile on the
mostly despondent, emaciated faces with sunken cheeks. Equally miserable were the small horses pulling the vehicles with ammunition,
food, and personal belongings. I was mentally comparing these
poor-looking Red Army soldiers with those of the Wehrmacht—
healthy, arrogant, marching in review—as I saw them in 1939, and
also as they were shown in newspapers conquering one country after another in 1940. Was the Red Army a match for them? These and
similar thoughts were crossing my mind on the way to Orel. Though
very tired, I sometimes would spend restless hours embracing a limb
of a tree before falling into deep sleep.

Finally, at the end of July or the very beginning of August, I
reached my destination point, the military training camp in the vicinity of Orel. Soon Josek Sharfartz, who left Gomel a few days after me,
also arrived. I was happy to have him with me, but it did not take long
before he was discharged due to his very poor eyesight. I never saw
him again; he must have perished during the war, like Salek Epstein
and Berek Bilander, otherwise I would have heard from them.

The camp was located in a deep forest, away from main roads. During my stay there it was never bombed. I was issued a military outfit,
we slept in tents nicely masked, the place was kept clean, and everything seemed to indicate an orderly military training camp. I was glad
to have arrived here. Now I was going to become a Red Army soldier
and would be shown how to use a rifle and fight the Nazis.

Alas, there were few rifles, not enough for the numerous conscripts in that camp; in our unit we were using wooden imitations of

rifles. For lack of real guns of any kind and perhaps also of ammunition, there was no practice shooting. We were trained in the basic rules of marching in step with others in an orderly column, turning right, turning left in an even row. It was mostly infantry drill, which I did not find at that time very useful. As I realized later, however, there were some important exceptions to the dull exercises. The drill sergeant made me crawl. He kicked my behind with his heavy boot and was yelling: *"Zhopu nie podymay"* (Don't lift up your ass). Enforced with regularity and by constant repetition, his boot taught me a basic and, for an infantryman, very useful skill—crawling under enemy fire. The other useful thing I learned at that training camp was how to dig the right infantry trench with a personal foxhole inside. Yet another skill I acquired, and it was an important one for a foot soldier, was how to put on *portyanki* (foot bindings—square pieces of cloth wrapped around the feet instead of socks), so that they would smoothly envelop the soles of the feet just like well-fitting socks. This was not a simple matter for a city boy like myself. I should add that during the war, all four years of it, almost everybody in the Red Army—except perhaps top brass—wore *portyanki* instead of socks. I made thousands of miles on foot, wearing *portyanki*, and I never had a corn or blister on my feet.

Rumors spread in the camp that we would soon be sent as reinforcements to the Smolensk sector, where heavy fighting was going on as the Wehrmacht continued its offensive and the Red Army was engaged in counterattacks—seemingly futile attempts at stopping the German drive toward Moscow. On 8 August the Germans liquidated the Smolensk pocket and recorded more than three hundred thousand POWs there.

I was supposed to be trained as a wireless operator, but before I had even seen any radio equipment, a new turn of events put a stop to it.

There were several categories of people the Soviets did not trust enough to send to the front. As it turned out, to my surprise, I belonged to one of them. A refugee from Poland under German occupation—for that reason alone I was suspect. There were other untrustworthy categories in our training camp: Soviet-born Germans, kulaks and their sons in particular. One day, together with many such men, I was ordered to appear at the camp's center, where we were told about an impending transfer into military labor battalions. I was in shock and so were many others. I recall the reaction of a Soviet cadre officer, a lieutenant; Miller was his name, of German ancestry, born in Russia in the city of Engels on the Volga. He knew almost no German. He was now bitterly cursing in pure, juicy Russian. Though he had already been engaged in front-line battles and wanted to continue fighting the German Fascists, he was removed from his regular military unit and assigned to become a company commander in a labor battalion.

Like all other ordinary conscripts of the nontrustworthy categories—officers excepted—I was stripped of my new military uniform and shoes, provided just a couple of weeks earlier. Instead, I got a half-military, half-civilian "previously owned" uniform and a pair of old civilian shoes. The only decent thing was a greenish half-padded coat; it was in good condition, warm, and it served me well for well over a year not only as a coat but also as a blanket, and even—its sleeves—as a pillow.

5. In Labor Battalions

It was the end of August or the beginning of September 1941 when my labor battalion joined by others left the railroad station near Orel to begin what we came to call *krugosvetnoye puteshestvye vokrug zhopy* (the world-circling voyage around the ass). It was a voyage in freight trains—during the war, passenger trains were used mainly as hospitals—that was to cover more than two thousand kilometers and last for about a month. We were going back and forth, changing trains, waiting for trains, dispersing under or away from them during air strikes. The commanding officers of our labor battalions had no idea what to do with us, where to lead us; they had been trying in vain to communicate with their superiors and obtain instructions. And no wonder these were lacking. We were on the edge of a fast-oncoming storm.

On 25 August the Germans began their drive from the Gomel area toward Kiev. Their pincer movement led on 14 September to a complete encirclement of numerous Soviet divisions. When the battle of Kiev was over and they liquidated the huge pocket on 26 September, the Germans claimed to have taken 665,000 prisoners. The official Soviet war history, providing only fragmentary data, disputed these figures. According to the most recent information, based on archival sources of the Soviet Ministry of Defense, 452,720 men were encircled, including about 60,000 officers, and almost all of them were taken prisoner (see D. Volkogonov, *Stalin: Triumph and Tragedy*, op. cit., p. 429). While the German figures were inflated, the Kiev-encircling operation was the largest in World War II and it yielded them the largest number of Soviet POWs in a single battle. For the Red Army it was a defeat of catastrophic proportions.

Hitler's armies were advancing even faster in the southeast direction heading toward the Crimea. On 18 August the Wehrmacht established bridgeheads near Zaporozhye on the Dnieper River, and on 25 August they captured Dniepropetrovsk. Our work battalions were moving on the northeastern edges of that German onslaught, where the Luftwaffe was now spreading havoc among the hastily retreating remnants of the Red Army. And the enemy's supremacy in the air was absolute, since by that time the Soviet air force lost more than ninety-five percent of the aircraft it had when the war broke out.

This was why we were moving so erratically, in "circles around the ass": at first to the west—from Orel to Briansk; then to the southeast—from Briansk to Kursk; still farther south to Belgorod and Voroshilovgrad, where we turned north to Millerovo, to Rossosh, to Voronezh, and back to Kursk. While we were moving on the western side of the circle, we got very close to the attacking German troops. There was no front line and they could appear ahead of us at any moment. The next railroad station could have been already taken. I could not get out of my mind the fear of falling into their hands; I dreaded it more than being killed. Not far away from us, the Nazis were capturing vast numbers of prisoners.

Though officially a taboo in the Soviet press, the POW issue was a public secret. The Nazi propaganda was boasting about great German victories of which the masses of Soviet soldiers being turned into prisoners of war were, indeed, the best proof. In turn, the *politruks* (political instructors) in regular Red Army units as well as in our military labor battalions were making it perfectly clear what was in store for Soviet POWs. We were told both how the Nazis were mistreating them, which was indeed a fact, and what the Soviet punishment for letting oneself become a POW was, which was also true. We were informed about Stalin's orders to that effect. Commanders who surrendered to the enemy were to be considered intentional deserters, and their families subject to arrest for this crime. Families of Red Army soldiers who gave themselves up as POWs were to be denied government benefits and aid. There were already millions of POWs, but the very extent of the problem had never been officially acknowledged. Moreover, falling into the enemy's hands was considered almost tantamount to treason. Only, we were told, if somebody

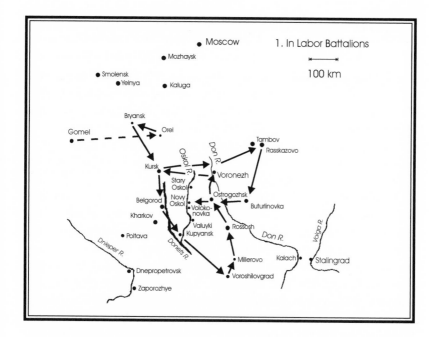

1. In Labor Battalions

100 km

was taken by the enemy while incapacitated due to injuries incurred in battle was it not dishonorable to become a POW. He who became a prisoner of war could be exonerated from guilt and shame, but only if he got out or was killed while trying to escape from a POW camp.

What we were not told by our *politruks*, but knew a good deal about from German leaflets and rumors, was that fate had played a practical joke on Stalin personally. His own son, Yakov, became a POW. The Germans were dropping leaflets with his photo over cities as well as over railroad stations and Red Army groupings. Loudspeakers installed close to them were repeating the news again and again.

While our train was running in circles, men were deserting the labor battalions. It was relatively easy to leave, and many did so. Some were going west, presumably to their homes that were already or were expected soon to be under German occupation. Others were mingling with the streams of refugees going east. I myself could have gone too, and perhaps joined Hanna in Kamensk Uralski, a place where many refugee-Westerners were living and working during the war. But I could not find it in my heart to just leave like that. I wrote Hanna about my decision to stay put.

It was amazing that our correspondence was not completely disrupted during this chaotic time. We were able to establish contact and sporadically communicate with each other by mail just a few weeks after we parted in Gomel. The military postal service was slow but the mail was moving. The trains were moving—the freight cars often damaged and half burned but moving. It was still, no matter how badly, a functioning communication and transportation system. To me it was an encouraging sign.

Our officers finally found the place where we were needed: Voronezh. It was a big city and a strategically important railroad junction on the east side of the Don River. At the end of September our labor battalion was encamped on the thirteenth kilometer of a major road between the Don River to the west and Voronezh to the east. Here we were to build field fortifications. The word "fortifications" would seem to imply building concrete bunkers for commanding posts, artillery, heavy machine guns, and so on. But there was neither cement nor equipment, not to mention time for such an undertaking. Instead, we were digging deep canallike ditches, which were to create obstacles for enemy tanks in case they had crossed the river. Behind and around the ditches was to be built a network of infantry trenches for troops in defense. The only equipment available to us were shovels and, later on, as winter was approaching, pickaxes to break the frozen surface of the earth.

In the very beginning we were sleeping on the ground right at the workplace. But we quickly built our living quarters—zemlyanki (dugouts, earthen huts) not far away from our workplaces. The one I lived in was wide enough to accommodate twenty people—ten on each side—but it was only about five feet in height, and even I, a short guy, had to bend when I tried to move around. The dugout was covered with foliage supported by tree branches serving as a roof. Tree branches were also used to strengthen and cover the "walls." We slept on wooden planks put on the "floor" and covered with straw or hay. There were no pillows or blankets; at night we covered ourselves with our greatcoats—in my case it was my warm green jacket.

In the middle of our dugout stood a burzhuyka—a small, round wood-burning iron stove—like the one on the *echelon* to the Urals. It was used for heating, making tea, cooking an extra meal of potatoes or gruel. Our food rations were inadequate, but those who had money or things to barter could get some additional food. I had neither. We worked twelve hours a day from sunrise to sunset with a short break for lunch. The work was exhausting, but I could manage as long as I was digging just infantry trenches and was not hustled by "double-quick!" cries. I was too short and physically not strong enough to expeditiously dig out a full shovel of heavy claylike earth, lift it, and throw it out from the bottom of an eight- or ten-foot deep antitank ditch. If not rushed too much by supervisors—*"Dovolno! Bros! Idi k nowomu myestu!"* (Enough! Stop it! Go to the next place!)—I would sometimes give my trenches, especially at outwardly projecting salients designed for machine gunners, a personal touch. Recalling what I learned in the Orel camp, I would make a niche, a sinkhole at the footing of the trench in the wall facing the enemy. The niche was for the gunner, or, for that matter, any infantryman, to serve as an added shelter where, under artillery fire, he could by squatting hide himself or just protect his head from splinters falling into the trench. If the earth was firm—clay was best for that—the niche could be made large enough to accommodate two or more people in sitting positions. If there was enough time and the means at hand would allow it, they could use planks and foliage to cover and support the walls of the trench. It would then turn into a blindage, or the niche, if enlarged in width and depth, could become a commanding post suitable perhaps to house a commanding officer and a telephone or wire operator, or a first aid nurse. Such mental images of possible uses of my "fortifications" made the tedious and boring work of digging trenches a little more bearable.

We rarely saw any officers. Our work was supervised by professional foremen, who, while strict, were quite fair. There were no enemy air raids over our workplace during the entire period of digging on the thirteenth kilometer. Everybody felt a nervous chill, however, listening to radio news about the Red Army again and again abandoning cities and territories. The Germans were coming closer and closer to Voronezh and, worse, to Moscow. To the northwest of us it was

Orel, which they took on 3 October, while ten days later, and much farther to the north, they captured Kalinin, less than one hundred miles from Moscow. Then, on 19 October, Stalin declared a state of siege in Moscow. Many government offices had been moved out of the capital to the east, but the official announcement that Stalin remained in Moscow was reassuring. However, other belated news had reached us soon afterward and, in particular, about the panic exodus of thousands of people from Moscow. The gloomy news had a devastating effect on the morale of our labor battalion, creating a mood of complete apathy. The digging almost stopped. *Naprasny trud* (needless work)—people were grumbling, our "fortifications" are just another exercise in futility. A *politruk* was rushed into our dugout, gave a hollow talk, and quickly left; he knew everybody detested his speeches.

As if to make our life even more miserable, the weather was turning from bad to worse. It was now raining, often nonstop day and night. Our clothes were permanently wet. There was mud everywhere, it was difficult to get in and out of the ditches, let alone dig the muddy earth. Our dugout did not provide a refuge either. To say that its roof made of foliage was leaking would be a great understatement. Water was pouring into our quarters and we were all wet; no matter how tired, I could hardly get a full night's sleep. The lulls in the rain were too short and our stove too inadequate to get our clothes dry.

The elements affected my health. Carbuncles, painful deep ulcers of the skin and underlying tissues, developed on my belly and spread to my buttocks. Although I was quite ill, it did not even cross my mind to go to a doctor. But it was quite a serious matter and I suffered from repeated outbreaks of carbuncles even years after the war.

Some other "trifles" began troubling me too. The "previously owned" shoes I got in the Orel training camp were by now completely worn out. One day, as I was digging in a muddy trench, pushing the spade with the left foot, the sole of my shoe fell off. Since I could not work without shoes, it was an emergency situation, the officer to whom I reported was willing to admit that. But new shoes or boots were in short supply in general, and not available at all for labor battalions. The people in the supply unit tried their best, but all they could come up with were two old, much oversized, left-footed boots, still in "pretty good" condition. What would I do, I wondered, deeply concerned about the state of my footwear. But after a while I said to myself, "Take it easy." I had learned by that time to comfort myself by looking for some bright sides in whatever was befalling me. "It was good the boots were oversized, not the other way around," I told myself. "By using double or thicker *portyanki* I'll keep my feet warm." And luckily, I got left-footed and not right-footed boots, in which case I would have a hard time pushing my left foot on the spade while digging.

One day, when it became impossible to dig in the mud, our *naczalniki* (bosses) decided to give us a bath. We went to the city on foot, some fifteen kilometers away, and were led to a *banya* (Russian steam bath). It was high time. Like the rest of the diggers, I was filthy and could smell my own sweat, and, what was worse, that of the others. I had gotten used to both and became quite immune to this and many other, even more unpleasant, odors, though I never lost my good sense of smell. The *banya* was a delight. The warm water, and there was plenty of it, as much as you wished, was so soothing that we left the place only after repeated orders. Our yellowed and very dirty underwear had in the meantime been taken to the *voshoboyka* for delousing, and afterward put out on benches. Then, surprise! I was looking for my underwear in vain, somebody had just stolen it. It was my only pair of underwear and there was no way it could be replaced. My request for another pair was flatly denied and during a good deal of the harsh 1941–1942 winter I had to do with no undergarment. Fortunately, part of that winter I would spend in a peasant hut in the Tambovski region, some two hundred miles northeast of Voronezh, to where we moved on foot in the beginning of December.

On 6 December, General Georgii Zhukov launched the 1941 winter counteroffensive, driving the Germans away from Moscow; they had been thrown back between 100 and 250 kilometers. The Wehrmacht was not invincible after all, it could be beaten and was getting a really good beating for the first time since the beginning of Hitler's eastern campaign. Stalin's words in his 3 July address—*"Budet prazdnik i na nashey ulitze"* (There will be a holiday on our street too)—were now ringing in my ears. Hitler was going to meet the fate of Napoleon under Moscow, I thought. Alas, to paraphrase another great World War II leader, it was just the end of the beginning, a very good end, but still, not the beginning of the end. It would take another terrible year for that and, in the meantime, fate had some awful surprises in store for me.

Who should be given credit for the German defeat under Moscow, General Zhukov or "General Winter"? I believe both, though how much each is still a matter of controversy. Be that as it may, the winter of 1941–1942 had been exceptionally severe. The Tambovski district, where our labor battalions were to stay for a while, was known for its harsh continental winters, and this one was worse than usual. My labor battalion was assigned quarters in a village near Rasskazovo at the southern edge of a large forest. We were lodged at the homes of local inhabitants. They were mostly collective farm workers, on the average incredibly poor, who did not mind, however, giving us shelter—this was a tradition going back at least to the Russian Civil War and revived by necessity during the war against Nazi Germany.

I had quite amicable relations with my *khozyaika* (hostess) and her son, Losha, a boy of ten or eleven. I slept on the top of a typical Russian village *pyechka* (oven). It was a small, narrow space between the oven and the ceiling, the warmest place in the large one-room hut. The tranquillity of the house and the village was enjoyable. There were no air raids, no sirens, no waking up from sleep with cursing calls, *podyem* (rouse), long before sunrise.

Though I got used to waking up early, I would not get up from my warm place until long after sunrise. Instead, I often daydreamed about the past, my home in Lodz, my life with Hanna in Gomel. I knew she had settled in those faraway Ural Mountains, but she wrote little about how she was managing all alone. Did she have warm winter clothes? Did she miss me as I was missing her?

In the early mornings my hostess would quietly begin her chores at the stove. I could hear as she went out to tend to her cow and a pig in the small adjoining cowshed. Before leaving for work in the kolkhoz, she would set out breakfast for the men, her Losha and me.

While food rations in the labor battalions were far from adequate, our bread was the envy of many collective farmers, who, as it was notorious with kolkhozes, had very little flour for their homemade bread and as a rule mixed it with potatoes, much more potatoes than flour. We were getting eight hundred grams of heavy black bread daily; the villagers called it "good soldier's bread." I would put my bread together with the grits and sometimes a piece of sugar on the hostess's shelf, and would, in turn, be invited to sit at the family table and share whatever was on it—bread, soup, potatoes, cabbage, gruel, or milk. But the best way to reciprocate the hospitality shown to me was to supply the house with what it most badly needed: heating fuel. Although there was a large forest range not far from the village, it was a criminal offense for the locals to collect brushwood there, let alone fell a tree. But I could not care less about civilian restrictions. After breakfast I would go to the forest, pulling a light sled with Losha sitting on it, a saw and an ax at his side, and on the way back we both would pull our load of wood. At home, I would chop it into smaller pieces, while Losha would stack it neatly under the roof's overhang. I spent about two months in that small, hospitable Russian house.

It was still deep winter when we were ordered to prepare, as best as we could—everyone for himself—for a long journey on foot. The first thing I had to take care of was footwear. To get a pair of *valenki* (warm felt boots) was out of the question, neither was it possible to obtain ordinary shoes or boots. The only solution I found was a pair of *lapti* (bast shoes) for which I paid with some of my bread rations.

Lapti were made from wooden fibers obtained from birch bark or from the bast of lime or elm trees. Removed in the early spring, when the tissue is soft and elastic, it was then woven into the shape of shoes. *Lapti*, when oversized, as they should be, so that the feet could be covered with one or two thick layers of *portyanki*, insulate from cold and provide excellent footwear on dry snow. Here is also their main drawback—they become useless when the snow gets wet, not to mention that they are good only for slow-paced walking. For centuries and probably until the 1920s *lapti* had been a staple, regularly produced by artisans and worn by Russian peasants. Afterward this kind of footwear largely disappeared, and most people, especially the young, seemed to be ashamed that it was ever worn. Most locals wore *valenki* in the winter. Even the poorest people, having only one pair of *valenki* for several members of the family, would rather share them than put on *lapti;* still, some wore them. I had to pay a rather high price for my *lapti,* because at that time few old-timers in remote villages knew the art of making them. At any rate, though I must have resembled a *bourlak* out of a Repin painting, *lapti* saved my feet from freezing during the ferocious winter of 1941–1942.

My warm military jacket was still in good condition, but was not long enough to cover my knees. This worried me, especially because—unbelievable as it may sound—there was no way I could get any undergarment in that poor village, and my civilian pants made of some satinlike, flimsy fabric provided little protection from cold. On departure, my *khozyaika* generously offered me some gifts—goods she still needed herself—an old shirt and a scarf. I also managed to get a much-used fur hat with flaps covering the ears, and a pair of tarpaulin mittens. So equipped, a small bag on my back, filled with dried bread, a piece of bacon, and some pieces of sugar, I was ready for my new journey.

In the beginning of March I left the Tambov district with my labor battalion. The Russian winter was still severe. The dirt roads, along which we were moving, like everything that was surrounding us up to the horizon, were covered with frozen snow that was sparkling in the sun. I could feel the crispness of the snow under my *lapti* in which I was walking as on a small, flat sled, slowly but firmly. I felt warm in my upper body, as my jacket as well as the backpack provided good protection from the cold. My feet were warm, but my knees were cold. While walking at first about fifteen miles daily, my knees were constantly inflamed, and this was getting even worse when I would enter a warm hut for an overnight stay. My knees and thighs looked and felt as if badly burned by the sun.

We were moving continuously in a southwest direction. As far as one could see it was all flatland or, I should say, it was all rye land which was covered by snow and dotted with hundreds of what looked from afar like large buildings. Coming closer I could see that what I took for buildings were huge stacks of rye shaped like rectangular boxes. The collective farmers managed to harvest the rye and to gather and bind it into sheaves, but, either because of a shortage of threshing machines or for some other reasons, these sheaves remained unthreshed and thus were stored tightly, pile upon pile, in huge heaps. It took some effort to pick out enough stalks of rye in order to make a hole big enough to burrow inside, but then one had a warm and cozy shelter. It was excellent for taking a nap or just to watch the field mice running around and feeding on the grain the collective farmers inadvertently left for them.

The weather changed suddenly and we got hit with a winter storm. The wind was now roaring with the force of a hurricane. At times it drew the blizzard low to the ground (that is why we called it *pozyemka,* from the Russian *zemlya*—ground—a blizzard accompanied by ground wind), and it became impossible to walk even with the wind behind, since it was strong enough to toss us out of the road into the open fields. Our misty eyes became covered with frost that turned into small icicles. The thick blizzard finally reduced visibility to virtually nil. Even the huge stacks of rye, at a distance of no more than fifteen feet away, would become invisible. Now not only my legs above the knees were hurting but also my hands were getting numb from the biting cold. I would put my fingers, in turns one after the other, into my mouth to thaw them until little by little they would begin to tingle, then throb with pain as warmth returned to them. Worse still, as it got extremely windy, it took just seconds for noses to freeze and for cheeks to turn whitish. I was often rubbing my nose and, especially, my cheeks with snow to get back some feeling in them.

Since villages were miles apart, those rye stacks were now our salvation. For about a week they provided us with shelter and also with some food—the same our cohabitants, the mice, so enjoyed. I would grate ears of rye, one after the other, with my hands and eat the kernels, chewing slowly and from time to time watering them in my mouth with an icicle.

Our long rest in the rye stacks came to an end finally together with the storm. An officer in a horse-drawn sledge was moving from one stack to another, assembling the men in his charge and trying in vain to form them into a column resembling a quasimilitary unit. But it was still not the end of the winter. Strong winds blowing around particles of snow were again blinding us, and at times slowed us to a stop. People would rest for a few minutes at the edge of some rye stack, putting their backs against it for protection from the cold wind. But it was extremely dangerous to fall asleep outside a stack, as it was a recipe for never waking up again. It was there that for the first time I saw people frozen to death.

In the second half of March 1942 we were still on the road walking slowly in a southwest direction. After we crossed the Don River, south of Voronezh, there was another sudden change in the weather. We could see and feel the signs of spring; mud and floods. My *lapti* became useless. I needed shoes badly, but these could not be obtained from my labor battalion. Again, the only sources of supply were local inhabitants, and in particular the *babushki*, the peasant-mothers who in such situations were often taking care of people like me. With nothing to barter, we had to rely on their kind hearts alone. The generosity of the peasant-mothers was boundless, and they acted spontaneously; if guided by any deliberate thought at all, one might call it "hypothetical reciprocity." "Take these shoes," a *babushka* told me, "they are my son's, perhaps your mother is doing the same thing for him." I did not respond. All I could think was: "Where is my mother now, is she still alive?"

A month after leaving Rasskazovo, our labor battalion finally arrived at its new workplace. We were again ordered to dig antitank trenches, initially close to the Donets River (also called *seversky* Donets, i.e., northern Donets), but after a while mostly along the Oskol River, on its east side, in the vicinity of Volokonovka. The Oskol is a tributary of the Donets, which in turn is a tributary of the Don River. The front lines were farther west, mostly along the Donets. Behind us was a supply railroad running north to south, parallel to the Oskol River. Our workplaces, between the towns of Novy Oskol and Volokonovka, were some 110 to 120 miles southwest of Voronezh, and some thirty miles northwest of Valuiki, an important railroad junction; both were still in Soviet hands. Some 80 miles to the southwest was Kharkov, the second largest city in the Ukraine, while some 60 miles to the west was the smaller city of Belgorod; both were captured by the Germans in October 1941.

The conditions here were quite different from those in the fall of 1941 at Voronezh. First of all, this time we were digging much closer to very active front lines. From the beginning of May we could hear the constant roaring of artillery. Secondly, as soon as we arrived at the digging sites, our labor battalion officers were replaced by smartly dressed NKVD commanders. Their stern faces expressing contempt, they treated us like convicted felons of penal battalions, from whom as much work as possible should be squeezed out no matter what. Working from sunrise to sunset, hungry, dirty, and exhausted, we slept on the ground, right on the edge of the ditches. Before sunrise we were roused by screams and kicks, given a piece of bread, some *kipiatok*, and hurried down into the ditches. Taking turns, our guards would not let us out of their sight, strictly enforcing their timetable for breaks and preventing any unscheduled interruptions. Standing at the edge of the antitank ditches and directing their booming voices at us, they were trying to scare and, at same time, to entice us to dig faster by a mixture of dirty curses and appeals to our honor and love of motherland. I was made to feel like a nothing, less than a speck of dust in the war machine.

The persistent artillery cannonade coming from the vicinity of Valuiki, southeast of the place where we had been digging, was an augural sign. On 9 May the Red Army began its ill-fated offensive in the direction of Kharkov, and it ended in disaster. The Germans, in their counteroffensive, which started eight days later, managed to encircle Marshal Timoshenko's armies. By 28 May the battle of Kharkov came to a close with about 240,000 taken prisoner of war, according to German sources. As we were still frantically digging the antitank ditches not very far away from the main battles, the sounds of war were coming closer and closer and so were the rumors of an imminent calamity. Our guards—there is no other name for the officers of the NKVD in charge of us and our work—went on a rampage, throwing at us all the dirty curses that can be found in the rich Russian vocabulary. They shortened our sleep time to six hours—from ten P.M. to four A.M. "The Red Army needs these fortifications badly and is going to take them over any moment," they were yelling while we were toiling and dripping with sweat at the bottom of the deep canallike ditches.

Why such ill treatment and mental abuse, I often wondered. Most of us exerted ourselves to the utmost, and the NKVD men had no need to behave like slave-drivers. Many years later I got something of an explanation as to why they had been in a constant state of ner-

vous agitation when I came across a documentary piece of a conversation between Stalin and General (later Marshal) Alexander
Vasilievsky. At two A.M. on 26 June 1942, having heard Vasilievsky's
routine report, Stalin stopped him from leaving and said: "Wait a
minute, I want to say something about the Kharkov defeat again. Today, when I asked the Southwestern staff if the enemy had been
halted at Kupyansk, and *how the building of the defences on the river Oskol was going*, I could get nothing sensible out of them . . . When are
they going to start obeying General Staff orders? They have to be reminded of this. Those who deserve it should be punished . . ." (Em-
phasis added. Quoted from D. Volkogonov, *Stalin: Triumph and
Tragedy*, op. cit., p. 432). While we were digging, mercilessly rushed
by the NKVD men, they were working under the menacing threats
of orders from Stalin himself. Stalin's watchful eye was everywhere,
including the digging of antitank ditches along the Oskol River.

6. Taken Prisoner

Timoshenko's May counteroffensive played perfectly well into the German High Command's hands. Having smashed and eliminated his main forces, the Wehrmacht could now move swiftly with their summer offensive of 1942. Code-named *Blau* (blue), it was planned to advance the Wehrmacht to the Volga, to the Caucasus, and to the Iranian border.

Did the Russians know about the German plans? It is now well known that they did, but nothing was done by the Soviet High Command to take advantage of that knowledge. On 20 June Marshal Timoshenko telephoned Stalin to tell him about documents taken from a German officer whose plane crashed behind Russian lines; the documents were the Wehrmacht plans with dates for the offensive. Stalin, suspecting a plant, refused to believe it and ordered Timoshenko to ignore the whole thing. At Hitler's headquarters the question was what to do with the timetable of the *Blau* operation now that, as it could be suspected, the Russians might be onto it. The decision was made to ignore that possibility, go ahead with the plan, and thus start operation *Blau* as originally scheduled.

The Germans had good reasons for their decision, because—short of an organized retreat, which Stalin forbade—there was little Timoshenko could do anyhow a week before their offensive. And so it began on 28 June, launched from the Kursk sector by General Hoth, commander of the 4th Panzer Army. Its aim was to encircle and destroy all Soviet forces west of the Don River. Two days later, the German Sixth Army under General Paulus began its offensive in the Belgorod sector. Having encountered little resistance, his troops would

soon move into the great east loop of the Don River and, after crossing it at Kalach, advance to Stalingrad on the Volga. Soviet troops,
whatever was left of them, failing to exploit the rivers Donets and Oskol as defense lines, were rapidly retreating. Voronezh was a key initial objective of the German summer offensive. Though they succeeded on 6 July in crossing the Don both south and north of
Voronezh, they could not take the entire city. Perhaps the digging
there of the antitank ditches by our labor battalions in the fall of 1941
was not an exercise in futility after all? I hope those ditches on the
thirteenth kilometer were of some use to the Red Army in preventing the fall of that strategic city, the midpoint between Moscow and
Stalingrad.

I learned much later about these movements and the general picture, of course. But at the end of June 1942 events started rolling fast
for me. It was the first week of July when our NKVD guards disappeared. They escaped unnoticed and we were left to ourselves in a
huge encirclement, together with thousands of regular Red Army
units now in a panicky retreat. We could attempt no organized
breakout. Abandoned by all our officers, our labor battalion quickly
disintegrated. People were going in all directions, those from territories already occupied by the Germans heading mostly home. I and
some others from our battalion found ourselves following in the footsteps of regular army units; they were defeated and their retreat became a rout. Some were pondering the possibility of joining partisans. We were, however, in forestless territory where there was no
natural habitat for partisans and, if they existed at all, nobody knew
where to look for them. We found ourselves in a kind of corridor between advancing German troops and under constant bombardment
by the Luftwaffe. German aircraft had the skies to themselves and
could strafe at will the remnants of a not so long ago fighting army.

During one such air strike, it was still not over when together with
other people from our labor battalion I rushed to horses just killed,
still bleeding, hot steam coming out of their open bellies. Squatting
close to one of them, I used my pocketknife to cut out pieces of flesh.
We cooked the meat in our small kettles (mess tins) on open fire,
and after days of hunger finally had our fill. Then we returned to the
horses, cut out some more meat, and put it into our kettles to have

on hand later. There was not much left of the two horses, mere skele-
tons, reddish bones and guts, over which swarms of flies were
buzzing, getting their fill. A few miles farther on we emptied our kettles on the ground and filled them with better meat. A local shep-
herd, trying to round up his flock of sheep into safety, came under
an air raid. He was now sharing with us the meat of the sheep killed
by the Luftwaffe.

Late that evening, I saw from afar, on an open flat field, a small
Soviet plane. Some people boarded, and then it quietly took off, turning eastward. I stood mesmerized by the very sight of the liftoff. It
was not envy, getting away by plane was not even in my dreams. I en-
vied the birds cruising high in the skies above me. Why could not I
escape on wings like they could?

As a matter of fact, I was not very far from the Don River, on the
east side of which the Red Army had managed to hold on and where
the situation stabilized somewhat at the end of July. To what extent
was this due to the extremely harsh measures undertaken by Stalin—
of which I learned much later—in his famous No. 227 decree known
as the "not one step backward"? "We have lost territories populated
by more than seventy million people," it said. "Retreating farther
means destroying ourselves and with us our homeland. Not a single
step back! Form penal battalions to direct middle and senior commanders there. Place them in difficult parts of the front to allow them
to expiate their sins against their homeland with blood . . . Form well-
armed guard units and place them at the rear of unstable divisions
and charge them to shoot the panicky and cowards on the spot in
cases of disorderly retreat."

I did not manage to cross the Don. Together with others, I was trying to get to the Don crossings as soon as possible, and we figured
that the shortest way was going to the northeast, but in hindsight this
was not the best decision, as it was also the shortest way to encounter
German troops moving in the southeasterly direction. The bridges
over the Don were already destroyed. But even before we could reach
any river crossing, we were overrun by German troops.

It was early morning, 8 July 1942. What I dreaded all these twelve
months since the German invasion of the Soviet Union had just happened: I was captured by the Germans!

The Germans made no distinction between regular soldiers and those from labor battalions. They herded us all into a field, where we were made to sit on the ground for long hours before they divided us into groups. I was among some three hundred prisoners marched to a place fenced off by barbed wire in the midst of which stood a barn where we were to be housed. As if being a Soviet POW was not trouble enough, I was a Jewish Soviet POW, and in the eyes of my captors I would be first of all, and above all, a Jew. The Wehrmacht had orders, issued before the eastern campaign began, how to handle commissars and Jews. Like that of the *Kommissarbefehl,* the order regarding Jews specified that captured Jews should be given "special treatment," which meant handling them not as POWs but as Jews. This did not mean, of course, that non-Jewish POWs were to be treated humanely or in accordance with international conventions. It was just that Jews, like commissars, were to be killed out of hand.

In postwar memoirs written by former German generals and in many books about them, one can find claims that some of those generals had not only strongly disapproved of the *Kommissarbefehl* and the order about the "special treatment" of Jewish POWs, but also tried to prevent their troops from engaging in such outrages damaging the good name of the Wehrmacht. There were perhaps such cases with regard to commissars. Thus, for instance, Marshal Fritz Erich von Manstein claims in his memoirs: " I had no alternative but to inform my superiors that the Commissar Order would not be implemented by anyone under my command" (*Lost Victories,* Novato, Cal.: Presidio Press, 1982, p. 180). Not a word in those memoirs about the treatment of Jews by the Wehrmacht, and this is not surprising. There is much evidence that troops commanded by some of the most prominent German generals were under orders, issued by themselves, to deal harshly with Jews. For example, on 10 October1941, Marshal Reichenau stated in his order that "the soldier must have full understanding of the necessity for harsh but just countermeasures against Jewish subhumanity." Copies of this order, which Hitler found to be "excellent," were sent by Marshal von Rundstedt, commander of the Southern Army Group, to the Eleventh and Seventeenth Armies, as well as to the First Panzer Army, for distribution. General Manstein, the future marshal, at that time the Eleventh

Army commander, elaborated on this in an order of his own, explaining that the Jew was the liaison between the Red Army on the front and the enemy in the rear. (See *Trial of the German Major War Criminals Before the International Military Tribunal,* Volume XX, Nuremberg, Germany, 1948, p. 642).

The "handling" of Jewish POWs, which I witnessed the first day of my imprisonment, was done by regular soldiers. As soon as we were pushed behind the barbed wire, I heard the dreadful German barking, which since the fall of 1939 had haunted me in my nightmares: *Jude, Jude?*! Hunting for Jews, this was the first thing they were occupied with in our POW camp. Among themselves, they were not talking about Jews, it was rather the weather, food, changing guard, and so on. I understood their conversations, but was cautious not to reveal that I spoke the German language, because that could have turned me immediately into a suspect. Looking for Jews as well as for commissars was just part of their duties, which some obviously liked and others did not seem to dislike. These were ordinary people, soldiers following wartime orders and, in addition, doing a little extra, not so ordinary a job.

Hannah Arendt coined the term "banality of evil" and it has become a commonplace, deceptive catchword. The perpetrators may have been "normal" and perhaps even "banal," but what about their deeds? To speak of "the banality of evil" is to trivialize evil.

A young Soviet Jew, my age if not younger, sitting on the ground close to me, responded mechanically to the German yelling and put up his hand. To this day I remember the face of that boy, I see his grayish, scared eyes. Before he was led beyond the barbed wire fence to be shot, he sat motionless while a Russian POW, a regular army officer, was hastily removing his shoes murmuring: "You have no need for them anymore."

The Germans could not tell a Jew from a non-Jew, so they tried to enlist Russians or Ukrainians to uncover Jews. They tempted hungry POWs with a loaf of bread for every Jew pointed out. In my presence two POWs were denounced as "looking Jewish" and, as it turned out, one of the suspects was indeed Jewish. As he claimed to be Belorussian, he was ordered to pull down his pants, and he failed the test. While he continued to deny being Jewish, he was mercilessly beaten and forced to dig his own grave before being shot. Five years later, when my son, Henryk, was born in Poland, I was adamant in my resolve not to have him circumcised.

I had so-called good "Aryan looks" and nobody as yet pointed a finger at me. Still, the very first day of my POW life I noticed a guy who knew me as a Jew. He was Ukrainian, a teacher who while in the labor battalion used to display his resentment of Jews. The moment I spotted him and our eyes met I told myself, "That's it, my time has come." But I was mistaken in my judgment of him. As I was waiting with bated breath for his next move, he came closer, looked at me reproachfully, and said, "Did you really think, you motherfucker, that I would be after you for a loaf of bread?" True, he did not like Jews, but to kill them, or watch them being killed? Besides, he was not a Judas. We became friends, Stepan and I, sharing afterward whatever there was to be shared. The same day, during the registration of POWs, I gave my name as Diomin Ivan Filipovich. It seemed to me a good Russian name I heard somewhere. I also liked it because there was no "r" in it. The letter "r," as I pronounced it, sounded somehow guttural, and this made me suspect of being Jewish. One of the tests the Russians sometimes used to uncover a Jew was asking to pronounce a word with an "r," for example: *kukuruza* (corn). For my birthplace I had chosen Kizel in the Molotovsky district. I picked that place because I knew it a little from the time I stayed there briefly with Hanna in 1940, and also because it was far away in the Urals under the Soviets. Recalling my first encounter with the Wehrmacht in 1939, I also made myself five years younger, born in 1926, I said, hoping that this might help in my release, but this time it made no difference. At any rate, from now on I was going to be Ivan and I was introducing myself as such to other POWs as well: Ivan, Vanya. I got rid of all my old documents and papers with one exception: two small photos, my mother's and Hanna's taken in Poland before the war. I kept them as a kind of a talisman, a sign of my true identity, lest I ever forget myself.

On the third day of captivity Hungarian soldiers took over control of our camp. We had no idea about the reason for the sudden change, but I was rather glad; nobody could be worse than the Germans, I thought. And, indeed, for the first time since in captivity we were given something to eat: small pieces of bread—white bread!

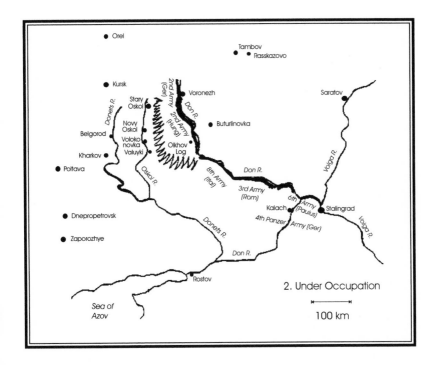

2. Under Occupation

100 km

Very soon, however, came disappointment. Not an hour had passed before I heard our new guards yelling at the top of their lungs in a strange language of which one word was nevertheless crystal clear: *Zsido, Zsido,* out! Had the order regarding the treatment of Jewish POWs been passed by the Wehrmacht to its allies, or had the Magyars invented their own version of "handling" Jewish POWs? This question came to me later. All I thought when I heard them yelling "Kikes, out" was that they might still find their *Zsido,* presumably the last one left here—me. They were not searching very hard, however, and some of them soon found other ways of amusing themselves at the expense of the non-Jewish POWs.

The German soldiers—our previous guards—whatever their treatment of the POWs had not played cat and mouse with their captives. By contrast, such were the favorite games of some of the *honveds* (Hungarian soldiers). They had an inexhaustible supply of these, and they seemed to derive sadistic pleasure from tormenting people. One guard—the other *honveds* called him Gypsy—would mount a horse and at a gallop turn it into the barn where we were sleeping on the floor, trampling people right and left. Another liked to play what he called the "hide and seek game." He would order ten or more POWs to go to the latrine at the same time, give them ten minutes for their relief, hide himself somewhere, emerge after five minutes, and, pretending the allotted time had already passed, whistle for them to run back at once while hitting the "laggards" with his rifle. A third guard's favorite was "the father and son game." He would pick up a pair of POWs, one very young, the other much older. "Give him a slap in his face," he would order the younger one, and then would mete out "fair punishment," hitting him hard "for having no respect for a father." In turn, he would order the older one to slap the youngster and would follow with an equally deserved punishment—"for abusing a child." I heard somebody say as if to himself, *"Koshke igrushki, a myshke slezki"* (For the cat it's a game, for the mouse tears).

The *honveds* made us all witness the execution of a POW. He was a young boy who escaped from the camp, but was almost immediately caught when he foolishly decided to have a bite in the village where our POW compound was located. The guards who caught him gave him a beating, but as he was brought back to the camp the commanding officer produced a show of "law and order" in the presence of all prisoners. The poor boy was charged and formally sentenced to be shot. The officer arrived, dressed solemnly for the occasion, followed by a firing squad. He gave a little speech in Hungarian and then ordered the soldiers of the firing squad to raise their rifles and aim at the boy. Before he was shot he turned to us, and as he cried out loudly, *"Proshchayte, tovarishchi"* (Farewell, comrades), an older POW standing to my left, tears in his eyes, whispered, *"Proshchay, synok"* (Farewell, son). The boy was buried right behind the latrine.

Our camp was just a temporary assembly point for prisoners of war. On the fifth day of captivity we were all moved on foot some thirty miles to the north, so that we would be closer to Voronezh, and to another, also transitional, but larger camp. That was where the Hungarians, for reasons unknown to me at the time, turned us over to the Germans. (I learned after the war, though I am not sure it had anything to do with our transfer, that in return for German equipment and arms, Hungary gave up its rights to prisoners and spoils.) Our new place was surrounded by a barbed-wire fence and in the middle of it stood pigsties already housing about twelve hundred POWs. German soldiers guarded the camp, where we were to become pawns of a game much more deadly than before, a game in which our very lives were at stake.

Hitler had not conquered the Ukraine to share its grain with Soviet POWs. No bread had been distributed in our camp for a long time. The local inhabitants were kept away from the barbed-wire fence, so that their efforts to smuggle bread or potatoes into the camp were, most of the time, frustrated. All we were getting to eat was watery soup with pieces of rotten meat, a diet that was literally decimating us. It was the flesh of dead horses killed and lying alongside the roads since the German air strikes in the first week of July that was now to become our staple. The horses, their swollen bellies and open wounds full of whitish maggots and other parasitic worms, were collected by POWs on adjacent roads, brought in wheelbarrows to the camp, cut into chunks and pieces, and thrown in a cauldron full of boiling water. People would eat anything to stay alive, and that "anything" became a mass killer just as the Germans wanted it to be— no waste of bullets and no possible effects on the morale of the *Soldaten* shooting POWs.

Death on the spot was the punishment for escape attempts, but some nevertheless tried. On two separate occasions I saw the end of those who had no luck: one prisoner was shot, the other hanged on a tree branch, both in front of all POWs, forced to witness the execution; the hanged man was dangling for hours for everybody to see. Still, there were also successful escapes and I made up my mind to try my luck too—I had nothing to lose, so I thought. I joined up with a group of POWs going to collect carcasses of the horses and, while outside the camp, made my dash for freedom. Alas, I was immediately caught. A German guard, hitting me with the butt of his rifle again and again, brought me back to the camp. As I was led to the tree to be hanged, I closed my eyes, I did not want to see my executioners; my mother and Hanna will never know where and how I perished, I thought. But I was not hanged by my neck. After a while, a

German soldier ordered me to put my arms behind my back, bound my hands together with a string, put a rope between my squeezed arms, and then—while a POW, who was to assist in the procedure, lifted me up—attached the rope to a branch of a tree and tightened it. I did not know how long I was dangling on that tree. At first I felt excruciating pain in my arms, then in all of my body. A trickle of blood came out of my nose and I lost consciousness.

Why had my life been spared? Was it because our guards were looking for a new kind of amusement? Or because someone in charge pitied the boy in half civilian garb, more a teenager than an adult soldier? Or was it the German weakness for blue eyes that saved me then—as Hanna would often say half jokingly years later? I will never know. Be that as it may, when I came to my senses I found myself at the barbed-wire fence, a German soldier kicking my aching body into the compound. As soon as I was inside, he threw a piece of cheese after me. The POW ordered to assist in the hanging was apologetically taking care of me.

The next couple of days were sunny and very hot. The policy of death by attrition and disease worked. All we could do while sitting on the ground, depressed by the waves of the Luftwaffe aircraft moving high over us in the southeast direction toward Stalingrad, was to take off our blouses and shirts and snap lice in the seams. Some had become so weak and apathetic that even this simple task was too much for them. Apart from killing lice, we could do little else to improve our unsanitary conditions. Very few were still seeking water to merely wet their faces. Many grew mustaches and beards so that they looked much older than they really were. I belonged to those who managed to hide old razor blades and shaved from time to time, either because they wanted, like myself, to look younger, or in order to preserve a little of their dignity, or for some other reason. I noticed a Tatar shaving his head with a piece of glass. He did it so well, all his hair cut off close to the skin and not the slightest scratch, that several guys, who cared more about their hygiene than possible cuts to their heads, wanted him to become their barber. As such he could have gotten a medal for a truly superb job. An artist in his new (or old?) profession, he would first be looking for a piece of thick glass, broken at a particular sharp angle, then, after testing it carefully on his fingernails, with a few strokes, beginning from the tip of the head and going down, he would show to all willing spectators a shining, bald nut.

Though lately we were receiving some bread every second day, we became more and more emaciated and sick. Almost everybody, including me, had severe diarrhea. I had stomach pains and my entire body was aching. We all had to go frequently, but access to the latrine was strictly regulated. Worse still, I began to feel extreme mental fatigue, which was a symptom of sickness of my mind more than my body. Trying to hide my identity, to pretend to be somebody else, was a cause of constant anxiety and tension. I was afraid that some words pronounced loudly in my sleep would expose me. "Did I talk at night?" I would ask my neighbors sleeping to the right and left of me. But even when not asleep I began daydreaming and would frequently ask myself: "Who am I, Vanya or Gavrylek (as mother called me) or Gabrys (as Hanna called me)?" And I had to touch the pocket on the left side of my blouse, where I kept their photos, to reassure myself.

POWs were dying like flies. Starvation and disease—mostly dysentery—were killing people at an accelerating pace. In just a little more than a month the population of our camp shrank from 1,500 to about 150. As I learned after the war, the Germans killed, mainly by starvation, 2.8 million young, healthy Soviet POWs in less than eight months of the first year of war. This policy was reversed only by the end of October 1942, when Hitler sanctioned the deployment of prisoners in German industry, construction, and mining. From the late fall of that year, most Soviet POWs were packed off for slave labor in the Reich, where they would ultimately be dying of hard work, starvation, and ill treatment. The same was probably going to happen to all of us, including myself, unless they kill me in the meantime for being a Jew, I thought. Indeed, it was in the second half of August when we heard rumors that all the transit camps to the north and south of ours—located in pigsties, barns, and stables—would be moved to one big camp and eventually to Germany. Another thing I did not know at that time was that during August 1942, more than 400,000 Jews were murdered in German-occupied Europe, mostly in Poland.

7. Escape: Surviving Under Occupation

The rumors proved true. Early one day we were given somewhat larger than usual portions of bread in addition to the ersatz coffee. A small column of our POWs was then formed and the guards led us on foot to a road going west. This was my last chance, I kept telling myself. I made up my mind days before and devoted all my thoughts to escape plans, which I shared only with Stepan, my "anti-Semitic" Ukrainian friend. He was not ready to join me or run by himself, but helped me with my plans. Walking on that dirt road, I was just waiting for the right place and moment to run for my freedom. Finally I noticed ahead what seemed to be some scrub or brushwood on the left side of the narrow road and, as we were ordered to sit down for a rest, while the guards were having a smoke, I jumped into what proved to be a dense corn growth. I heard shots, but fortunately the guards did not bother to chase after me. I was free, if this was the right word, since I was still deep in occupied territories with only vague plans of what to do next.

At first I hid in fields or among trees and, as it was still summer, slept in haystacks. I remember them so well, they emitted an intoxicating heavenly smell. This could not last long, however, I had to come out into the open. But where to go and what chances did I have under German occupation? I was in jeopardy on two accounts, as an escapee POW and as a Jew.

As it turned out, the situation on the first account was not as bad as I initially thought. I was not the only escapee around, though for security reasons everybody pretended never to have seen a fugitive from a German camp. What was most important, we had the sympathy of the local population. We, strangers in their midst, could count on their support. For one thing, most of the local population had no love for the German invaders, quite the opposite. On the other hand, the Soviet regime as such, loved by some and hated by others, was not far to the east and could return at any time. The historical memory of the civil war, when the "Whites" were replacing the "Reds" and vice versa on an almost daily basis, was not forgotten yet. But above all, the Red Army was the army of their husbands, fathers, and sons, and so were its POWs. Whatever the claims of the Soviet propaganda, people knew that there were millions of POWs and figured quite rightly that their own loved ones might also be among them or join their ranks in the future.

In comparison with other escapee POWs, however, I was at a disadvantage. To begin with, my Russian was bookish and with a foreign accent. A somewhat mitigating circumstance was the fact that this was mixed Russian/Ukrainian border territory, while I myself, "coming from the Urals," could not possibly speak "normally." The best way to deal with that drawback was to talk as little as possible, which was not easy for me. Next, it was kolkhoz—collective farm—country all over, an asset I counted on in my escape plans. The problem was, I never worked on a farm. All this paled, however, in comparison with my greatest handicap. Would I be tolerated as a Jew? Who would help me, who would dare to protect a Jew, even if willing, an offense punishable by death. I knew that expecting help from anybody would be too much to hope for. I had to go on hiding my identity not only from the Germans but from the local population as well.

It was not difficult to find employment. The German propaganda promised what many villagers had dreamed about—to break up the kolkhozes and restore private farming. It was a wish I heard numerous times both under occupation and while in the army: "Comes the war to an end," Red Army soldiers said among themselves, "and they"—meaning the Soviets—"will undo the kolkhozes." But it was not an easy matter even if the Germans intended to keep their vague pledge. I witnessed one such attempt, initiated by some new activists in a kolkhoz under occupation. As men were in the Soviet army, the general meeting was attended mostly by women and chaired by the *starosta* (elder), a new position and title substituting for the old one, the "chairman." Listening to the initially cautious, convoluted manner of speech, I wondered how many of them were really serious about disbanding the collective farm. Some women left no doubts that they were against or wished to postpone the whole thing. *"Bez khoziaina dom sirota"* (In the absence of the master the house is an orphan), one was saying, while some others were giggling cheerfully in agreement.

Apart from the absence of the men, there were numerous, extremely difficult problems the activists would face in undoing the kolkhoz. These were not discussed, however, only hinted at. Instead, what seemed at first amazing to me, a heated debate erupted about a horse, the only one left in the kolkhoz. It was an old, overworked horse, which was why neither the Soviets nor the Germans took it away from them. But ownership of that horse, born after the village had been collectivized, excited—especially the older men—very much. Who should get the horse? "Obviously not Peter, who was taking care of it before he left the kolkhoz for the army, nor his family, which in the old times never owned a horse. It should go to somebody whose family used to own horses in the old days, but, on the other hand, there were several such families and only one horse." It was enough to make the poor horse laugh, but to these people it was a dead serious issue. And, indeed, it was, as I realized the more I listened to them. The matter of horse ownership symbolized the troubled waters of the kolkhoz system. Collectivization was forced down the throats of the peasants, and most of them detested it. But the road back to private farming was bumpy and full of hard choices. The scene of that kolkhoz meeting would vividly come back to me whenever, in later years, I pondered professionally over the problems of collective versus private ownership.

The Germans, for their part, had shown no intention whatsoever to dismantle the kolkhozes. Like the Soviet regime before them, they soon found out that the collective farms were an excellent tool for pumping grain and livestock out of the villages. Passing through villages, I would ask people how the occupiers were behaving and, typically, I would get the following answer: "Never mind, they do not take ours, only what belongs to the state." The collective farmers considered to be theirs only what they produced on their small private plots—kitchen gardens—adjacent to their houses; the rest, which was the bulk of the collective farm's output—most of the crops and most of its livestock—was always taken by the state. No change in that regard, it was just the state had changed. For the same reasons, they had no moral scruples about stealing from "their" kolkhoz; they stole more from it under occupation, because, with the Party gone, it became easier to steal and avoid punishment.

I do not mean to imply that it made no difference to the kolkhoz folks who was their lord and master. Far from it. The Germans were foreign invaders to whom they and their countrymen were subhuman. Most people, both Russians and Ukrainians, had they gotten their wishes, would have the Germans gone as soon as possible. But it was summer 1942, and these practical people knew that this was just wishful thinking. They were mesmerized by the might of the Germans, which both terribly impressed and depressed them. It was common knowledge, of course, how far the German summer offensive had led them. The whole of the Ukraine, including the Donbas (the Donets industrial basin), became occupied territory. A German Army Group crossed the Kerch Peninsula and entered the Caucasus. General Paulus's Sixth Army reached the Volga River near the outskirts of Stalingrad. True, in spite of Hitler's repeated victory claims, the city had not fallen yet. The Red Army resisted and ferocious street fighting still continued. Overall, however, it was a time of the triumphal march of a most terrible foreign conqueror.

Since there were few men on the collective farms, there were plenty of jobs available. And so I worked as a farmhand. With no experience, however, I was often suspected—not necessarily of being a Jew, though this happened too—and viewed as a somewhat strange boy. "In what forest have you been born?" I would be asked scornfully, or "You must be a city boy," another derisive comment. The case that brought much discredit upon me had to do with how I handled a pair of oxen. These docile, slow, but powerful animals were for lack of horses commonly used in the fields and as draft animals. The way to direct them was to call *tsob* or *tsebe,* and they would obediently turn right or left. One day I was given these instructions together with a pair of oxen already harnessed to a cart, which was put on a sledge because the road was snow-covered. My task was simple—just to deliver straw from one place to another. I had difficulty, however, handling the oxen and began yelling simultaneously *tsob-tsebe*. This drove my poor oxen to a frenzy. Normally very slow, they went into a stampede down the sloped road. The sledge hit a tree and got damaged. And so was my reputation. .

For similar reasons, I had to change workplaces frequently, going from one village to another. The villages were Russian and Ukrainian, side by side, and people were used to transients. I felt more at ease as I gained some experience in farmwork. I was moving in circles, to the south of Voronezh, in an area between the Oskol River and the Don River, but rather closer to the latter, hoping that I would eventually cross the front lines into Soviet-held territory, though I had no idea how. At the same time, I tried to avoid places where army units were stationed. What I could not avoid entirely was the new local police, eager to serve. Eluding them was a constant headache. They would have had a fine time catching a Jew.

I was dressed and behaved not much differently than other sixteen-year-old local boys. The Germans, and there were very few around, were usually unable to recognize a Jew unless he was a carbon copy of a *Stürmer* picture. One morning, however, I was stopped by a Ukrainian policeman in a village to which I came the day before. The local police knew everybody in the village by name. Most inhabitants were related to each other, former Communists and present German collaborators alike, often shielding even distant family members. They also tolerated the presence of transients with identification papers. I was perspiring heavily—trying to hide how terribly frightened I was—when I presented my identification. It was a fake document which, together with Stepan, my "anti-Semitic" Ukrainian friend, I prepared in the POW camp. The document issued by the chairman of kolkhoz Volokonovka certified that Diomin Ivan Filipovich, born 16 February 1926, in Kizel, Molotovsky district, was temporarily employed as a cowherd in that kolkhoz. It was dated 15 June 1942 and had a round stamp on it, which we made using a pyatak (a five-kopek coin). When preparing the "document," I picked both the name Volokonovka and the date it had allegedly been issued because it was the place and time our labor battalion was staying just before the German summer offensive began. My ID was probably as good as any average document issued in the kolkhozes for collective farmers, who under the Soviets were as a rule not given domestic passports so that leaving the kolkhoz would be more difficult for them. But as I was handing it to the policeman I realized how foolish it was to stick to the name Diomin from the POW camp. What if it was entered into a real registry, and the Germans, looking for Diomin, the escapee POW, notified the local police? It was also stupid of me to put into my ID the name Volokonovka, a place by now under occupation. I was no doubt in peril, but as fear makes danger greater than it is, I saw myself already at the police station reading a wanted poster. I should have rather picked the name of a POW who died in the camp. Well, as with other afterthoughts, these, too, came somewhat late. The policeman began asking questions. "I see you are from the Molotovsky district, what are you doing here?" I gave him my standard story: "I am too old for an orphanage so I live with Auntie Tanya in the city of Buturlinovka, but I went for a visit to my grandmother for the summer to help with the work on her plot—she lives in Volokonovka close to the Oskol River. Everything was okay, then at the end of June fighting began there and my grandma said that I'd better return to Auntie Tanya. But they say Buturlinovka is under the Soviets or perhaps there is fighting there too, so I am working in the kolkhoz for a while." The policeman was not satisfied with my answer and told me to follow him to the police office. In the meantime, a small group of onlookers gathered around us, among them the *khozyaika* at whose place I had breakfast, and who was impressed by a well-behaved boy discreetly crossing himself before and after eating. She turned to the policeman by name and said calmly but firmly: "Let the boy go, ours are also wandering somewhere." "Yes," he answered meekly, "you are quite right," and he let me go. The sign of crossing myself proved to be my best ID.

Mothers whose sons were in the army had generally been helping me in many ways. They would provide me with shelter, food, and wash my shirts and underwear. More than once I saw a mother looking at me tenderly, as holding back tears or shedding them profusely, she would whisper: "Perhaps your mother is now taking care of my boy." Such words would make my throat tight with emotion. I would have liked to take my mother's photo out of my pocket and show it to those loving mothers, but I had to restrain myself from doing so. Would they still be smiling gently at me if they knew that I was Jewish?

Was there any Jewish population on the territory where I was wandering around? Farther west, in the big cities as well as in shtetls of the Ukraine, a considerable proportion of the population was Jewish. I was under the impression, however, that there were few Jews living in the territory between Oskol (or perhaps even Donets) and the Don River, dotted mostly by villages and few towns.

The closest and biggest Jewish center was in Kharkov, west of the Donets. According to the 1939 census, it had a Jewish population of 130,000, one-sixth of its total. Only after the war did I learn about the fate of the Kharkov Jews. In the summer of 1941, when the Germans were approaching the city, many of its inhabitants fled, including the bulk of the Jewish population. The city, after its capture in October 1941, was under a military government. This meant that all decrees concerning the city, including those affecting Jews, were issued by the Wehrmacht. On its orders, hostages were taken and were shot or hanged, most of them Jews. A month later *Sonderkommando* 4a arrived and the annihilation of the Jews of Kharkov began. On 14 December 1941 in an announcement published over the signature of the military governor, the city's Jews were herded into a ghetto. Three weeks afterward came the mass slaughter of the Kharkov Jews in the Drobitski Yar (Drobitski ravine), where they were murdered in pits that had been prepared in advance; gas vans were also used in the killings. A report issued by the special committee which after the war investigated Nazi crimes in Kharkov and opened the burial pits in the Drobitski ravine stated that fifteen thousand people had been murdered there. However, according to evidence given at the trial of the officers of *Sonderkommando* 4a, the actual number of victims was 21,685. This figure includes all the Jews killed from the beginning of the German occupation until early January 1942, when the liquidation of the Jews of Kharkov was completed (Israel Gutman, ed., *Encyclopedia of the Holocaust,* Vol. 2, New York: Macmillan, 1990, pp. 796–97).

Because the local inhabitants had few if any Jewish neighbors, they had not developed that sixth sense in "smelling out Jews," which was so common in Poland or frequent in some parts of the Soviet Union.

I had, however, encounters with two people who, if not certain that they were "smelling a Jew" in me, still smelled something fishy; both were transients from big cities, perhaps escapee POWs like myself. The first tried to check out my pronunciation of the letter "r." Say *kukuruza*, he turned to me with a malignant smile on his face. I gave him a stern look and the guy pretended he was joking; the "r" rolling in my throat reminded him, he said, of people of aristocratic stock. The second encounter was more serious. Together with other kolkhoz boys we both worked in a nearby forest felling trees and chopping wood. Each time we met face-to-face, the guy, with no reason at all, would sneer at me, *"Ty evreyskoye nasenye"* (You kike's spawn). This was becoming dangerous as, repeated again and again, it could easily be overheard by others. In desperation, I finally decided to stand up to him. Next time, when nobody could hear and see us, I caught him by the lapels of his coat and, forcing myself to look relaxed, said to him: "Kike, you call me? Tell this to the police. Let's go to the police station." He was taken by surprise: *"da bros ty, net, ya tolko shutil"* (drop it, I was only kidding). I would not let go of his lapels, waiting for him to repeat that he did not really mean it. The gamble worked—he was mumbling apologies.

I wrote that there were no Jews in the area where I was wandering, but to be precise I should have said that I met no Soviet Jews there. This qualification is necessary, because as a matter of fact I got to see many other Jews, Hungarian Jews. And, as an eyewitness, I want to give a somewhat fuller account about how they were tormented by their compatriots.

First, however, a few words about Hitler's allies on the southern Soviet front. Hungary and Romania became German allies for the purpose of aggrandizement. Both countries later had to pay a heavy price for that alliance. When the German advance toward Stalingrad petered out in the fall of 1942, the front lines were held, along with the Wehrmacht, by Hungarians, Romanians, and Italians; there was also somewhere a Spanish so-called "Blue Division." The territory in the rear of the front lines on the Don River was divided accordingly for some administrative purposes. I must also mention here that all the occupied territories were generally divided into two zones. The first, adjoining the front lines, was governed by respective military administrations, while the second, which comprised the hinterland, was administered by a German civil administration. I had been wandering within the first zone, mostly in the sector occupied by the Hungarian Army south of Voronezh on the middle Don. The front lines around and under Stalingrad on the Volga were held exclusively by the Germans, specifically by Paulus's Sixth Army supported by the Fourth Panzer Army. From Stalingrad the front line receded to the Don and ran along that river to Voronezh. In between, again going northwest, were the Third Romanian Army, the Eighth Italian Army, the Second Hungarian Army, and, in the Voronezh sector, the Second German Army.

I never went so far south as to encounter Romanians, but I heard they were no better than the Hungarians. On the other hand, the Italians I met impressed me as being humane. This was perhaps due to a scene I witnessed that was both amusing and illuminating. I was sitting at a table in a Ukrainian hut when an Italian soldier carrying a rifle entered the room and asked for some cabbage. The *khozyaika*'s response was a definite no, and when he persisted she aimed a broom at him. And what did he do? He left, shaking his head. I was taken by his humble behavior; such a scene could not have happened with an armed German or Hungarian soldier. And the behavior of the Italian soldier was probably not something out of the ordinary. The *khozyaika* must have had some experience with these characters or she would not have been so quick with her broom.

Frm the end of September or the beginning of October I lived in the village of Olkhov Log under Hungarian administration. The Hungarian Army was in charge of a 130-mile stretch on the Don River. In Olkhov Log, which was a large village some forty miles west of that river, was stationed a Hungarian Army supply unit. I stayed at a tiny house of a Russian widow, whose grown-up children had left her: two for the Red Army, another for work in the Donbas. The location of the hut, away from the main road, the police station, and the military suited me well, though I did not like the *khozyaika*. She was gossipy, which did not bother me much—in a short time I heard something about every neighbor—but she was also mischievous and would poke her nose into anybody's private affairs. She was especially down on her next-door neighbor, who was both well-off and much younger than herself. "Her husband, who escaped with the Reds," she told me, "was a big fish in the Party and Marusya, his wife, would always put on airs, but now she is *nizhe travy tishe vody* (lower than grass quieter than water). My *khozyaika* disliked me as well, and she had good reasons for that—she was disappointed in me as a handyman. I was too much of a city boy, who could not properly repair a roof or mend a broken window. She nevertheless tolerated me, because I would bring home all the meager pay from work for the kolkhoz— grain, sunflower seeds, sometimes a little sunflower oil. I would also, whenever I had a chance, steal hay or straw from the kolkhoz, and bring home firewood from the nearby forest.

Almost through the entire month of October and well into November I worked day after day in that forest for the Hungarian supply unit, which provided its army with timber and wood products, particularly charcoal. The kolkhoz was under obligation to deliver free labor services, and I was assigned to the forest. Thus, under the supervision of Hungarian soldiers, who treated me rather well, I assisted in the making of charcoal. It was in that forest that I saw Hungarian Jews for the first time.

They were conscripts drafted into the Hungarian Army though not as *honveds* bearing arms. Instead, they were herded into special units called *Munkaszolgalat*, in essence labor service battalions dressed in military garb but without shoulder straps, badges, and the other usual military insignia. In that forest they were felling trees, carrying them, chopping wood, and generally doing most of the hardest and dirtiest work, for instance, cutting down and pulling heavy trees out of mud. While they would often be ordered, maliciously, to do the latter, they were at the same time required to keep themselves meticulously clean and were punished for having muddied shoes. Their supervisors, often ordinary *honveds*, treated them as a rule sadistically. Constant swearing and profanities directed at them were the mildest form of abuse.

Although my job, by comparison, was an easy one, our common supervisors were having fun yelling: "Ivan"—that was me—"show the damn kikes how to work." When I was sitting and resting at lunch break, the Hungarian Jews had most of their time filled with degrading and cruel exercises: They were forced to somersault, snake-crawl, frog-leap—all this was called, "scientifically," calisthenics. The maliciousness of the *honveds* toward their fellow countrymen seemed to have no limits, and yet the same men were capable of quite humane behavior toward the Russian boy (me), not to mention their dogs. Those Jews who became so exhausted that they could not perform the crazy exercises anymore were often ordered to strip naked and were put for hours into iron barrels with freezing water, to "cool off." I felt a double affinity with them—as a Jew and as a labor battalion worker, which I had been not so long ago. But also on the latter score, I had been incomparably better off. Even our NKVD supervisors required only hard work from us, and work that was not demeaning; with them it was strictly business, tough business but not mischievous games; their cruelty was impersonal and they never abused us physically. A couple of months later, I saw the Jews of the Hungarian labor battalions again under even more ominous conditions.

Winter was fast approaching and the work in the forest came to a standstill. I was now busy helping my *khozyaika* feed her cow, pig, and chicken, chopping wood and, most important, carrying buckets of water from the nearby river. This was quite a chore, as first thing in the morning I had to crush the thick ice, often with the help of a pickax, and then, two heavy buckets of water in my hands, walk uphill on a slippery footpath. But now each passing day my thoughts were getting lighter as the roar of war was fast approaching, this time from the east. And as the turbulent, tragic, and most unforgettable year of my life, 1942, was coming to an end, I saw finally light at the end of the tunnel.

On 19 November a major Soviet offensive under Stalingrad had began. It was a two-pronged attack on the flanks of Paulus's Sixth Army—on the Fourth Romanian Army and parts of the German Fourth Panzer Army south of Stalingrad, and on the Third Romanian Army north of that city. Three days later, these armies having been overrun, Soviet spearheads met at Kalach on the Don, thus closing the ring around Paulus's army. The Germans and their allies suffered an enormous loss—about 330,000 men had been trapped in a huge "cauldron." Manstein, who failed in his attempt at rescuing the Sixth Army, claims (F. E. von Manstein, *Lost Victories*, op. cit., p. 296) that the 300,000-plus figure is exaggerated, but his estimates of

200,000 to 220,000 men in the pocket seem to have discounted many non-German soldiers. According to the official Soviet announcement, those 330,000 men had been encircled in November. Between 23 November and 10 January, when the liquidation of the Stalingrad pocket began, 140,000 men had died in the fighting, or were taken prisoners. By 10 January, according to the general quartermaster of Paulus's army, there were 195,000 men to be supplied in the pocket. Bloody battles were waged until the end of January, when the remnants of the Sixth German Army, 91,000—including Paulus himself, in the meantime promoted to field marshal, his generals, and 2,500 other officers—surrendered, which meant that about 100,000 men had been killed or died between 10 January and 2 February. Let me add that Paulus himself, in a letter sent to Manstein, dated 26 November, wrote of "the odd 300,000 men entrusted to my charge" (F. E. von Manstein, *Lost Victories,* Appendix 1, p. 553).

The Wehrmacht's *wunderbar* (wonderful) days in Russia were over. Continuing its winter offensive, the Red Army launched an attack against the Italian, Hungarian, and German troops northwest of Stalingrad. The Fritzes and their allies were running like rabbits now. In the winter, the thickly frozen Don River constituted no obstacle whatever and was easily crossed. And so, it was the Hungarians who felt the next blow. On 12 January 1943 Soviet troops smashed through the lines of the Second Hungarian Army.

As the front on the Don River south of Voronezh was collapsing, the Hungarians in our village, led by their junior officers, lost their heads. The small supply unit stationed in Olkhov Log was moving back and forth. It was so sweet to see the *honveds* in a panic. I was on alert that my liberation would come any moment now. But this was not going to happen yet. The villagers were told about an "orderly retreat" of the local military unit, which in participation with the local police was to supervise the evacuation to the west of volunteers/collaborators, and also youth of conscription age, as well as all transients, including people like myself. On the eve of the evacuation day, the police, going from house to house, warned of dire consequences for anyone attempting to evade their orders.

That evening I made a fool of myself, and did something that could easily have cost me my life. Horrified at the prospect of be-

ing driven to the west, while Soviet troops would now any day liberate Olkhov Log, I thought I had at least a chance to let Hanna
know that I was alive by leaving a letter to be sent to her by mail when
the village was liberated. Good idea, but whom should I entrust with
a letter addressed to a Miss Rabinowicz? I wrote the letter hastily and
was equally quick in going to the next-door neighbor of whom all I
knew was what my *khozyaika* said about her, namely that she was the
wife of a communist activist. I told her that as a transient I was ordered to join other evacuees going west—that much she already
knew—and that I was a Jew, hiding my identity. I begged her to do
me a great favor. After the liberation of Olkhov Log would she send
the letter that I wrote to my family so they would know that as of 25
January 1943 I was still alive? The moment I put my letter on the
table to which I was initially invited with a smile, I saw the neighbor's face turning pale. She got up and just chased me out of her
house, promising nothing. Momentarily I felt I did the most stupid
and dangerous thing possible. My dead secret, which I had been so
jealously hiding from the whole world for over half a year, I just dis-
closed on the spur of the moment to a complete stranger. I was now
terribly afraid that she would go to the police to report me, but it
was too late for regrets. She did not notify the police, but neither
did she send the letter, otherwise Hanna would have gotten it; mail
service, as I have already indicated, worked well under the Soviets
in wartime.

The next day, before sunrise, I responded to a knock at the door
followed by an order: Police, get out! With my heart pounding I was
led to an assembly point where a small crowd of people, some
guarded by *honved*s, others not, was already waiting. I was made to
join the first group.

As we were moving on foot on a main road leading west, our small
column was being joined by more and more people who were
guarded or accompanied by *honved*s. We passed the village of
Tatarino, and in another small place, Pirogovo, we joined a large column of unguarded civilians on foot and in horse-drawn carts. These
were in part refugees, local inhabitants fleeing from the battle zone,
some from Ostrogozhsk in the northeast, but mostly policemen and
other collaborators with their families. Thus guarded, I found my-

self in a strange, motley crowd of local people, voluntarily and not so voluntarily being evacuated to the west "for their own good." It was getting cold, and worse, my shoes were in disrepair and, as road dirt was getting inside the soles, I had to stop every now and then to rearrange my *portyanki*. The guards were becoming angry with me, and one of them in particular could not resist hitting me each time with the butt of his rifle. Luckily, before long it began to snow heavily and our guarded column was first given a couple of hours for rest and then put into a nearby barn for an overnight stay. Next day, when we arrived in the late afternoon in Alekseyevka, a relatively large town, we saw a place crowded with retreating *honved*s of the Second Army. It was clearly shown on their faces, uniforms, equipment, and general bearing that they were a defeated, decimated army.

I was still a captive exposed to the *honved*s' whims, beatings, and a possible bullet from their rifles. I shuddered, however, at the very sight of the Hungarian Jews, the Jews of the *Munkaszolgalat* again. They were dragging their feet under heavy loads on their backs, many carrying not only their personal belongings but also some of the tools of their work, because they were denied space in the *honved*s' wagons. I wanted to give them a sign of sympathy, whisper to them some encouraging word, but did not dare utter a sound.

The following day we were put in the middle of the column. Behind us was the crowd of "free" civilians, in front, the retreating *honved*s with their Jews. We were to keep pace with the head column and, as my shoe problems hindered the march, I was being hit even more often by the angry guard. It was a very long and terribly cold day before we were ordered to a barn for an overnight stay.

It was still dark, before sunrise, when we got roused from our sleep by an unusual commotion, a multitude of voices cursing in Hungarian the "Jewish fucking s.o.b.'s," their whorish mothers, and so on. I had no idea what the cause of that tumult was until, after getting the "coffee" and daily portions of bread, we were led onto the road. I could not believe my eyes. I saw again the Hungarian Jews and understood what the commotion and cursing were all about. The Hungarian Jews were lying along the road, scores of them, frozen to death, as their fellow countrymen had kept them in the open during a terribly cold night. The *honved*s, who in their "orderly retreat" had no use for their Jews anymore, now, free of many, if not all of them, would try to disengage themselves quicker from the pursuing Russians.

But what was I doing in the midst of these damned *honveds* escaping westward? I must get rid of them as soon as possible. The sight of the frozen Jews sped up my resolve. But it did more than that. As the column got ready for its daily march, the angry guard beckoned to me and pointing his finger at the frozen Jews, said: "Get yourself a pair of good shoes." And I did just that. The frozen Jew gave up his shoes and socks easily, they passed from feet to feet as between siblings. The shoes, while a little too big, fit when I put my *portyanki* over the socks, which I now wore for the first time in more than a year. The guard, as he was inspecting my new shoes, was evidently gratified with himself. I felt no shame at what I did.

At night, lying on straw in another barn, I could not fall asleep. I thought about what I did to that frozen Jew. What was the difference, I was asking myself, between you and the Russian officer in the German POW camp who took the shoes off the feet of that Jewish boy before he was led to be shot? I could detect a dissimilarity as between the dead and the living, but whatever the difference, a dilemma was on my mind. I was too young, however, and in mortal danger myself, to have pangs of conscience for long. And so I spent a good deal of the rest of that night thinking about when and how to make a dash for freedom.

The heavy snow was blinding and artillery explosions in the back of us were coming closer and closer—it was high time to try to escape. All I now needed was the right place and moment. It came in a small town on a narrow street with sharp curves. When we turned at a ninety-degree angle, and the guard behind us momentarily lost sight of the column ahead of him, I slipped out and ran to a nearby house, knocking urgently on its door. It opened immediately and a woman, leaning forward, pushed into my hands some cooked potatoes. She was at her window, saw the poor men under guard and was looking for a chance to give them some food, when I came to her door. But I was not after potatoes. Surprised, as I entered the room and closed the door behind me, she pleaded: "Go, they will come after you and they will kill me too!" "I will stay just a few minutes," I told her while I was chewing the potatoes slowly, very slowly, delaying my exit. She in turn, looking again out of the window, her fears somewhat subsided, said to me calmly: "The street is already empty, not a living soul there, but before you go in this awful weather, have more potatoes with some warm milk, who knows when you will get your next meal."

It was early afternoon, and the main road intersection downtown was crowded with horse-drawn wagons and panicky people, civilians carrying their belongings and lightly armed *honveds* all going westward and hindering the push forward as many tried to get ahead of each other. I decided, of course, to go east, but at the same time to stay off main roads. I turned to a deserted dirt road. A few miles ahead was a kolkhoz in a Ukrainian village. As I entered the village I met a small boy who, all excited, told me cheerfully, "No soldiers in our place, nobody home, everybody at the meeting." I was somewhat surprised, a meeting, with everybody (or many) attending, at this time of the year, while the sound of gunfire was coming closer and closer. But the boy was not kidding. The collective farmers, mostly women, gathered at the kolkhoz's storage facilities, shouting loudly at each other, but mostly at the *starosta* (village elder), who together with a few other men—some seemed to be cripples—were sitting in front of them on a bench at a table covered with papers. They were deliberating whether or not the kolkhoz should distribute some of the foodstuffs kept in collective storage, basically grain and sunflower oil. Should the village become a battleground, it would be safer, many argued, to keep the stuff dispersed among individual members in their homes. In fact, they wanted to get a hand on what they had produced themselves, before it was too late, as they anticipated that with the return of the Soviets, the old ways of exploiting the kolkhoz would be restored. The *starosta*'s counterargument was that the storage facilities, having brick walls, were the safest in case of shooting or fire. "It is yours, at the right time, you'll get it all." This was greeted with such sarcastic remarks as "spare your throat," "castles in the air," "better an egg today than a hen tomorrow," and laughter and scorn.

After it was decided to immediately distribute the goods in question, I approached the *starosta*, asking him to allow me to stay in the kolkhoz overnight and perhaps another few days until it became safer for me to return home. He refused and started shouting at me, saying that he was forbidden to let strangers stay in the village. But at this point some kolkhoz women began yelling and outright threatening him: "You seem to forget that your days are over." I was thrilled with delight hearing this courageous talk; after all, the village was still under occupation! But the *starosta* was not sure of himself anymore and yielded at once. I was formally allowed to stay, and the *khozyaika* who volunteered to take me to her home was given some grits and oil on account of feeding me.

Night fell. Covered with my greenish jacket, I was resting on top of a traditional Russian oven, enjoying the warmth and coziness emanating from it, and listening to the sound of nearby firearms, when I suddenly heard the kicking of boots at the door. Several German frontline soldiers burst into this one-room house and, noticing my half-military jacket, pointed their semiautomatics at me and brutally pulled me down, barking: "*Soldat, russische Soldat!*" At this moment my hostess began frantically waving them away: "*Yakyzh vin soldat, tsesh moy synok!*" (What soldier, this is my little son!) That brave, short Ukrainian woman with a big heart saved my life. I am ashamed to admit that I do not even know her name, though I will never forget her.

The Germans had some milk and left as they came, on foot. They were perhaps a rear guard of a retreating unit, their motor vehicle on the outskirts of the village; or maybe, running from the Russians, they just got lost and cropped up in the village accidentally, I can only speculate. At any rate, these were the last German soldiers I was to see under occupation. Early the next morning, as I opened the door and walked onto the sparkling snow to bring water from the well, I had the impression of a new beginning. There was no shooting to be heard, the air was crisp, the straw roofs of the little huts were covered with white snow, and the entire village slept in its tranquillity, as if depicted on a postcard. "Don't be afraid of them," my hostess consoled me, "they are gone and will not come back, damn Germans." She spat in the direction they had gone. "As for you, have breakfast and go home, somebody is waiting for you."

As soon as I left the village and the dirt road leading out of it, I was again in the midst of army units moving west. But this time it was a delightful sight. Arriving mostly in trucks were Red Army soldiers armed with submachine guns, wearing winter hats with earflaps, sheepskin coats, and felt boots. The soldiers were waving back to the local inhabitants, who went out to welcome their liberators. It was 5 February 1943, near the town of Stary Oskol. The spearheads of the Soviet army, tank and armored units, were already much ahead, moving with lightning speed toward Kharkov and farther to the southwest, in an attempt to cut off and annihilate the German southern wing of the army retreating from the Caucasus and the Kerch Peninsula.

Before turning to a new chapter in my life, I must take up once more the story of the Hungarian Jews forced into the military labor battalions. Ever since I witnessed their plight and saw many of them tormented and later frozen to death, I have felt a kind of kinship with them. Was their lot known? What has been written about them? I wondered frequently. After researching the matter, what I have found in a good part of the literature proved to be frustrating. I got the impression of confusion and much whitewash. The fact that the German onslaught on Hungarian Jews came only in the summer of 1944, and that until that time they were incomparably better off than, say, Polish or German Jews, seems to have tempted many writers, unwittingly perhaps, to present the deeds of the Horty regime in the previous period in a too-favorable light, and, in particular, to gloss over the atrocities committed by the Hungarian Army and its officers against the Jews, who were herded into special units called, as if in derision, "labor service." For example, in a book published just after the war, when wartime memory of recent events should have been still fresh, the following assessment of the situation of Hungarian Jews in 1942–1943 is made: "At this time . . . Hungary stood like the refuge of the persecuted: of Jews and escaped prisoners of war alike . . . Hungarian Jews through their leaders advised the fulfillment of all German demands, only to avoid the horrors of a German occupation. . . . They asked only for lenient treatment of Jews called up for compulsory military labor." (J. Czebe and T. Petho, *Hungary in World War II: A Military History of the Years of War,* Budapest, 1946, p. 29). Fifty years later similar assessments are still present even in some of the Holocaust literature. I was quite surprised to find the following tip given to interviewers of the Holocaust survivors: "When interviewing survivors from Hungary, remember that many were not affected by the war until 1944" (*The Newsletter of the Survivors of the Shoa Visual History Foundation,* Los

Angeles March 1996). Even an authority of Elie Wiesel's caliber is not free of that kind of assessment. He describes the treatment of Hungarian Jews under Horty after the 1941 expulsions to Galicia were suspended: "Things had been relatively quiet for the Jews since Admiral Horty had taken power in Hungary . . . Exempted from military service, young Jewish males were drafted into the *Munkaszolgalat*, a kind of auxiliary force that accompanied the troops as quartermasters, digging antitank trenches in summer and cutting wood in winter. They did not complain unduly, nor did their families" (Elie Wiesel, *All Rivers Run to the Sea: Memoirs,* New York: Alfred A. Knopf, 1955, p. 29). Luckily, however, I found quite a few sources that corroborate my own evidence and provide data on numbers and the fate of Hungarian Jews in those military labor battalions. To quote just one such source: "The Jewish labor battalions, mostly commanded by rabidly anti-Semitic officers, were sent to the Ukraine. Of the roughly 40,000 sent, some 5,000 returned in 1943, and a few thousand were taken prisoner or escaped to the Russians. The rest were killed, mostly by Hungarian and German troops, or starved and beaten to death. The result was that young Jewish men were simply not there when the German onslaught on Hungarian Jewry came in 1944" (Y. Bauer, *Jews for Sale? Nazi-Jewish Negotiations, 1933–1945*, New Haven: Yale University Press, 1994, p. 148). According to other sources, in the winter of 1942–43 the number of Hungarian Jews on the eastern front had reached 50,000 and it is estimated that 40,000 to 43,000 of them died during the retreat, while several hundred were taken prisoner by the Russians.

Even at the lower estimates, if one takes into account that those 40,000 had in most cases families—mothers, fathers, sisters, brothers, aunts, uncles, and cousins—one easily arrives at a figure of about 200,000, about one-third of the total Hungarian Jewry at that time, more or less directly affected. Of course, like Jews elsewhere during the war, they had probably only vague notions about the fate of their loved ones and of the enormity of the crime in which "their" successive governments participated. For the latter, no possible excuse can be found and there should be no exoneration.

8. Liberation: The NKVD Verification Camp

On 6 February 1943 I celebrated the first day of my freedom in Stary Oskol. The railroad station was a heap of charred wreckage after the fighting a day or two earlier. Together with another liberated POW, we went looking for spoils on the freight trains, which came under fire and could not get away. Some oil tankers and gasoline barrels were still in flames, but many cars were full of goodies. We picked what was most valuable to our *khozyaika*, at whose hut we stayed and who told us exactly what she most needed: flour. This was going to be our gift to the hostess. With two big sacks of wheat flour on our backs, we became welcome guests. Soon plates full of scrambled eggs appeared on the table, followed by the most delicious *bliny* (pancakes) I ever ate. Our *khozyaika* entertained us even with a bottle of smelly moonshine.

A couple of days later I went to the newly established office of the city's military commandant to ask what to do next. I was not the only one there. Several other people, former Red Army soldiers and POWs who managed to get out of German hands, were already sitting on benches waiting to be admitted to the commandant's room. The atmosphere was unfriendly and tense. Some were saying nervously in low voices that former POWs suspected of desertion or collaboration with the Germans were sometimes shot on the spot without any court. They exaggerate, I thought, it couldn't be like that. I entered the commandant's office smiling, but he did not reciprocate, and our conversation was very brief. He told me, like he did all the others, to go to the city of Kalach on the Don, to an NKVD camp *na provyerku* (for a "checkup"). What is there to "check up"? I asked, and to my surprise heard his answer: "Haven't you just been with the Germans? There will be a thorough checkup on your conduct." When I asked my next question about the means of transportation to Kalach, he turned his wry face to me. "By what means? *Na swoikh, na dvoikh.*" (On horse of ten toes.) I got a similar answer when I inquired about food rations: "Provide yourself."

Kalach on the Don, located some forty miles west of Stalingrad, was far away from Stary Oskol. I was neither clothed nor physically or mentally prepared for such a journey on foot in the midst of another cold, harsh winter. Fortunately, many Red Army trucks, going eastward to pick up supplies for frontline troops, were mostly empty and their drivers were willing to give a ride and have a chat and a smoke with recently liberated POWs. As soon as I left the city in the company of two other travelers going, like myself, to the special NKVD camp "for checking," we waved at a passing light truck, the driver stopped, and I clambered up into the box. The two others sat in the front next to the driver.

The first hundred miles of our voyage, though not smooth, were uneventful. As we came closer to the Don River, we found ourselves on vast steppe tracts, all snow-covered and sparsely dotted with small villages. The only people on the road on foot whom we saw from time to time were German, Romanian, Italian, and Hungarian POWs, long lines of them trudging eastward. It was now their turn! They walked wearily, scarves and blankets wrapped round their heads and backs, rugs wrapped over their boots or shoes, or perhaps just over their bare feet. Very few armed Russian soldiers accompanied them. There was really no need to guard them, as there was nowhere for them to escape.

Almost at the end of our journey, in the eastern loop of the Don River, our half truck's engine refused to respond to the driver's curses. Taking turns, all four of us got busy trying to crank the old, stubborn engine, but to no avail. As we stood on the road, leaning on the truck, we were approached by a group of unguarded Hungarian POWs who looked even more miserable than those prisoners of war we saw passing from our truck. One of the Hungarians, the blanket on his back covered with frosty snow, icicles hanging around his eyes and from his nose, asked in half Russian, half Hungarian:

"Pozhaluystya skazhite, hova Sziberia?" (Please, tell us the direction to Siberia?) Poor guy, he had not yet reached the Volga.

Twenty years later, in Warsaw, a friend of mine mentioned the episode with those Hungarian POWs to a popular Polish writer, Wojciech Zukrowski. He was interested in the story, as he was preparing a novel, its plot centering on Hungary during World War II. We met and I described to him in detail the time, place, and the appearance of those poor, miserable Hungarian POWs. About a year later, I received a copy of Zukrowski's book *Kamienne Tablice* (Tables of stone) with a nice personal dedication. Hanna, always the avid reader, read it first and I heard her laughing herself into fits. "Look what he did to your story," she called to me. I turned to the relevant pages of the novel and could not believe my eyes. As the author described it, not far from Stalingrad a Hungarian military unit, in clean uniforms, was marching into captivity; they knew they were going to Siberia, but with admirable dignity were keeping their heads high, looking forward to a brighter future. What *licentia poetica* can do!

The NKVD "verification" camp was located on a guarded poultry farm on the outskirts of the city of Kalach on the east side of the Don River. Inmates, housed in chicken coops, were all from the recently liberated territories—policemen, *starostas* (village headmen), priests, draft dodgers, deserters, escapee POWs—all alike under suspicion of collaboration with the enemy. The chicken coops were extremely overcrowded. We slept on floors covered sparsely with straw. At night people were stepping over the bodies of snoring men. Even in daytime, moving from place to place, one would inevitably tread on someone's legs. Only lice had complete freedom of movement; the place was crawling with them and they were creeping into all our private parts. There were no washing facilities of any kind inside the chicken houses. As the doors were kept closed, both for security reasons and because of the cold winter, the air inside was foul and full of smoke; at times the stench was overwhelming. Going out to the latrines, where, while relieving ourselves, one could get a breath of fresh air, was strictly regulated. Worst of all, however, was hunger. The food was meager, about a pound of claylike bread and tealike hot water in the evening, and two *balandas* (watery soups), one for breakfast, the other for lunch. The most frequent word one could hear was *pozhrat-by* (to devour something). Newcomers asking, *"Kak kormyat?"* (How's the food?) would typically be answered: *"Zhyt budesh, no yebat ne zakhochesh"* (You'll live, but fuck you will not).

Funny thing! In the German POW camp, where I was literally starving, I never had dreams about food. Now, on a meager but not yet a starvation diet—which I somewhat supplemented by bartering my *makhorka* (an inferior kind of tobacco) for bread—I would in my dreams almost night after night find myself in a bakery full of bread and its aromatic smells. I would devour loaf after loaf of all the kinds of bread I ever ate in my life, and being hungry still, would eat more and more of it. To awake from those dreams and, after having gorged myself on that delicious bread, feel very hungry was such a disappointment! That's how I celebrated my twenty-second birthday.

My investigator was in his thirties, had decent manners, and treated me rather politely. He began by filling out a kind of questionnaire, and this took a long time, almost the entire first interrogation, because of the somewhat unusual data of my biography. "Name?" I was trying briefly to explain that Diomin Ivan Filipovich was a fake name, and why I changed my name. It aroused his suspicion. "What, then, is your real name?" There was again some difficulty with my patronymic: Mayer-Chaim. "What?" I repeated. "What kind of a name is that? It's Mikhail, so say it!" As he wrote down, "Temkin, Gavryil Mikhailovich," I said to myself: "Have it your way." And so, from then on, it remains with me in all my documents. "Where were you born?" was another problematic item, but the interrogator seemed to be satisfied with my answer; being born in Lodz, Poland, seemed to have "explained" both my accented Russian and why I was—as I told him—transferred from the regular army into labor battalions. Knowledge of foreign languages was the next hitch; my interrogator sounded as if he had finally caught me lying: "Your knowledge of the German language was of help under occupation, wasn't it?" I replied to this, stressing every word: "I never pronounced even a single sentence in German, neither in the POW camp nor in all those months under occupation." His last question: "Who might tell us how you conducted yourself under occupation?" "I think," I said, "it might be best to ask the people in the village of Olkhov Log, where I was staying for quite a while, almost until liberation; of course, they knew me under my assumed name of Diomin Ivan Filipovich." As the interrogation seemed to have come to an end, I asked if I could write a letter to my wife, Hanna, who had been evacuated from Gomel to Kamensk Uralski. My interrogator wrote something down in his notes and, after a pause, told me to remind him about it next time I was summoned.

The next time was more than two weeks later. I had a fever and felt lousy, but I had to face my interrogator pretending I was okay. "First, some old business we have to take care of," he said, putting before me a handwritten sheet of paper. "This is the record of our previous conversation. Read it carefully and, if anything is not to your liking, tell me before you sign it." Indeed, I did not like a few things, particularly what he ascribed to me: "Knowledge of the German language was helpful under occupation." He corrected this and some other phrases, and, after I put my signature on the bottom of that "document," thinking the interrogation was all over, I heard him saying: "Well, now that we have the questionnaire behind us, let's turn to serious matters." Alarmed and confused, I did not wait for the questioning and, rather anticipating it, referred to what I naïvely believed would prove that under any circumstances I could not have been a German collaborator. "You seem to suspect," I said, "that I might have collaborated with the Germans, but that has not been the case, and could not have happened anyway, if not for any other reason than just because I am a Jew!" My interrogator burst out laughing. He could have proved, if need be, that I was an elephant and not just a collaborator of the German Fascists. But he did not pursue his previous line of questioning. Instead, he wanted to know about life in prewar Poland, not just my life, but about living conditions in the country in general. He seemed really interested—not as an interrogator, just as a Soviet man—in the kind of life people were living abroad. "It was good in capitalist Poland, wasn't it? There was plenty of food and everything in the stores? Each family in the cities had its own apartment?" All questions, not a single statement on his part. I was taken aback and, as I regained my composure, was cautiously trying to dampen the outburst of the NKVD man's admiration for life in capitalist Poland. The second-time interrogation ended with his promise to send my letter to Hanna. "Bring it to me and it will be sent by military mail service."

I had not given any letter to my interrogator, because I was afraid it might entrap Hanna in some trouble with the NKVD. Yet, on the basis of the interrogation, my own and that of my comrades from the chicken house, I was under the impression that we were indeed in a kind of "filtration" camp and that our NKVD investigators were after real collaborators only. That impression, in hindsight, seems quite reasonable. Had the interrogators been given set quotas of "guilty"— as was often the case in "regular" NKVD investigations—I would have probably never gotten out of the poultry farm. I was no doubt a good candidate for the category "guilty unless proven innocent," and would have had no chance whatsoever to prove the latter. As the Russian saying goes, *Dokazhi chto ty ne verblud* (Prove that you are not a camel). "The army needs reinforcements badly"—these were probably the orders under which NKVD investigators operated in Kalach on the Don camp.

I should add here some figures which, while writing this memoir, became known to me thanks to the opening of archives in Russia. In August 1942 Stalin sanctioned the construction of three special concentration camps where the NKVD could "check" former POWs and German collaborators. In 1943, the troops of the NKVD, who were responsible for security in the rear of the active Red Army, in the process of cleaning up the territory liberated from the enemy, arrested 931,549 people to be "checked." Of these, 582,515 were servicemen and 349,034 were civilians. "Of the total number, 80,296 have been unmasked and detained as spies, traitors, members of punitive squads, deserters, bandits and similar criminal elements." (See D. Volkogonov, *Stalin: Triumph and Tragedy*, pp. 439, 446.)

9. Typhus: Hospital in Kalach

In the meantime, I became ill. Typhus, which had always been rampant in Russia during times of war and famine, erupted in the chicken houses, and I, too, succumbed to it. I felt hot, weak, ceased to be hungry and—unheard of in my experience—did not care anymore about my bread rations. "Store it or barter for *makhorka* (tobacco), those who survive typhus get hungry like wolves," I had been cautioned, but I was giving away bread as if for me there was no tomorrow. With rickettsial fever, I was taken to a quarantine room, packed with likewise sick people, lice crawling over their faces and sometimes even getting into their eyes. There I spent several days in broken sleep until, completely unconscious, I was taken to a hospital in the city.

When I eventually opened my eyes, I was lying in a bed on a white sheet, covered with a clean, warm blanket. "Where am I?" I asked my neighbors. "*Chort vozhmi*" (Gosh), one of them exclaimed, "he woke up for good; we thought you had died, and were looking for somebody who could say a prayer for your soul." A friendly face of a young woman, a white kerchief on her head, leaned over me as she put her palm on my forehead, then gazed at me and said: *"Chto bylo, to proshlo"* (Whatever it was, it's over by now). She encouraged me to drink a little something, which turned out to be American-supplied powdered milk, but I felt no desire for food.

I wrote the letter to Hanna, the first one since I became a POW. It was short, only a few words awkwardly scribbled with a still-unsteady hand. Days and nights were passing, and I began slowly to convalesce, the unmistakable sign of which was getting hungry, very hungry.

Our hospital ward was separated from those housing the wounded. So, fortunately, I was spared the constant sight of men who lost their legs, arms, hands, or eyes. Our ward was for typhus cases only and was populated mostly by the inmates of the poultry farm, but also by regular army soldiers who were victims of the same disease. It was easy though to distinguish one from the other. Those still on the NKVD books were on the average less animated than the free army soldiers. I tried to raise the spirits of some I knew as former POWs as well as to reassure myself. "They will let us go as soon as they make sure we are innocent, won't they?" But my comrades were pessimistic. "You are perhaps innocent, but no doubt naïve," said one, while the other added: "*Byla by spina, naydetsya i vina*" (As long as you have a back, there will be a load for it).

The food in the hospital, considering severe wartime shortages, was, if not adequate, quite tasty: We were getting soup, millet kasha with real American butter in it, scrambled eggs made of American egg powder, fruit tea with sugar, and a tiny piece of white bread with a spoon of American lard on it for dessert. However, instead of "real" bread, there was zwieback (toasted biscuit). It was considered to be dietary and most appropriate for those hospitalized. But young men recovering from typhus were permanently hungry on that diet and were complaining, especially about the bread substitute; zwieback would have been good as a snack for nibbling, but not as a staple food.

Still, all those already out of bed seemed to have been happy with their hospital stay. The regular army soldiers, having survived a terrible disease, were now enjoying a unique furlough, unique because turning out wounded or sick in a hospital had been the only legally available furlough a soldier could have gotten during all the years of war. In addition, those regular army soldiers could expect an extension of that furlough, as they would be permitted to go home for a couple of weeks, like some of the seriously wounded recuperating in other wards. The reason for that generosity toward those not seriously wounded, but just sick? Quite simple. Those recovering from typhus would still be carriers of that disease, harboring it in their organs for many weeks and thus capable of spreading it to others. And so it was a protective measure intended to shield the army by keeping away potential "causative agents" of such diseases as typhus. The matter of furloughs was much on the mind of regular army soldiers, while for us, the poultry farm inmates, it was rather an unpleasant subject even to listen to. Somebody belonging to this group, playing the wit, quoted a phrase which he ascribed to Lenin: "Generally speaking, we are all here dead men on a furlough"— meaning on furlough from life eternal. But this sounded to me more like a quote from some religious writer, and I doubted it was really a Lenin saying.

At any rate, except for those still very sick, all the other patients in our ward, including people from the poultry farm like myself, were having a rather good time in the hospital, free for a while from front duties as well as from the dreaded NKVD men. I was reading books and newspapers, especially enjoying the writings of Ilya Ehrenburg, Boris Gorbatov, Konstantin Simonov, Alexander Tvardovski, and Wanda Wasilewska—mainly war dispatches, but also some wartime novels and poems. Among the latter, most popular was *Vassily Tyorkin* by Tvardovski. The hero—a private with common sense and a gay character, fighting a war not for glory but for life on earth—was liked by everybody. The patients in our ward were always asking for their favorite reading materials, some new comic and tragic adventures of Vassily Tyorkin. Newspapers were available, and I found reports about the work of Jewish intellectuals and artists in an antifascist committee led by Mikhoels, the outstanding Jewish actor and director of the Yiddish State Theater in Moscow, later so tragically killed on Stalin's orders. We listened to the radio, to frontline and world news, to the beautiful old Russian and new wartime songs.

Above all, however, we were engaging in interesting chats, sometimes lasting all day. "Let's tell each other about life before the war," someone would suggest, and there was no shortage of storytellers. As a rule they were rather nostalgic and bragged about the past. Typically they would tell how everything was in the stores, how on days off they would go out necking with the most charming girls, go to the movies, have the most delicious ice cream—in short it was *zhizn malina* (life—a raspberry). From those who were married, one could sometimes hear a worrying sigh: *Zhena bez muzha—vdovy khuzhe* (A wife with no husband—worse off than a widow). But most would listen with admiration, some like children with their mouths slightly open, to all kinds of life stories, the more unusual—as long as they were "true"—the better. "Tell us, Gavryusha," I would be asked, "about life in that faraway country, Poland—but something really interesting." Skeptics and connoisseurs were not satisfied, however, with my story. I would have to tell more next time, they demanded, and explain how it felt leaving Poland for Russia and why I ended up in the mess I was in. And many were nodding their heads approvingly when somebody judged me, *umnaya golova, da duraku dostalas* (a wise head given to a fool).

Too many inmates were having a jolly good time in the hospital for too long, and the NKVD finally decided to clear up the situation. They came up with several truly "Solomonic decisions." First of all, most who survived in the hospital, I among them, were to be cleared of charges. However, while we were not considered—at least for the time being—potential enemy agents, we still remained potential "causative agents" of typhus. For that reason we would not be ordered back to the chicken houses. Instead, NKVD men installed themselves in a hospital room, where most of us, ordered in one at a time, would listen to the same verdict consisting of three words: *Vozvratit' v stroy* (To be returned into service). What about a leave home? We all got a clear, though perhaps not quite logical, answer to that question: *Otpusk domoy vam, kak ne v sostavye Krasnoy Armii, ne polagayetsya* (Not being in the ranks of the Red Army, you have no right to a furlough). Thus, soldiers who got sick in the army, now, as a precaution against the spread of typhus in its ranks, would be heading home (to carry the typhus home?). At the same time, by the twisted bureaucratic logic of the NKVD, those in their charge were being sent to the army, though possibly still carriers of that dreadful disease. However, probably to cover their backs, the NKVD men were not sending us to the front by train, which would have brought us there quickly. Instead, we were to reach it in very small groups, on foot, a couple hundred miles away, with no fixed time limit. I was in a group of three. Two of us, Sergey and I, both were hospital patients with typhus, the third, Misha, a healthy army sergeant. He was put in charge, given our papers, provided with ration cards for food at military supply depots on the way, and ordered to arrive in "reasonable" time at the point of destination.

It was early spring, the weather was gorgeous, but I was sour. Another dreadful voyage on foot while I was still very weak, permanently hungry, and unsteady on my feet! It would take weeks to cover on foot the distance of 300 to 350 miles. And how would I manage to walk all those miles, day after day, in my woeful condition? Misha, however, the healthy guy in charge of the two *slabo-silnye* (weaklings), was in an upbeat mood and making fun of my worries. "Stupid, it wasn't for nothing they named you Gavrylo (the proverbial fool). What are you afraid of, you'll miss the bus and you'll be too late for your funeral? Had they taken you to the front by train, you would have been there next day and, in your condition, you would be gone a day after. Listen to me, both of you good-for-nothings, death is patient and will get us anyway. In the meantime, you'll see, *"Na babushkinom atestate my zazhivyem"* (On Granny's vouchers, we'll live and prosper). Misha was smart and, as it turned out, he was not bluffing about his promise. What he meant, however, by "grandmothers" was not clear to me until we actually entered cossack country in the large bend of the Don River.

Before turning to that voyage, I must mention what, in hindsight, I think was the main reason for our speedy discharge from the NKVD verification camp. The Red Army needed reinforcements much more desperately than I could have imagined.

When we left Kalach on the Don River, the last act of the high drama between the Donets and the Dnieper was already over. It began with Stalin's bold plan, probably his greatest blunder as a strategist. After the defeat of the Germans at Stalingrad, and the disintegration of their allies—the Romanians, the Italians, and the Hungarians—a two hundred–mile gap from Voroshilovgrad on the Donets to Voronezh on the Don was yawning and into it Stalin had been driving strong mobile forces since the end of January 1943. They crossed the Donets River and, in the beginning of February, reached out toward the Dnieper and southward to the Sea of Azov. The objective of Stalin's bold plan was to overtake the Germans before they got to that huge river, and encircle and annihilate them east of the Dnieper. Moreover, as an extension of this plan, he conceived a new grand operation in which his troops would cross the Dnieper, move south toward the Black Sea, block the approaches out of the Crimea, and thus cut off the entire southern group of the

Wehrmacht. That bold if not reckless plan code-named Star involved a penetration of about 150 miles on top of the near 250 miles Soviet troops had already advanced from under Stalingrad. Operation Star was frustrated mainly by Marshal Manstein's clever strategy of improvised blows against the Soviet breakthrough west of the Donets River. By the end of February, his mobile divisions had caught between pincers the Soviet Sixth Army plus an armored corps—the powerful spearhead of General Nikolai Vatutin's army group—subsequently smashing them west of the Donets River.

After the war I was thrilled to see, in a Soviet military history book, a map titled "The year 1943—the radical turning point in the war (19 November 1942–December 1943)." On the map were big arrows running uninterruptedly westward from the Volga through the Don, Donets, Dnieper, and beyond. Of course, it is true that 1943, on the whole, had been the war's breakthrough year, and that the victorious Red Army reached at the end of that year the points indicated on the map. To pretend, however, that it was a year of an uninterrupted march forward borders on falsification of military history. The fact is that the Soviet 1942–43 winter offensive was driven a couple of hundred miles back after its spearheads were cut off by Manstein, who gave an entire Soviet army an awful thrashing west of the Donets River, which indeed became the front line for the next several months, from the beginning of March to mid-July 1943. Only years after the war were these facts acknowledged, and still rather in general terms, by semiofficial Soviet sources: "The attacks of the enemy's seven tank and motorized divisions against the flanks and rear of the Sixth Army and Popov's group forced our troops into a desperate fighting retreat south of Kharkov and then across the Donets . . . By 4 March the enemy had regrouped and delivered a deep thrust in the Kharkov-Belgorod direction. The situation grew steadily worse every day and finally became critical in the extreme" (S. M. Shtemenko, *The Soviet General Staff at War (1941–1945),* Book One, Moscow: Progress Publishers, 1985, p. 175). How critical? According to German sources, more than six hundred tanks, four hundred guns, and six hundred antitank guns had been destroyed; twenty-three thousand Soviet dead littered the battlefield. These added to the wounded meant an effective loss of one hundred thousand Soviet troops. Only nine thousand were taken prisoner, a comparatively low figure, which indicates that a considerable number of troops managed to make good their escape across the frozen Donets, but without weapons, vehicles, and equipment. The Germans could claim a little revenge for Stalingrad.

The magnitude of that defeat was, of course, unknown to me at the time I left Kalach, though I heard rumors about the havoc the Germans spread among Soviet troops between the Dnieper and the Donets. I also knew that since mid-March the front line ran again along the Donets River, with Kharkov and Belgorod recaptured by the Wehrmacht. That was where we were heading at the very beginning of April 1943.

10. The Not-So-Quiet Don

The sight of the region through which we were now wandering brought back to my mind the stories I heard in my childhood about its inhabitants. This was Don cossacks country. My parents used to tell us children about the cruelty of the cossacks, recalling vividly incidents of how they mistreated Jews in the city of Lodz before World War I. Even more gruesome were the stories of the evil deeds they committed on the Jews of the shtetl of Komarow, my father's hometown, during the Soviet-Polish war in the summer of 1920. The Red Army was advancing toward Warsaw to hasten a revolution in Europe, while some units of that army, by now "Red" cossacks, engaged on the way in pogroms. At that time Komarow had a population of about three thousand, of which sixty-five percent were Jews. The survivors of the pogrom—among them my grandmother and some of her children—were still filled with horror years later when they recalled the indiscriminate killings, rapes, and looting, and the desecration of the Komarow synagogue.

Pogroms—the savage killing of Jews by the cossacks—had a long tradition going back to the sixteenth and seventeenth centuries, and in particular to Bogdan Khmelnitsky (1595–1657), who led his Ukrainian warriors in successful bloody rebellions against the Poles. His "free warrior" have-nots revenged themselves on the haves, butchering anyone dressed in Polish style and lynching Catholics, but the Jews were always their favorite target. From then on, the cossacks emulated their forebears. Thousands of Jewish men, women, and children had been slaughtered whenever the cossacks came close to their hamlets. No wonder that the fear of cossacks was so deeply embedded in the Jewish psyche.

The Don cossacks had their own hero, Stenka Razin (?–1671), renowned and immortalized in folklore. While Bogdan and his Ukrainian cossacks finally swore submission to the tsar, Stenka became a rebel leader against tsarist domination and, having been finally caught, was brought to Moscow, where his tempestuous head was cut off in Red Square. It is said that before the bandit became revolutionary, leading his cossacks against the tsar, he and his band would go in their *chaiki* (boats) up the Don to the point where it flows closest to the Volga, drag the vessels across the elbow of land between the two rivers, and there, with Russian commercial traffic before their eyes, turn to piracy. As the city of Kalach stood at that point, our trio was entering on foot places perhaps treaded by Stenka Razin and his band of cossack pirates some 280 years earlier.

Cossack warriors were usually fighting somewhere for or against somebody and something. The men's military duties left women to do much of the farmwork. Cossack villages were always populated by women. As the cossacks were not permitted to bring womenfolk on expeditions, their wives stayed home awaiting their return. Women were a pastime, like drinking and fighting. But the womenfolk were as free as the men to change partners, and participated as freely in cossack orgies of drink and sex—at least that was what eyewitnesses had reported. The cossacks' attitude toward women is well depicted in a famous folktale about Stenka Razin. During one of his pirate expeditions he made a Persian woman of great beauty his mistress, but could not take her home with him. So, after a last night of feasting and passion on the banks of the Volga, he lifted up the unsuspecting woman, carried her to the water's edge, and threw her into the river. As he did so, Stenka declared to the mother of Russian rivers: "I have had so much from you and given you nothing, now I offer you the thing dearest to me. Volga-Mother, accept my gift!" So much for folklore.

The effects of World War I and the Civil War in terms of cossack lives had been horrific, and the losses were greatest among the young. A generation before, young men had outnumbered the young women. By 1920, there were only four men to every seven girls between the ages of seventeen and twenty-four. As the battles of the Civil War raged back and forth in Don cossack territory, brother fought brother. Sholokhov, in his masterly epic ironically named *The*

Quiet Don tracks the wavering of his cossack hero between the Red and White causes. Most cossacks were on the side of the Whites, but there were also Red cossacks, for example, in the well-known First Cavalry Army, which included Don and Kuban cossacks commanded by Semyon Budienny. However, the Reds had no trust in their cossacks. When Trotsky in the summer of 1919 inspected the new Cossack Corps of the Red Army, he judged its leader, Budienny, to be "the Stenka Razin of today." But he was none too sure of his reliability. "Where he leads his gang," he wrote, "there will they go; for the Reds today, tomorrow for the Whites." The cossacks, even the Red ones, were likewise distrustful of the new regime. When the time comes, says one of Babel's *Red Cavalry* characters, the Bolshevik rule will "rub them down with a brush of iron."

A decade later and the steel broom had been set in motion. Collectivizing the cossacks was to reduce them in effect to serfdom, a condition from which they had originally escaped to become free men. No wonder they resisted more fiercely than others. Thousands of cossacks, again mostly young men, were shot or dragged off to forced labor camps and forced settlements in Siberia.

Another decade passed, and when Hitler invaded the Soviet Union in 1941, 100,000 cossacks were serving in the Red Army. Tens of thousands more were conscripted as the war progressed. On the other hand, under German tutelage the cossack regiments of Krasnov were formed to fight against the Soviets. And as the German conquest of the Don and the Kuban proceeded in the summer of 1942, cossack collaborators began to appear. Many of them accompanied the German Army's retreat from under Stalingrad later. Joining those who defected or volunteered in POW camps, they had been welded into cossack divisions along—or merged—with so-called *Osttruppen* (Eastern Troops) to fight on the German side. As I walked through the Don cossack villages, liberated just three months before, I had the impression that all the male youth of conscription age and younger left together with the Germans—or perhaps earlier—voluntarily or involuntarily.

I saw there a region not much different from many other Russian and Ukrainian places. It was open steppe with few good roads, almost no cities or towns, a land of sparsely scattered villages, some of which in the past used to be *stanitsa*s (fortified villages) along the Don, Chir,

Khoper, and other rivers. The houses here were larger and more comfortable than elsewhere, and the livestock more visible, a sign of relatively higher living standards, but not remarkably different from the Soviet countryside I saw elsewhere. What was unusual and striking was the sight of the *Cossachki* (cossack women).

They stood in front of their houses, singly or in small groups, chatting, and, as the three of us were passing, politely waving at us with loud invitations to stay with them for dinner and overnight. It was a scene that would repeat itself with almost no variations in many cossack villages. Never before or after had I seen ordinary women behaving like that. True, many were by no means ordinary. Young, shapely, attractive—perhaps one of the finest physical types one can find in Russia—these women seemed to be starved for sex, showing their sensuality freely. There was no pretending, no flirtation, no kidding around about "serious" or "lasting" relationships, just a smile expressing a liking of the companionship and the need for a sexual partner. And to my surprise I could not find anything undignified in their demeanor, it all seemed so natural. Diogenes, the ancient cynic, is said to have carried a lantern in daytime looking for a "man," someone who had the true human virtues. The *Cossachki* were not in a position to be choosy, they were looking for a "man"— any man deserving that name not in a moral just in a physical sense—but, because of an extreme scarcity of that species, they had no less difficulty than Diogenes.

Misha, a handsome, muscular man full of glee, was obviously most desirable, though either Sergey or I would also be welcome by those left with no other choice—half a loaf is better than none. But the three of us decided to stay together. That decision would evoke protests. Each of the ladies wanted a man for herself, and so they would follow with competitive bids, one saying she had lots of eggs and a couple of chickens to offer, the other had just slaughtered a pig, and so on. As Misha was inflexible, they could not hide their disappointment. "Why all together? It'll be more comfortable for everyone to stay at a different home." But Misha would make it clear no such arrangement was negotiable, our trio was indivisible. He was gracious enough to protect the two weaklings in his charge without making fun of them.

Once a particular invitation had been accepted, everything else was quite predictable and unpretentious. For dinner the four of us would have borsch, potatoes, gruel, pickles, meat, and moonshine. We often slept in the same large kitchen room, the three of us on straw or hay on the floor, the *Cossachka* on her bed or on the top of the oven. Misha would soon join her, and the other two of us, before falling asleep, would hear their voices, giggling, and heavy breathing. In the morning, our hostess, all smiles, would serve the three of us a sumptuous breakfast. But if Misha did not come up to expectations, we would be getting no breakfast at all; our *Cossachka* would demonstrate disappointment, busying herself with chores in the yard.

Misha was often complaining of being completely exhausted. Though sometimes he just boasted of his exploits, judging from the noises in the middle of the night, he was perhaps not exaggerating much. At any rate, when he needed some rest, he would refuse all invitations from young women. We were then looking instead for a house of an older lady, but it had to be a house with a cow, Misha would insist. *Korova na dvore, kharch na stole* (A cow in the yard, food on the table).

11. In the Reserve Regiment

The month of April was coming to an end. Good food, fresh air, and leisure put Sergey and me back on our feet. We regained our physical strength, while Misha, whom we owed much for our recuperation, may have lost a couple of pounds. In accordance with the *putevka* (traveling orders) issued by the NKVD, he brought us to the *zapasnoy polk* (reserve regiment) stationed at the northern tip of the Donets basin, where so-called "marching companies" were being formed and dispatched to the nearby front lines on the Donets River.

I stayed in that reserve regiment only a couple of days, just enough to be enlisted as private of the 4th *Marshevaya Rota* (marching company), go through a refreshing shower in a field *banya* (bath), and receive a new military uniform, shoes, a knapsacklike bag, a spare pair of underwear, and a soft cap to cover the top of the head. There were no helmets, which anyway were as a rule discarded by field soldiers in frontline conditions because they were uncomfortable. I had seen helmets being used for cooking potatoes in our labor battalion. For one tall guy in our squad, whom everyone called "Baldy" because of his closely shaved head, even that soft cap seemed to be too heavy. "I have enough worries on my head and must keep it cool," he would cut off any inquiries. He was ten years older than me and had already managed to get wounded twice. He lost touch with his frontline unit, which was why he turned out to be in the reserve regiment. Befriending me in a kind of an uncle-nephew relationship, he, not very talkative, whispered into my ear as if it were a state secret: "They won't keep us long in reserve." He was the first among us to treat lightly the fact that because of a shortage of rifles, our squad remained unarmed. "That shit is clumsy, heavy, and of little use, we'll get ourselves submachine guns."

He would answer my questions with a reassurance. "Keep close to me, you have a lot to learn." In that he was quite right and, moreover, what I needed to learn could come only from experience.

As I did not smoke, I would give Baldy my tobacco. He was grateful, and used the occasion to give a talk on the unfairness of the distribution of rations in the army. "Two things," he said, "bread and tobacco, should be distributed according to needs, and not according to the silly equal stomach principle. Take bread, the food most important for a human being. Is it fair to give everybody, a big guy like myself and a small guy like you—no offense, Gavryusha—the same daily *payok* (ration)?" I had to admit that he needed much more bread than I, though I, too, needed more food, not necessarily bread. Still, Baldy was very careful in sharing with me our soup equally. We ate from the same *kotelok* (mess tin), using approximately the same size wooden spoons. We would eat by turns, I a spoonful then he a spoonful, and so on, slowly, as becoming among comrades. Having finished the soup or kasha, we would lick clean our personal spoons and put them back in place, where they were customarily kept—behind the top of the right or left boot. Frontline soldiers would sometimes, in panicky retreats, throw away their heavy rifles, but never their spoons.

Baldy was probably the only one in our 4th Marching Company to completely ignore a propaganda lecture on the theme "You'll soon have the honor of fighting for our motherland." He did not show up for the talk. Apart from that major theme, the *politruk* was answering questions raised by some young conscripts, most of whom were from the territories liberated during the winter offensive. "What about military training? We had none." As I was in the same boat, my ears were on alert when the *politruk* replied, *"Nichevo, tam nauchat"* (Never mind, there you'll learn).

One morning, before going with my platoon for the drill with wooden rifles, I was ordered to appear immediately at the *osobyi otdel* (special section that was responsible for counterintelligence and security within the Soviet armed forces). An officer in an NKVD-like uniform had in front of him a file with the papers Misha had brought from Kalach. "Where were you born? When did you enter the Soviet Union? In what labor battalion did you serve before becoming a POW? When and where were you liberated?" Having compared my answers with what he had in his file, he was again questioning me about Poland. "Was your former citizenship Polish?" Finally he crossed out something on a paper in front of him, and I was dismissed. I had no idea what it was that he crossed out. Only a couple of weeks later would I learn that it was my name.

Why had my name been crossed out? Even today, writing these memoirs, I can provide only an educated guess. The last time I read a newspaper before coming to the reserve regiment was the beginning of April, when I left the Kalach hospital. If I had been better informed, I would have known the Soviet version of a terrible story which the NKVD man in that regiment knew for sure. On 13 April 1943 the Germans announced the uncovering of mass graves of thousands of Polish officers in the Katyn forest near Smolensk. The Germans charged the Soviet authorities with murder and appointed a multinational medical commission to probe the matter. The Soviet authorities flatly rejected these charges, claiming that the murder had been committed by the Germans after they occupied the area in July 1941. In mid-April 1943, when the Polish government-in-exile demanded that an investigation of the Katyn killings be made by the International Red Cross, the Soviet Union reacted by severing relations with the government-in-exile. This was announced on 25 April. It was to have far-reaching effects on relations between the Soviet Union and Poland. Now, a half a century later, the Katyn massacre is already well-documented history. There is no doubt that it was done by the NKVD on Stalin's orders.

Of course, the officer of the special section in the reserve regiment was well informed about the breaking of Soviet-Polish relations. And he was a vigilant NKVD officer. Coming across a former Polish citizen with family ties in German-occupied territories, he evidently needed instructions what to do about the "special case." That was probably why he crossed my name off the list of the 4th Marching Company.

My mother Helena (left), and Hanna. Photos were taken in prewar Poland. I kept them throughout the war and concealed them while in German captivity.

My father Chaim, born in 1887, around 1914. The author in 1939.

From left to right, front: my brother Moses and I. Middle: my sister Pola. Second row: my brother Jakub, cousin Renia, my father and mother. Photo taken in the countryside near Lodz, summer 1926. Except for Jakub and me, they all perished in the Holocaust.

With Hanna in the countryside. Summer 1938.

September 1939. A German soldier is amusing himself by cutting the beard of an old Polish Jew and humiliating him. (Jewish Historical Institute, Warsaw, Poland)

A Jew of Lodz wearing the Star of David. (YIVO archive)

A Jew being frisked and
mocked by German sol-
diers on a street of Lodz.
(YIVO archive)

In front of the office of
the Eldest of the Jews
clamboring for help.
(YIVO archive)

A ghetto bridge at rush hour. (YIVO archive)

Children working in the Lodz ghetto.(Photographer: Mendel Grossman.
YIVO archive)

Deportations out of the Lodz ghetto, 1942. (Photographer: Mendel Grossman. YIVO archive)

Deportees passing the ruins of the Old City Synagogue on Wolborska Street. (YIVO archive)

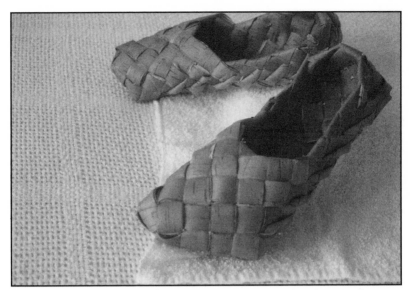

Lapti (bast shoes). I wore a similar pair while in a labor battalion in February-March 1942. They saved my feet from freezing. (Halina Zawadzka)

From left to right: Timoshkin, the author, and Titov. Hungary, November-December 1944.

With senior lieutenant Rochlis—the divisional translator.

Colonel Shevchenko in front of a field map with staff officers of the 458 Rifle Regiment. I stand in middle row fifth from right.

With my friend Andrey Kravchenko, shortly before he was killed in November 1944. On the left is Urazmukhambetov.

With the reconnaissance platoon, Budapest, February 1945. Not all survived the end of the war unhurt. Out of this group, two of my comrades were killed and two were seriously wounded.

Infantry and tanks of the 2d Ukrainian Front in the last day of street fighting in the battle for Budapest, 13 February 1945. (Planeta Publishers, Moscow)

A Soviet antiaircraft gun and crew positioned in a Budapest square to attack Luftwaffe, February 1945. (Planeta Publishers, Moscow)

An hour of rest in Budapest, January 1945. From left to right: Alekseyev, Philipenko, the author.

Red Army Infantry attacking the approaches to the Imperial Bridge over the Danube during the fighting for Vienna, 1945. (Planeta Publishers, Moscow)

Submachine gunners of 2d Ukrainian Front break through to the Danube Canal in the battle for Vienna, April 1945. (Planeta Publishers, Moscow)

With Alekseyev. May 1945, in Austria.

A Victory Toast—May 9, 1945. From left to right: Timoshkin, the author, Volgin, and Titov.

My son Henryk born
February 15, 1947 and
daughter Helena born July
8, 1951 in Poland.

With my wife Hanna back in Lodz, 1946.

With the "Tsarina of the Fields"

12. On the Bridgehead: My Real War Begins

The officer of the special section told me nothing about what he intended to do with me. A couple of hours after I left his office, at night on 4 May 1943, the reserve regiment was awakened: 4th Company to get up! With no roll call we were hurriedly marched out to the front.

The front lines, after the successful German counterattacks followed by their recapture of Kharkov in mid-March 1943, were to the southeast of that city, where they ran along the Donets River. Both German and Russian troops, having been exhausted, were now engaged mostly in skirmishes, with savage fighting erupting only at the bridgeheads held by the Red Army on the west bank of the Donets. The leadership of the Soviet Southwestern Army Group tried to enlarge and reinforce those bridgeheads as potential springboards for a future offensive. And it was one such bridgehead toward which our 4th Marching Company was heading as a complement for the 458 Rifle Regiment stationed in the vicinity of Raygorodok. Our bridgehead was located southeast of the Izyum bend of the Donets, to the east of Slavyansk, a strategically important city at a road junction and the northwestern gate to the Donbas. That city as well as the Izyum-Slavyansk highway, running north-south on the west side of the Donets and parallel to it, were in German hands. The enemy also occupied Kramatorsk, an industrial center a little bit farther to the southeast.

It was morning, 5 May, when our marching company arrived at the eastern bank of the Donets, but to get to the bridgehead we had to wait until dusk. The bridge was destroyed and what was left of it could

not be repaired. Small boats were used for transporting reinforcements, ammunition, and food to the bridgehead, and the wounded
back to the rear. To facilitate the crossing, a steel cable almost touching the water had been stretched across the river; two oarsmen on
one or the other side of the boat would grab the cable instead of the
oars, to propel the boat forward. During daytime, however, it was impossible to cross the river safely because a Focke-Wulf reconnais-
sance-observation plane was hovering constantly over it, directing the
enemy's artillery fire. Indeed, heavy shells quite often raised gush-
ing fountains of water while splinters from the destroyed bridge were
spreading all over. The Luftwaffe could still fly the skies, and even
"stand"over the river with impunity, because we had no antiaircraft
guns. The reconnaissance plane was high enough, where it was in
no danger of being hit by a rifle bullet. Though some more experienced soldiers in our company used to get on their backs and shoot
their rifles or machine guns at German aircraft, this was strictly forbidden at the river crossing lest we would turn ourselves into easy targets. There was not a single Soviet plane to bother the Focke-Wulf.
Only at night would some ancient PO-2s dare to cross the front lines
and drop their loads of bombs on enemy rear positions. The PO-2,
dating back to 1927, was a small wood and canvas plane with a five-
cylinder engine. It was amazing that, for lack of anything better, these
relics were used for night bombing. It was nicknamed *Kukuruznik*
(from the word *kukuruza*, meaning corn), because it could fly only
slowly—sixty miles per hour—and low, not much higher than corn,
and was best perhaps for spreading pesticides over corn fields.

While we waited not far from the river crossing, a *politruk* organized a question-and-answer meeting. Our squad was still without rifles, and the sergeant in charge asked when and where we would get
them. *"Nye voryuy, tam naydyosh"* (Don't worry, you'll find them
there)—was the answer, as the *politruk* pointed his hand toward the
other side of the river.

I will never forget that night at the bridgehead, the night before
going into action for the first time. That night is strangely associated
in my memory with a frightful impression made on me by a book,
The Real War, which I had read in my early childhood. It was a dark,
moonless night but the shooting lit up the area brightly. Flares across

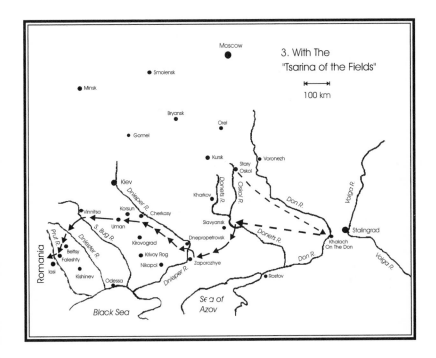

3. With The
"Tsarina of the Fields"

100 km

the skies provided glaring though unsteady light. Flashes from nearby shrapnel-shell explosions illuminated for split seconds the fearful faces of my comrades standing close to each other in a narrow trench. Shells threw out piles of earth and scattered it together with splinters all around. I was confused, not being able to distinguish mortar from artillery fire, ours from the enemy's. Whenever I heard a shell flying in the air I feared it was going to explode in front of me. My ear was not yet trained to quickly estimate whether it would fall short or would be an overshot. Likewise, I did not know that one never hears a direct hit at all. There seemed to be no end at all to that long, terrifying night. Machine-gun and rifle bullets were buzzing in the air from midnight to dawn. Before dawn this had rather intensified because—though I didn't know it at that time—the Germans were becoming nervous about a possible Russian attack and were thus shooting wildly. I felt completely lost as the barking of machine guns and the fitful light of tracer ammunition seemed

to be coming from all directions. Had we been encircled and would
have to turn to an all-round defense? Could the worst happen to me,
that is, not that I would be killed or wounded but that I would be
captured by the Germans and become a POW again? Thoughts were
flashing through my head like the flashes of the gunfire coming from
all sides. If the world around me that night had been just strange, or
outlandish, I would have said I felt like Alice in Wonderland. Alas, it
was the world of *the real war,* and I was in the midst of it.

The *politruk* was right. There were plenty of rifles, ammunition,
and hand grenades left by the dead and wounded in the field and
trenches, and I was soon to "learn on the job" how to use them. I had
not seen yet the first sunrise on the bridgehead when, before daybreak, and with no support from our artillery behind the river, our
company was rushed into an attack on enemy positions, at a place
where the sappers cleared an opening through the barbed wire and
the mine field. In the dusky light I could at first see only some silently
moving shadows of my comrades and I kept close to Baldy. We were
led by a junior lieutenant, who worked his way forward with his platoon through the opening in the barbed wire. The sappers were sitting there, showing him the narrow passageway cleared of mines. We
were supposed to engage in a hand-to-hand fight and, as soon as we
passed the barbed wire, everybody on our side began shooting wildly.
I did likewise, not aiming at anybody or anything in particular, because visibility was poor, and even if it were excellent, I would not
have performed any better, as I never practiced shooting from a real
rifle to a target. Be that as it may, the Germans were not caught by
surprise. Their heavy machine guns began to crackle and mowed
down our soldiers, killing and wounding at least half a dozen in our
platoon alone. Baldy got what he wanted, a submachine gun taken
from a fallen soldier, but had no chance of using it before the platoon commander ordered us to crawl back. It was high time, because
by then we were also under heavy mortar fire.

As soon as we returned to our forward trenches, our big guns behind the river began pounding German positions, and a sporadic artillery duel back and forth lasted for several hours. In the late afternoon we got a hot meal, as much as everybody could eat, because
our platoon had shrunk. While getting ready for a longer rest, we

were roused from a sleeplike state and ordered to prepare for a new attack before sunset. It was again like it was in the early morning, but with a significant difference. It began with an artillery barrage of the German positions by our big guns, located on the other side of the river, and mortars located on the bridgehead itself. Under this cover we raced through the path cleared of mines toward the German foremost trenches, which we reached rather easily, because the barbed-wire obstacles in front of them were ripped to pieces by our artillery and, most important, we were met by no resistance at all. Yet, before jumping into the enemy trenches, we threw in lots of hand grenades just in case, but nobody was there, dead or alive. The German infantrymen, and above all their commanding officers, were still tacticians much superior to ours. Evidently expecting the evening attack by the *Russkis*, they withdrew in time from their forward trenches while leaving their heavy machine-gun posts on the flanks of our passageway; they kept silent so we had not noticed their very existence. Our junior lieutenant, emboldened by the successful, in his judgment, penetration of enemy lines, ordered another push forward. However, as soon as we climbed out of the abandoned German trenches, all hell broke loose. The up-to-now-silent heavy machine guns began their barking and mowing job, mortar shells were exploding all around, and German marksmen appeared from nowhere. Baldy fell in front of me, his head a bloody mess. He was killed instantly by a stream of machine-gun bullets. I was close to him, but—perhaps because I was much shorter—only my cap, blown off my head, had bullet holes in it. There were more killed and wounded, our commanding officer among the latter. Following the first fleeing soldiers, the rest of our platoon and indeed the rest of our company—the entire lot had taken to their heels.

My second night at the bridgehead was quite different. I just slept through it like a log, dead to the world. But the wheels of war would not come to a standstill. There was night business as usual. Fresh supplies of ammunition, food, and a new reinforcement for our 458 Rifle Regiment, about two hundred men strong to replace those killed and wounded, had to be brought to the bridgehead again. This place was a bloody meat grinder taking its heavy toll every day. The newcomers would join those who went through the attacks of the last few

days. They would often wonder why the survivors were so uncom-
municative, sleepy, just waiting apathetically for the order to attack
again, and wished it would never come. Then when we, the survivors
of yesterday's fights, were in deep sleep, there was the night business
of disposing of the dead and taking care of the wounded. The dead,
those who could be retrieved, would often get buried where they
were killed, just out of sight, their graves marked by small wooden
planks with their names and date of death. Baldy's body was left behind the German lines. Before putting on bandages, those lightly
wounded would "disinfect" the wounds and cuts on their hands by
just pissing on them. We had brave nurses and medical orderlies,
mostly girls, who sometimes became casualties themselves, because
they would often follow in our footsteps as we went to the attack. They
were dedicated and would try their best to patch up the wounded.
Unfortunately, unlike their German counterparts, they had no dis-
infectants and, worse, the means of transporting the wounded were
horrible. The wounded able to walk had to get to the bank of the
river, where a first aid station was located, on their own.

As for the severely wounded, the medical orderlies would put
them on a kind of toboggan on wheels, which was pulled to the river
by harnessed dogs. The wounded brought to the river at daytime had
to wait until darkness to get to the other side. By the time the severely
wounded arrived at the hospital in horse-drawn ambulances, their
wounds were often already infected and gangrene had set in. The
surgeons had no choice but to amputate a leg or arm; no wonder so
many surgeons became magnificent experts in the art of limb am-
putation. Many lives could have been saved by prompt medical attention, and far fewer amputees would have been seen in the cities
of the Soviet Union after the war.

A couple of days later, during a somewhat longer lull in the fighting, I had a chance to take a closer look at a part of our bridgehead.
It was covered by trenches, which in a zigzag pattern were running
parallel to the river and were interconnected by a network of corri-
dors. Shell craters all over the place were round, mostly not very
deep. Some of the deeper ditches were filled on the bottom with rain
or underground water, which was used for washing. Closer to the
river were the 80mm mortar batteries that often changed position

to avoid detection. The regiment's 45mm antitank guns were kept on the eastern side of the Donets.

Our "quarters" in the forward front lines were, by comparison with ordinary trenches, truly amazing. The old-timers had dug themselves in superbly, in deep, narrow trenches, often with niches—deep recesses in the wall facing the Germans. It was a small labyrinth of trenches, dugouts, and a few underground wooden bunkers, the bigger ones housing commanding officers, telephone operators, nurses, and medical orderlies—all together. Somewhat behind our forward lines were located the posts of our heavy machine guns. The German trenches, in a huge Sovkhoz fruit farm full of apple trees, were quite close to ours, in some places a mere 150 to 200 yards away. In between was a mine field, "guarded" on both sides by bundles of barbed wire.

During lulls in the fighting our most forward front lines were also relatively the safest, and for a simple reason. While trenches in the rear were always under at least sporadic German artillery and mortar shelling, shooting at our forward positions carried the risk of putting their own troops under friendly fire. It was not a safe place for everyone, however, and we had many casualties even during longer daytime lulls in the fighting. The victims were new, inexperienced recruits who had been brought to the front line before sunrise. They had no inkling of the appalling end that lay in store for many of them. The majority came from the formerly occupied territories, where they were drafted immediately after liberation and sent to fighting units almost completely untrained. Mostly kids, eighteen or nineteen years old, they appeared to be even younger because they were small and skinny—probably effects of living their early childhood through collectivization and the starvation that went along with it. I had chats with some of them, born in 1925, in the kolkhozes of Belorussia, where potatoes had been their staple diet. They were glad to be in the army, and the answer, when asked why, was similar: "To gorge oneself on *khlebushka* (diminutive of bread)." At lunchtime they would eat soup and kasha first, leaving bread for dessert. Why? *"Da vied' khleb po sebye khorosh"* (You know, bread is good by itself).

Deceived by the relative calm of the place, and told that the Germans were less than some one hundred yards away, the newcomers wanted to check out the situation for themselves. Though warned not to stick their heads out of the trenches, they nevertheless would often be overwhelmed by a childish curiosity: *"Davayposmotrim na Fritza"* (Let's take a glance at Fritz). But Fritz would not oblige; instead, a sniper would send a bullet into the curious's head. Indeed, lots of casualties had been inflicted by those German marksmen, sitting in their foxholes, under an apple tree or in its branches, and just waiting for the inexperienced youngsters.

There was another group of soldiers among whom the rate of casualties was enormous, and this because of inadequate communication equipment. As a rule, communications between forward units, heavy machine-gun nests, mortar batteries, and observation and command posts were by telephone; wireless communication was available only to the battalion commander and up. This was why being a telephone operator was so dangerous, especially for those pulling their heavy wire spools while working feverishly under enemy fire to reestablish communication.

I had been in combat, in bloody attacks which, on and off, lasted about two weeks. Whenever I go back in my memory to those days, I have before my eyes dead and wounded people lying on the ground in most unnatural positions, covered with earth and blood, sometimes in their own guts, and my senses recall the sweet stench of corpses. Even later, having seen scores of dead and wounded people, I never got used to that smell, though I learned to distinguish between the odor of human corpses and that of horse carcasses.

Those two weeks included some ten days of savage fighting during which our regiment's cost per day in killed and wounded was about two hundred men. Almost every second day the reserve regiment would pump in another two hundred men of a marching company to replenish the losses at our bridgehead. It follows that, despite reinforcements, the total net loss incurred in those ten days was about one thousand men, which our 458 Rifle Regiment could hardly afford any longer. This was probably the main reason that our attacks aimed at enlarging the bridgehead had been halted. With exceedingly heavy losses the attacks produced no territorial gains; we made no progress whatsoever.

Part of the reason was that we were most often the attacking side, while the Germans did not bother to counterattack. More important is the fact that the Red Army, especially its foot soldiers and their commanding officers, was still learning how to fight the Germans. A huge percentage of the privates had not served in the army. They were often trained—some not at all—with wooden shotguns, as there were shortages of rifles at the training camps. Mostly youngsters of eighteen and nineteen, they were sent to the front with no heavy weapons, many even with no rifles at all. The latter, it can be argued, was nothing out of the ordinary in Russian history. To cite a historian's figures, in World War I the Russian army ran out of its supply of weapons and for a period of time, in 1915, up to twenty-five percent of Russian soldiers were sent to the front unarmed, with instructions to pick up what they could from the dead (see N. V. Riasanovsky, *A History of Russia,* New York: Oxford University Press, 1969, p. 464).

It goes without saying that in World War II, the Russian army fought under much more difficult conditions. And even after Stalingrad, in May 1943, many commanders of those young recruits were still equally inexperienced young officers, mostly cadets from short-term officer training courses.The result was that, as at the bridgehead, the Germans were just waiting in their well-entrenched positions for our frontal attacks, and must have enjoyed watching our poor and not too clever junior lieutenant as he led us into their trap. Our infantry had to pay far too high a toll in blood on account of the soldiers' and officers' lack of combat experience.

In the final analysis, however, the enormous casualties in the futile fight at the bridgehead were due to the sad fact that—it still pains me to think about it—our higher-ups had, as a rule, with exceptions, of course, perhaps many exceptions, little regard for the lives of their soldiers; they did not count losses. But then, there is something about it in the old Russian sayings that people grow like mushrooms or like grass without sowing.

The next episode in my life as a Red Army soldier has always reminded me of Gogol's *Dead Souls.* Chichikov, the scoundrel of that satirical novel, was buying up dead souls—serfs were referred to as "souls" in Russia—to sell these serfs later as if they were alive. In my case, no complex machinations were involved, though there was an enigma about the character being dead or alive, and it also centered on a piece of an official paper with a name on it, the name Temkin, Gavryil Mikhailovich.

It all began with a bureaucratic blunder. In the reserve regiment the NKVD officer of the special section crossed my name off the official list of the 4th Marching Company going to the front. A short time afterward, when the scribbler-clerk of our 458 Rifle Regiment got the list of new arrivals, he noticed a name crossed out. What was he supposed to do? To keep the regiment's personnel records in order, he wrote in the blank space of the last column, opposite my name, a single word: *ubit* (killed). If words could kill, there would be no problem for the regiment's bureaucracy. The problem was that after I had officially been killed, the supply of food rations for Private Temkin should have been stopped. But the very existence of that private as well as his name was not detected for the next two weeks as long as fierce fighting was going on, and the number of daily food rations delivered to the bridgehead was as a rule in excess of the number of soldiers still alive there. The situation changed radically after the fighting had come to a standstill and a roll call revealed the existence of a *lishnyi rot*—a superfluous mouth. I was the one too many. And the sergeant-major responsible for supplies launched an investigation in order to solve the "is he dead or alive" puzzle. It was perhaps silly to try to bring a dead man back to life in a place where so many live men were quickly turning into dead ones. But it was a serious matter, especially for nonbelievers. A dead man—blessed be his soul—had just been resurrected and, on top of everything, was requesting food rations, which were in short supply. I was ordered to leave the bridgehead and appear at the regiment's headquarters next day at 1300 sharp.

The regiment's headquarters consisted of one large and three much smaller wooden bunkers in the ground, exposing only their roofs made of beams and thick layers of earth covered on top with foliage for camouflage. The larger bunker was the HQ proper, housing some of the P.N.Shs. (assistants to the chief of staff), and in particular P.N.Sh. No. 1 (the operations assistant), also telephone and radio operators, orderlies, and a clerk-scribbler. The three smaller bunkers were personal quarters of the regiment's commander, his *zampolit* (political deputy), and the *nachshtab* (chief of staff).

It was a sunny, quiet day, and Zampolit (lieutenant-colonel) Fiedotov, before whom I was ordered to appear, was sitting at a table in front of his bunker. I saluted, pronounced the usual "Krasnoarmeets (Red Army private) Temkin according to your orders," in response to which came the "at ease!" His eyes inspected me all over, but he had a friendly face and with a gesture of his hand invited me to sit across from him at the table. "You passed the field test, the battalion commander cited you for courage," he began, "tell me how things are at the bridgehead, speak your mind." Noticing my hesitation, he raised his hand. *"Nyet! Nyet! Nye boysya, pravdu govori"* (No! No! Don't be afraid, tell the truth). I did what he asked for, but as his face became more and more gloomy, I was not sure anymore that he really wanted to hear the truth as I saw it. He urged me, however, to continue just cautioning: *"Chestno govori"* (Speak honestly).

After half an hour or so, his orderly put biscuits on an aluminum plate and two aluminum mugs into which he poured hot, sweet tea on the table. "Help yourself," I was invited, and the *zampolit*, now all smiles, was asking different kinds of questions, beginning with *"Kak ty k'nam popalsya?"* (How did you happen to have come to us?) He could not hide his amusement and stop laughing as he listened to my description of the conversation with the special section officer in the reserve regiment and how I went with the 4th Marching Company to the front afterward. In turn, I was rather surprised hearing the *zampolit*'s comments, clearly indicative that he was not only a cultured man with a good sense of humor, but also frank enough to express views which may have been politically incorrect in front of a private. He kept asking more and more about my education, knowledge of foreign languages—he himself knew some Polish and German—life in Poland and under German occupation, and especially the POW and the NKVD period; "a fine mess you got yourself in," I heard not for the first time. Finally, with a glance at his wristwatch, the *zampolit* ordered me to come again the next day at the same time. "Get some food and find a sleeping place for him," he told his orderly.

13. The Regiment's Translator

Heavy thoughts were passing through my head as I was waiting the next day for Lieutenant-Colonel Fiedotov to appear. "What are 'they' going to do with me? 'They' know by now that I was not the guy who would become a deserter fleeing to the Germans, but will 'they' ever trust me? And who are 'they'—Fiedotov himself, his higher-ups, how high up?" I had a feeling the *zampolit*'s sympathies were with me. But I also knew that the institution of officer-and-commissar dual command had been officially abolished, and military commanders were given sole authority, though political departments remained in the Red Army. *Zampolits*, like all other *politruks*, lost much of their previous influence; the power of any *zampolit* vis-à-vis the military commander depended on personal relations between them.

What the *zampolit* had in store for me was at first short and simple. "We have a proposition: You either go back to the reserve regiment or you stay with us to fight the Nazis, it's your choice." I did not hesitate for a moment, I would, of course, stay. "That's what 'we' expected of you," I was told before the *zampolit* outlined a rather complex arrangement "they" had for me. I had a good working knowledge of German, and the *khozyain* (boss-commander of the regiment) had approved his suggestion to put me in the vacant position of the regiment's translator. Since this had been an officer's position, for at least a lieutenant, it was the intention of the *nachalstvo* (bosses) to send me as soon as possible to a three-month cadet school for men already in military service, which would give me the rank of an officer. In the meantime I would be loosely attached to the *razviedka* (the regiment's reconnaissance platoon), take part on a voluntary basis in its actions, cooperate with P.N.Sh. 3 (the chief of staff's assistant responsible for reconnaissance), but take direct orders only from the *nachshtab* (chief of staff).

Almost everything described by Zampolit Fiedotov, with one significant exception, came true. General Mikhaylov, the commander of the 78 Rifle Division, issued a warrant sanctioning my appointment as translator in the 458 Rifle Regiment. Somewhat later Hanna began receiving most of my monthly pay regularly, which was due not according to rank but to position held. During the next two years I was consecutively promoted through the ranks of junior sergeant, sergeant, senior sergeant, and, finally, *starshyna* (master sergeant), but I did not become an officer. I had been awarded medals and high orders. My regimental and divisional *nachalstwo* made several attempts to send me to cadet or other officer school, but to no avail. They were repeatedly refused, evidently because of my "original sin"—a refugee from Poland under German occupation. Each time I was told about it, I felt, of course, disappointed, but not discouraged or having second thoughts about my resolve to remain where I was and to be useful in the struggle against the Nazis. This was my just war, everything else was *chepuha*—a trifle.

At the end of May 1943 only one battalion was left on the bridgehead, in a strictly defensive position. The other two infantry battalions of our 458 Rifle Regiment were moved to the north, on the east side of the Donets. It was now position warfare, more precisely, "trench warfare" with few skirmishes along the front held by our 78 Rifle Division and perhaps the entire army of which we were part.

At a time like this, *razviedka* becomes very busy, trying as often as possible to capture a *yazik*, literally a tongue (meaning, here, to capture a German prisoner and "make his tongue loose"). While aerial reconnaissance was a reliable source of information about movements of enemy troops and reserves, field commanders favored, especially at trench warfare times, the "tongue" method as generating useful tactical intelligence on enemy groupings, their capabilities and intentions. Indeed, the interrogation of a captured prisoner and the documents found on him could provide much specific reliable information: his battalion and regimental numbers, what other enemy units were in front of us, where they came from, how they were positioned, who was on their flanks and rear, if and when they received reinforcements, what their strength was—manpower, artillery, tank support—where exactly they were located, means of communication, and other details.

The task of interrogating German prisoners, making their tongues loose, became much easier after Stalingrad than before, when some were stubbornly refusing to reveal any information beyond what could be found in their soldier books or other papers they carried. Together with their lost victories, the soldiers of the Wehrmacht were losing their arrogance.

I volunteered to go with our *razviedka* on a "tongue" hunt. It was my first experience of that kind, and it turned out to be nasty. A German mine-laying party had been spotted at about midnight on the bridgehead. We were waiting for them in a sort of an ambush in a narrow ravine in no-man's land. As they came closer, three of them, some of our guys rather amateurishly opened fire from submachine guns, wounding one of them while the others escaped. We put gauze into the wounded prisoner's mouth and tied his hands, but had to pull him because he either could not or refused to walk. In the meantime the two who escaped must have alerted their comrades, because the Germans were raking the ravine with machine-gun fire and mortar shells by now, trying to cut us off from our forward lines.

The ravine was situated parallel to those lines and, though it was a longer way back and probably full of mines, we used it as a cover, running along the bottom of a small stream and pulling our prisoner by his legs. While we ran, his head was bumping on the stones along the stream. But we noticed the damage that occurred only when we finally entered our trenches. He was bleeding from his mouth. "Looks bad, doesn't he?" said a medical orderly pushing swabs into the prisoner's gaping head wounds, but our "tongue" remained mute; he was already dead. We were strongly reprimanded for so stupidly losing a prisoner. The documents found on him provided little new information.

I now shared food and living quarters with the *razviedka,* and our relations grew into friendship based on mutual help. I did not hide my Jewishness from them, but neither did I advertise it. Since I was not religiously observant, there was not much interest in me as a Jew. Some knew that I was Jewish and felt sympathy for the plight of my family whenever I mentioned it. Others knew but did not care, being more curious about my Polish origin. A foreign country and yet a neighbor about which they heard a lot of good and bad things, Poland always provided an interesting topic. Still some others just would not believe that "such a nice guy" could be Jewish. Jewish jokes were being told, though not that often. For example, before an attack on enemy positions, an officer tries to cheer up two Jewish soldiers: *"Vperiod orly!"* (Forward eagles!) to which they reply, *"My nye orly, my lvy*—We aren't eagles, we are lions—Lev Abramovich and Lev Moiseyevich."

Much more popular among Russian soldiers were so-called *natsmen* jokes (*natsmen*, national minorities, usually Asian). A *natsmen* in his broken Russian is complaining about the unfairness of war: *"Voyna nekhorosh"* (War is no good). Why? he is asked. He replies, "A loaf of bread is given to four soldiers, two soldiers have to share a pot of kasha, while everybody has to carry a whole rifle." In another joke, a platoon of *natsmen* is ordered to attack and take a hill, but they refuse. To encourage them, the officer repeats his order in the name of motherland— *"Rodina prykazyvayet"*—but to no avail. Finally, the officer beseeches by all that's holy—Stalin himself— *"Stalin prykazyvayet"*—to which comes a positive response: *"Kotelok kasha, vysotka nasha"*—a pot of kasha and the hill is ours. Plainly disliked *natsmen*s were Georgians and Armenians. Those who had a dark complexion and a protruding nose were often called *Armyashki* (derogatory for Armenian). There were no Georgians or Armenians in our *razviedka*, and we had only one *natsmen*, Urazmukhambetov, a Kazakh, and everybody was fond of him.

The reconnaissance platoon was closely knit by common fate and struggle, but above all by many similar personal characteristics. The latter was to a great extent due to the general selection criteria for admission to the *razviedka*, but even more so by the requirements and recruitment methods of Senior Lieutenant Andrey Kravchenko, our P.N.Sh. 3, assistant to the regiment's chief of staff responsible for reconnaissance. He had a quick mind, was a good-humored, handsome, swarthy man in his late twenties. He probably inherited the cheerfulness from his Ukrainian father, and his dark skin from his Tatar mother. A brave, sometimes reckless man, Kravchenko was looking for similar characters for his *razviedka* and was excellent in nosing for them. What he could not do was to select the platoon commanders for the *razviedka*, because these were positions held by officers sent from schools or reserves. "They were good for nothing," he would complain, asking the bosses not to send any replacements. Whether there was actually a platoon commander or not, he often preferred to lead his men himself. He was fair but strict with people and it was difficult to fool him. Far from being a disciplinarian, Kravchenko was very demanding of his soldiers, as he was of himself. He was also strict about his authority.

From where did Kravchenko get his characters? His main source of potential candidates were *shtrafnye battaliony* (penal battalions), or, rather, the few remnants left in them after the punishment term was over. During the war, convicted murderers, bandits, robbers, and other assorted criminals were given the choice of joining a penal battalion to be sent to the front and thrown into the most dangerous battles. Whoever survived a three-month term in a penal battalion would have his name cleared and would be enrolled into a regular Soviet army unit. This was where Kravchenko was looking for and finding volunteers for the *razviedka*.

Most of the time his recruits would turn out to be competent for the job and would willingly follow wherever he led them. Moreover, many were good not only for the *razviedka*; they were exceptional in their comradeship and loyalty. Titov, with whom I became friends, was such an example. Like most others selected by Kravchenko for the *razviedka*, Titov was a former criminal. He came to us from a penal battalion, to which he went in order to nullify a ten-year jail sentence for murder. He professed homicide but not murder, and seemed to have no remorse—"the guy deserved to be killed." His past a mystery to me, Titov nevertheless impressed me with being a very decent human being, though he generally distrusted people. Expressing his life philosophy, he used to caution me, *"Gavryusha, sviet khorosh, no lyudi bladi"* (The world is good but people are whores). I will later say more about him.

Escapades for a "tongue" and similar adventures excepting, life in the *razviedka* was less dangerous in comparison with that of front-

line infantry. It was also more comfortable, because the reconnaissance platoon was a small—never more than fifteen to eighteen men
strong—and in many respects an independent unit. It could pick its
own quarters, had full control over its food rations, and was doing
its own cooking and so on. While there was never open talk about
this, I had been aware that some of these characters, in order to sup-
plement the meager food rations, would at times engage in stealing
from military supply units, though never those of our own regiment
or division; if caught, they faced court-martial and execution. The
fact that quite a few old-timers were still around in the same platoon,
some throughout a two-year period, is perhaps indicative of a casualty rate on the average not higher than in ordinary infantry units.
I will just mention the fate of some of my close friends, the "class of
May 1943," with whom I was together on almost a daily basis from
that date. Trofimov and Zubov, killed December 1943; Kravchenko,
our P.N.Sh. 3, killed October 1944; Pyrla and Efremov, killed March
1945; Lisevich, wounded March 1945; Balachev, wounded April
1945; Titov, Urazmukhambetov, Timoshkin, and Mikriukov survived
the war unwounded.

I had been fortunate to make some real friends among these and
others of my comrades in arms. And I wished I would always have
friends as reliable. Long after the war I retained the habit of taking
measure of a friend by asking myself: "Would I want him as a foxhole
buddy?" I knew this was asking too much, and that one should only
wish never to have any of his friends be forced to undergo such a test;
still that became my highest, ultimate criterion of friendship.

According to the assignment given to me by my boss, Major
Buldyshkin, the regiment's chief of staff, my daily task, especially during trench warfare conditions, was to provide him with information
for his reports which he had to send to the headquarters of the division each evening. For that purpose I would gather from the
razviedka, and from Kravchenko in particular, whatever data and estimates they had. But mostly I was relying on my own information
collected by keeping my ears alert and my eyes wide open.

As a soldier in the front line I could see only a small fighting area,
while the broader picture, the tactical let alone the strategic pattern
of a front line or a battle, was hidden from my sight. My new position introduced some significant changes in this regard. Like all

officers in the regiment, I was provided by Lieutenant—later on se-nior lieutenant—Tarasov, P.N.Sh. 6—cartography assistant to the chief of staff—with excellent, up-to-date field maps. Nota bene, ours were, in my opinion, much better than the German ones, and this goes also for the maps of Romania, Hungary, and Austria, which we used later in 1944–45. With the help of a field map, I would first fa-miliarize myself with the shape of the terrain held by the Germans in front of us and in their immediate rear, in particular hills, valleys, patches of woodland or forested areas, single buildings standing alone outside a village, the location of the smallest streams, lakes, and watering places for livestock, and nearby wells. This would provide me with a picture of potentially favorable places for artillery, mortar, machine-gun, command and observation posts, and so on. Finally, glued to my binoculars, I would observe artillery flashes, watch and listen to the points from which machine-gun fire originated, where artillery and mortar shells were actually coming from, and their fre-quency. All these bits of information, a compilation of those of the *razviedka* reconnaissance with my own, would provide the framework for my daily reports. An updated situation map attached, they nor-mally contained estimates of the enemy's fighting strength vis-à-vis our regiment, the location of his artillery, mortar, and machine-gun nests, the calibers and approximate numbers of shells he had actu-ally fired during the past twenty-four hours.

At this point I must add that the German reconnaissance had one great advantage over us in getting military intelligence about their enemy—they would eavesdrop. We had no acoustic detecting equip-ment whatsoever. Worse still, their job of eavesdropping was made relatively easy by the inexperience and carelessness of our wireless operators. The compact battery-operated radio, carried like a knap-sack to provide two-way communication in the field, was still a tech-nological novelty in Soviet infantry units. The result was that our in-experienced radio operators communicating with each other were often inadvertently revealing top secrets to the enemy. Their mes-sages were rarely coded, and the thing that they tried not to disclose was the names of the "bosses," but our radio operators were some-times so clumsy that they pointedly revealed just that. For instance, one would begin transmitting a message with the words "Roger!

Roger!" *"Khozyayn prykazal"* (The boss ordered), then the receiving operator would ask *"Kakoy khozyayn?"* (What boss?) and in response would come: *"Durak! Petrov konyechno"* (Stupid! Petrov, of course). After the war I was astonished to read about the advantages the Germans derived from this inexperience and lack of vigilance even at the top of the Soviet army.

Regarding this lack of vigilance an incident occurred involving the First Ukrainian Army Group, which came under Marshal Zhukov's command after General Vatutin was seriously wounded in an ambush at the end of February 1944 (he died of the wounds in mid-April). Specifically, in the last week of March 1944, Zhukov expected Manstein's First Panzer Army to break out northeast of Kamenets Podolsky toward the south, over the Dniester River. He therefore moved his main forces southward to intercept the Germans there. But the enemy struck instead to the west, toward Bukhach, in part because Manstein was in the fortunate position of knowing Zhukov's intentions.

Paul Carell—in *Scorched Earth: The Russian-German War 1941–1944,* Boston: Little, Brown, 1970, p. 445—describes how Manstein listened to and commented on Zhukov's orders: Zhukov commanded: First Tank Army will thrust to the Dniester in the direction of Chernovtsy. "Good," acknowledged Manstein. Zhukov's next order was: Fourth Tank Army will wait until its infantry divisions have moved up. "Better still," commented Manstein. The Germans also succeeded in listening in to the quartermaster signals of Zhukov's First and Fourth Tank Armies and in decoding them. As a result, Manstein learned almost as much about those two armies as Marshal Zhukov himself. Twice daily Manstein's HQ was kept accurately informed about the number of battle-worthy tanks possessed by each Soviet tank brigade. It was an ideal form of reconnaissance. Manstein, for all intents and purposes, was sitting at Zhukov's map table.

But let me return to my own reconnaissance reports, as I was learning to prepare them in the late spring of 1943. Having done what I could, I would hand in my notes together with a daily situation map to Senior Lieutenant—later on captain—Philipenko, P.N.Sh. 1 (operations assistant to the chief of staff), who was in fact responsible for the report and would send it out to the division, but not before it went through the editorship of the chief of staff. Major Buldyshkin's corrections mainly overstated the enemy's strength in order to justify requests for reinforcements, additional equipment, and ammunition. The same was done, however, at the division's HQ and probably all the way up to armies and army groups.

In fairness, I should mention that I learned after the war that the Germans, like the Soviets, though perhaps to a lesser degree, also quite often and for similar reasons claimed their enemy significantly superior in numbers.

But I am more familiar with the exaggerated estimates by our side, figures sometimes inflated out of any proportion, of German forces attacking and/or destroyed, the enemy's unbelievably high casualties in dead, wounded, tanks, artillery, and other equipment. Though such figures were often used for propaganda purposes, perhaps also in feuding among generals, I could not believe they would be taken seriously. After all, the higher-up generals knew too well, also from their own experience, the practice of cooking up estimates of the enemy's strength and casualties, not to discount those estimates significantly and perhaps even more than warranted. That was my thinking, influenced in part by the fact that we had not been receiving anything extra due to Major Buldyshkin's editing of the regiment's reports.

All that was probably true in general, but with significant exceptions, as I came to realize, noticing that many inflated figures had sometimes actually become the basis of fateful decisions even at the highest military levels. To illustrate the point, I will return to the operation code-named Star undertaken at the end of January 1943 as it was described after the war by General Shtemenko, who at the time of Star headed the operations department of the Soviet army's GHQ (Sergey Shtemenko, *The Soviet General Staff at War, 1941–1945*, pp. 100–101). He summarizes the official results of the first phase of the 1942–43 winter offensive: The Soviet army had smashed 120 enemy divisions; more than 200,000 officers and men, up to 13,000 pieces of ordnance, not to mention other materiel, had been captured; our troops had advanced nearly 400 kilometers. According to Shtemenko, these extremely impressive figures, which had been published in the supreme commander's order of 25 January 1943, gave grounds for an important conclusion. It was considered indisputable that the initiative the Red Army had seized at Stalingrad was being firmly maintained, and that the enemy had no chance of regaining it. Moreover, it was regarded unlikely that Hitler's army would in the near future undertake any significant counteraction east of the Dnieper or in the center of the strategic front. This assessment of the situation led to the decision to continue with the offensive without a pause—wrote General Shtemenko—explaining the background of the ill-fated operation Star, timed to begin on 1 February 1943 and involving an additional penetration of almost 250 kilometers by an exhausted Soviet army without reserves.

Soon I got to know more about the staff officers of the 458 Rifle Regiment's headquarters. Our new regimental commander, Lieutenant-Colonel Shevchenko—promoted after a while to the rank of full colonel—was not very educated, but had good military experience and a lot of common sense. A broad smile on his face, showing all his steel-capped teeth, he ruled the regiment with a firm hand, and quite successfully, until the end of the war. He was generally liked because he treated his men fairly—myself included. Only once during the two years I was under his command did Colonel Shevchenko get mad at me. The matter was about my foul language. It took a long time and much teasing from my comrades—"In what forest were you born that you don't speak like a human being"—before I began using swear words like everybody else. One day, however, it happened while we were already in Hungary and a campaign of "reintroducing cultural behavior" was in full swing, Colonel Shevchenko caught me swearing like a trooper. It was one of those moments when I, the apprentice, could finally show off my skill in using the rich Russian vocabulary, in which the word "fuck" substitutes for punctuation marks. Surprised, as if he had never in his life heard such language, the colonel gave me a dressing-down: *"Chto? Rugat'sya budesh? Desyat' sutok aresta—eb' tvoyu mat'!"* (What? Cursing? I am giving you ten days arrest for that, you motherfucker!) Not so much abashed as amused by the awkward rebuke, I stood at attention and, of course, in silence, but the smirk on my face had probably not escaped the commander's notice. Since under frontline conditions arrests were not practical,

Colonel Shevchenko's sentence was changed to a fine. For the next three months my monthly salary, which Hanna had been receiving, was cut by ten percent; she was not notified why.

The relations between Major Buldyshkin, the regiment's chief of staff, and Captain Philipenko, his operations assistant, were correct, though not too friendly. They worked closely together almost to the end of the war. Captain Philipenko, a handsome man of mild manners, had more military knowledge and was also intellectually better equipped than his superior. Major Buldyshkin was pompous, in many ways typical of a high-ranking, well-connected Soviet bureaucrat. *Druzhba dhruzhboy, a sluzhba sluzhboy* (Duty before friendship) was his favorite saying, which he would repeat at any opportunity, and without a reason as well. He liked to hear himself called the "chief of staff" instead of Major Buldyshkin. He disliked questions. *Mnogo budyesh znat', skoro sostaryshsya* (To know too much is to get old too quickly) was his typical reply to my inquiries. No doubt fond of me, he favored me with an inscription on his photo which he gave me shortly before he was wounded in April 1945: To My Translator.

Philipenko and Tarasov, the regiment's staff officers, became my good friends. Since Senior Lieutenant Tarasov, the well-educated and easygoing P.N.Sh. 6, was much less busy than Philipenko, I had long evening chats with him about history, literature, world affairs—everything except politics. *Zampolit* Fiedotov had been transferred and I lost sight of him; I have only a vague recollection of his replacement.

14. Politruks, Propaganda, Entertainment

Apart from the *zampolit,* the other two polit-propaganda officers at the regimental level were the *partorg* (the party organization representative) and the *komsorg* (the Komsomol representative). There were also *politruk*s in each battalion and company. What good did they do in affecting the morale of the soldiers?

Our first *partorg* was generally disliked, though not because of his stupid, stale, vague propaganda. The soldiers did not mind his silly slogans, they just ignored them, but they could not forgive a certain trait of his character. He had the habit of nosing around in places where cooks were preparing soup in big cauldrons, and right there, in the open and unashamed, would treat himself to a can of American-supplied meat, one of the very few cans to go into the soup for an entire infantry battalion. Of course, it is hard to trust where there is no respect. "He ought to be ashamed," many would comment, while the cynics reflected: *Styd nye dym, glaza nye vyyest* (Shame isn't smoke, it won't eat out the eyes). Though the *partorg* was, indeed, dead to shame, the poor guy still did not deserve to be killed for lack of character, as he was actually struck by shell splinters in mid-July 1943. The *komsorg,* on the other hand, was generally liked, particularly by the younger soldiers, perhaps because his enthusiastic though naïve speeches were genuine, strikingly sincere, and his optimism echoed their own dreams about the future—the victorious war is soon coming to an end, we return home where everybody's waiting, there is lots of food, ice cream, pretty girls, movies—everybody is going to be happy, exactly *kak polozheno* (as it should be).

Field commanders who had no sympathy for polit-propaganda kept political officers at arm's length. I heard some field commanders openly ridiculing the work of these officers as a waste of time that could better be used for military training. Yet some of them were quite capable of bringing about a desired improvement in mood and behavior, in raising the morale of the troops. I myself witnessed polit-propaganda officers who were not only able speakers but also had the gift of giving their speeches a spiritual meaning, infusing in their listeners a sense of honor, duty, and courage before major battles. These officers performed a function to some extent like that carried out by the clergy in other armies. But ours was still the *Red* Army. While polit-propaganda officers, on higher orders, had ceased to be outright foes of religion, they were far from encouraging it. Religious people, and there were many religious people in the Red Army, were deprived of the possibility of open prayers. True, during the war Stalin permitted the opening of churches in big cities, which by itself belied the myth that the Soviets had succeeded in eradicating religion, but the new policy had changed little in the countryside and still less in the army.

I recall how village lads, before going into battle, would whisper the Lord's Prayer and cross themselves repeatedly. There was no such thing, however, as religious service in the field as in other armies, no chaplain to give the soldiers general absolution to calm their nerves and offer some solace before the battle. I heard the wounded and dying yelling or murmuring *"Gospody pomiluy"* (Lord, have mercy). But there were no priests to assist the dying on the battlefields or in hospitals, no requiems for the departed souls. And this was a gap which even the best *politruks* could not bridge. Some may have become good in the art of appealing to patriotic feelings and nationalistic sentiments, but they could do little to fulfill the spiritual needs of the Red Army soldiers coming mostly from peasant families with strong religious traditions.

Many *politruks* would insist on collective reading of the news even at times when there was no shortage of newspapers. But the thing soldiers really enjoyed reading collectively, sharing loudly enthusiastic comments, was the adventures of Vassily Tyorkin. They were always hungry for new episodes of the hero's story. Fortunately, Tvardovsky was prolific enough to deliver new episodes of this serialized narrative poem, written in the attractive, humorous, and folksy style that the soldiers loved, systematically until the end of the war.

During that trench warfare period, our regiment got some professional entertainment, much enjoyed by the soldiers. The most enthusiastic was always the soldiers' reception of shows produced by the army's traveling dance and song ensemble. We also watched several patriotic movies preceded by interesting albeit always too short newsreels. Listening to the battle cries in the historical movies and even in some of the newsreels, I wondered why I had never heard them in combat on the bridgehead.

Senior Lieutenant Rochlis, who held the position of translator in our 78 Infantry Division, visited me quite often from the end of May on. He was a thoughtful man and we became friends. As it turned out, we had many things in common—not just the knowledge of the German language, of which he had a much better command, or the translation business in which we both had little experience. He was a Moscow Jew with many relatives in places presently occupied by the Germans, and this became the main topic of our intimate conversations.

One day, in the beginning of July, Rochlis came to our regiment in a half truck loaded with some strange equipment and accompanied by a polit-propaganda man from the corps or army headquarters. I was to get them to the bridgehead and as close as possible to the front lines, which was no big deal, because the bridge had in the meantime been rebuilt and German artillery fire was almost nonexistent. As soon as we arrived at an appropriate spot, the technicians quickly pulled out wires attached to several loudspeakers, which they hung on stumps of trees and directed toward the Germans. Then the show began. Our enemy, for an opening, was treated to some Russian music and songs the Germans were known to like very much, such as "Volga, Volga, Our Mother River," among others.

Following a short intermission, Rochlis took over, turning to the real theme of the spectacle. In his clear, scholarly German, he first read from a manifesto of the "Free Germany Committee," which was prominently displayed in the Soviet press after it was formed in Moscow; it was an appeal to the German people to rid Germany of Hitler. Next, Rochlis recited the popular German verse: *Es geht alles*

Voruber, es geht alles Vorbei, nach jedem Dezember kommt wieder ein Mai (Everything is passing, everything goes by, after every December May comes again). As the Germans kept silent, Rochlis—a megaphone in his hand—continued loud and clear: "May has already passed and what can you look for ahead? Don't count on a summer offensive. What happened to you in December will be repeated this summer. It is only going to get worse, much worse, if you follow your mad Führer. Run over to us, you'll be treated well and you'll save your lives. Don't let Germany be destroyed, join the *Frei Deutschland* movement headed by German patriots." At this point the Germans had perhaps heard enough and decided to silence the loudspeakers by delivering a barrage of machine-gun and mortar fire. The show was over; Rochlis and his party returned to the Divisional HQ satisfied with their performance.

15. Toward the Dnieper—Zaporozhye

On 5 July Hitler's armies launched their 1943 offensive dubbed Citadel, the third summer offensive since their invasion of the Soviet Union. This time, however, the strategic situation was quite different not only in comparison with 1941, but also from that of a year earlier, when I became a POW. The Germans were by now seriously weakened as a result of Stalingrad and its aftermath. They also fell out of their fortune in North Africa, and their own industrial centers in Germany were being pounded by American and English aircraft. All this meant that a transfer of significant forces from the West to the eastern front for a large-scale offensive operation was out of the question. The 1943 summer offensive was thus concentrated on a relatively small front line at the Kursk salient, where the Germans introduced technological novelties: brand-new, heavily armored tanks and self-propelled guns—Tigers, Ferdinands, Panthers, and other weapons, such as flame-throwing tanks. These new weapons were supposed to turn the 1943 summer offensive into a decisive German victory. It was a large gamble for them.

On the Red Army side, things had changed much for the better. The troops were by now massively supplied with arms and equipment, which at least in quantity surpassed what the enemy could put in the field. Our military leadership improved greatly as the war progressed. And so did the fighting spirit after Stalingrad; the feeling of confidence that success inspires was more and more noticeable among both our commanding officers and ordinary soldiers.

There were by now some highly regarded top generals, among whom the leading figure was Marshal Georgii Zhukov. They became proficient in ways of using and coordinating large masses of artillery, tanks, and aircraft. And what was no less important, they had learned how to avoid disastrous mistakes such as the one made a year earlier when Marshal Semen Timoshenko had been ordered to launch a preemptive strike on Kharkov, a strike that simply played into German hands.

This time Soviet troops at the Kursk salient were patiently waiting in several deeply echeloned and fortified zones for the enemy attack, ready to sustain the first thrust of the German blitz. Another very important difference from what took place a year earlier was that Soviet military leadership obtained key intelligence information on Citadel, which the Germans later claimed was coming from some kind of "betrayal at the Führer's headquarters." Be that as it may, in the battle of Kursk, Soviet troops were not taken by surprise. They were on full alert, though had, of course, no knowledge of where, exactly, the Germans would concentrate their main thrust, which army's attack would be the striking one, and which would merely have the task of covering flanks.

The Citadel plan was simple enough. The German positions were to the north, west, and south of the Kursk salient, so their plan was the well-tried recipe of a pincer operation. The objective was to encircle the Soviet forces in the Kursk area by means of a rapid thrust of two attacking armies, one in the northern direction from the Belgorod sector, the other in the southern direction from Orel. Hitler expected that his new *Wunderwaffen*—especially the Tigers and the Ferdinands—would bring a decisive turn in the war; indeed Soviet T-34 tanks that would happen to come into their sight were as good as finished. But those miracles of engineering, as they were called by the Germans, were few in number and, most important, had their vulnerable spots. Soviet troops in the Kursk salient quickly learned how to withstand their attacks. The Battle of Kursk was to become the greatest of all tank battles, on a scale unprecedented in the history of armored warfare. It was also one of the bloodiest. However, fighting back, the Soviet armies regained their previous positions and, after bringing up reinforcements and supplies, delivered their own crushing blows, destroying a good deal of the powerful German forces involved in operation Citadel. It is generally agreed that the Battle of Kursk was the turning point of the German-Russian war.

At this time, as part of the 78 Rifle Division, my regiment held positions to the south of the Kursk salient, and we were not involved in that fighting. We were kept in reserve on alert, just in case. The rest of what I call the trench-warfare period was used to bring our regiment up to strength after the bloody attacks at the bridgehead, and for intensive training; the same was going on in other regiments of the division.

When the Soviet summer offensive commenced in the second half of August 1943, our 78 Infantry Division was among the troops of the Southwestern Army Group (I prefer the term "group" instead of "front," because the latter when used to designate a group of armies—not a fixed location—is somewhat confusing). That army group, under General Rodion Malinovsky, had been deployed between the Steppe Army Group commanded by General Ivan Konev in the north and the Southern Army Group under General Fedor Tolbukhin in the south. It launched the first attack of the offensive on 13 August 1943. The task of the Southwestern Army Group, as made clear to us by our *politruk*s, was to liberate the Donbas and, in close cooperation with the Southern Army Group, advance to the Dnieper River.

It was fierce fighting in the Donbas, especially during the first three weeks, until on 6 September our troops finally captured Kramatorsk and Konstantinovka, the latter taken by our division. I was with the *razviedka* as we broke into that city. Burnt-out tanks littered the battlefields around Konstantinovka, mostly our own T-34s, some of the crews' charred, shrunken bodies still not removed, lying close to their tanks, left behind as worthless scrap.

The T-34 was a very good medium tank, superior to many German panzers of the same class, especially in maneuverability. Another advantage of this tank vis-à-vis the German was its broad tracks, allowing for much better movement on snow- or mud-covered ground. Still, we called the T-34s *spichechnye korobki* (matchboxes), and for two reasons. Firstly, they caught fire easily. When hit at vulnerable places they would instantaneously ignite, often incinerating their crews. The second reason for comparing them to boxes of matches was more positive: Since Stalingrad they were being produced on a mass scale. Indeed, the T-34s were to become a main weapon of Soviet victories. What they probably needed most in the second half of 1943 was a Russian Guderian.

The bloody fighting around Kramatorsk and Konstantinovka hindered our offensive. But even afterward our advance toward the Dnieper, though steady, was rather slow. It had taken us about four weeks to cover a distance of some two hundred miles between Kramatorsk and the Dnieper at Zaporozhye. I am speaking, of course, of the advance made by our 78 Division, but the same goes for the entire Southwestern Army Group and its neighbors on the flanks.

I must, of course, agree with the generally held view that the Soviet advance was slowed by the fierce resistance of German panzer troops under the skillful leadership of Marshal Manstein. In postwar German literature one can find glorifying words for what was achieved due to that resistance. To quote one such source: "Mid-September saw the start of the boldest withdrawal in military history. About a million German troops were pulled out of a 600-mile front, over six Dnieper bridges, and again fanned out to hold a 400-mile line on the near bank" (P. Carell, *Scorched Earth*, p. 322). I do not intend, of course, to question facts. However, there are always two sides to a coin. Based on my own experience and observations, I would like to point out a not-insignificant reason why our advance slowed down .

It can probably be said without exaggeration that at the time of our push toward the Dnieper, moreover, until the end of the war, the Soviet army was made up of two categories of military units. As the war progressed, the first category became a modern, well-equipped and trained, first-class fighting force. It included tank and air armies, tank and mechanized corps, artillery corps and divisions, air corps and air divisions, and others. To this category belonged also all kinds of "guards" forces, Stalin's favorite crack units: guards armies, guards tank armies, guards tank and mechanized corps, guards rifle corps, independent guards rifle divisions, and so on. He kept the guards troops for key assignments in offensive operations, and for counterattacks in defense. All guards units were granted special conditions of service. Their command and administrative officers received one and a half times, and all other ranks twice, the usual pay (which for nonofficers was not very much anyway), better uniforms, and more food rations. Some of the crack troops had a good deal of American military equipment. The first category armies also had plenty of American-made trucks and jeep field vehicles.

The second category, embracing the quantitatively main Soviet forces, was ordinary infantry armies, infantry corps, and infantry divisions. This was the *Tsaritsa Poley* (Tsarina of the Fields), as it was patronizingly called. Only a small section of the Soviet infantry, particularly the guards troops, was motorized; the vast majority were foot soldiers. The ordinary infantry divisions, when engaged in heavy fighting, especially at times of major offensives, would, of course, get outside support like tanks, self-propelled artillery, heavy long-range guns, air force, and even *katyusha* support (a Russian nickname for the formidable multirocket launchers, which the Germans, in turn, nicknamed "Stalin organs"). By themselves, however, the equipment, uniforms, and food supplies of ordinary infantry were much worse by comparison with those of guards infantry troops. We were especially sensitive to the unequal treatment with regard to food rations, perhaps even oversensitive mainly because most of the time we could eat more than we got. Strict military supplies such as ammunition were a top priority and, as a rule, at the expense of food supplies, which were quite often scaled down for military units of secondary importance such as those of the *Tsaritsa Poley.*

In general, it has been my impression that the ordinary Red Army rifle divisions of World War II were by themselves not much different from their Russian counterparts of World War I; they had probably many similar weaknesses and strengths. Among the first, I would mention a relative lack of military initiative and of military discipline, unless the latter was enforced with a firm hand. The weaknesses, however, were to a great extent offset by the amazing endurance of the Russian soldier, who during World War II fought toughly and could carry on without most of the things other armies regarded as basic necessities. No other army in the world could possibly withstand two years of horrible suffering inflicted by the cruelest enemy imaginable and still be able to turn the tables against him.

Insight into the matter of proportions between the two army categories can be obtained by a glance at the composition of the Southwestern Army Group, which on 1 September 1943 was as follows:

Armies:
>   combined arms: 6
>   air: 1

Corps:
>   rifle: 11
>   cavalry: 1
>   tank: 1
>   mechanized: 1

Divisions:
>   rifle: 41
>   cavalry: 3

Brigades:
>   motorized: 1
>   tank and assault gun: 3
>   artillery divisions: 3
>   AA (antiaircraft) divisions: 3
>   mortar brigades (ind.): 1
>   MRL (multiple rocket launcher) brigades (ind.): 1
>   TD (tank destroyer) artillery brigades (ind.): 2
>   air corps: 2
>   air divisions: 9
>   engineer brigades: 6

The 78 Rifle Division, of which my 458 Rifle Regiment was part
and parcel, was one of those forty-one rifle divisions listed above.
We were in the service of the *Tsaritsa Poley,* carrying a good deal on
our backs—not an insignificant reason that our push toward the
Dnieper was slow. As I recall, even PTRs, shoulder-fired antitank rifles, which were long-barreled and heavy, were sometimes carried
by two men because of a shortage of horse-drawn vehicles. These
crude weapons, effective against tanks at close range, whose handling required courage and coolness, were still in use in our regiment in the fall of 1943. In addition to the very heavy antitank

grenades applied by hand, the PTRs were the only personal antitank weapon at the disposal of a Soviet infantryman. At that time, German infantry was already equipped with the much more sophisticated *Panzerfaust*, an early bazooka-type weapon, very handy for personal tank-infantry combat.

Another Soviet antitank "weapon"—small dogs with antitank mines attached to their chests—was not used anymore. I heard eyewitnesses describing how a small dog, running directly toward an oncoming German tank, beneath its machine-gun fire, would "deliver" the mine under the tank, where it would explode, killing, of course, also the poor dog. Their use as antitank "weapons" had been discontinued, due mainly to training difficulties. The dogs had to be trained to run against roaring and firing tanks to get their daily food. Still, as I already mentioned, dogs continued in service of medical orderlies. And they were used in cities and towns to help in clearing mines.

In our regiment, however, "man's best friend" was not the dog but the horse. Our light 45mm antitank guns, which along with the 76mm artillery pieces were most essential for fighting enemy tanks, were up to the end of the war horse-drawn. Mortars had to be moved on horse-drawn carts. The same situation held for supplying ammunition, food, and fodder to the regiment, and the transportation of the wounded to hospitals. Our commanding officers, Colonel Shevchenko, his *zampolit*, Major Buldyshkin, his P.N.Sh.s (assistants), and all battalion commanders rode horses, while most other commanders used horse-drawn carts for themselves and their personal belongings. There was not a single motor vehicle in our regiment until the summer of 1944, when Colonel Shevchenko, the commander of the regiment, and Major Buldyshkin, his chief of staff, got themselves military jeeps, the only ones in our regiment until the end of the war. It is often said in military history books that during World War II the role of the horse was over. Perhaps so, but not quite in our regiment and not, I think, in the numerous rifle divisions of which the Red Army's *Tsaritsa Poley* was made up.

Sometimes I walked with the *razviedka* in front of the regiment in reconnaissance, at other times behind it, with our knapsacks, ammunition, and other supplies in a horse-drawn cart. Unless on parade or on solemn occasions such as victoriously entering a city or town, Soviet foot soldiers rarely marched in an orderly fashion, but when they did they often sang very nice old and new songs and marches, initiated by the yelling from time to time of some sergeant-instigator: *"Zapievay!"* (Set the tune!) I also liked to listen to a completely different tune, the quiet, central-Asian-sounding melody an Uzbek from some supply unit chanted all day long in his subdued voice. The melody was always the same, but the lyrics were his own. He composed the words himself, and they reflected what he was seeing or feeling at a given moment: a stream he was passing, a hill or a bird he was watching, his home in Tashkent, or Samarkand, or Bukhara he saw in his dreams, and so on.

After Konstantinovka, our regiment was progressing on the average at the rate of fifteen miles daily, sometimes much less or more depending on the enemy's resistance. But here is the main point: The enemy was motorized and we were on foot. This meant that in the early morning, the German main force under our attack would withdraw in their trucks, leaving only a rear guard, a couple of armored fighting vehicles, or just a motorcycle unit with machine gunners, to keep our entire regiment busy for a while. It would take the German main force an hour or so to distance themselves from their pursuers, and have a whole day for a rest, or for whatever they had to do not being bothered by the Ivans. In the meantime, we would engage in a skirmish with the Fritzes' rear guard, and it would sometimes take until noon to make them run, then we would walk until evening to find the German main force in its new, prepared-in-advance positions. It became almost a routine: all night wild shooting, then early in the morning their main force would depart in trucks, while we would be "chasing" them throughout the next day on foot, fighting on the way with their small rear guards. As I recall, we encountered strong German troop resistance, lasting perhaps a week, only north of the highway running east-west from Donetsk to Dniepropetrovsk, which they wanted to control as long as possible in order to "evacuate" goods and people from the Donbas.

Indeed, they had plenty of time to implement what became known as operation "scorched earth." Before I turn to this, however, I will describe an episode of which I have a vivid recollection.

One early morning—it must have been the end of September or the very beginning of October—my attention was drawn to a dramatic scene. The night shooting had just come to an end, when about a dozen enemy soldiers emerged from the woods. Hands up and clutching white flags of surrender, they cautiously approached our trenches, and then began screaming in the purest Russian: *"Bratcy, nye strelyayte! My svoi, Russkye."* (Brothers [affectionate], don't shoot! We are your own people, Russians.) At first our soldiers were startled. *Vlasovcy*! (Vlasovites!) they murmured to each other. After a while, however, in an outbreak of anger, berating them for "serving our enemies," many ran toward the Vlasovites to beat them up and roared themselves hoarse: *"Podletsy, izmienniki, nashu krov prolivali, svolochi!"* (Scoundrels, traitors, turncoats, you spilled our blood, scum!) As it turned out, two were *Hivis* (acronym for *Hilfswillige*—volunteer helpers in noncombatant service in the German Army), the others were indeed from the *Osttruppen,* volunteers fighting on the German side in detachments associated with Vlasov's name. Vlasov was the former Soviet general, commander of a front army in the Volkhov district, where he was taken prisoner by the Germans in July 1942. In captivity, he offered his services to the Wehrmacht. The bulk of the Osttruppen was composed of POWs who survived the horrors of the German prisoner of war camps. Vlasov dreamed of an independent Russia, liberated from the Bolsheviks, but under the Nazis he did not have any chance for that. Fighting on the German side, his soldiers had not been provided even with uniforms resembling anything Russian. They were wearing *Feldgrau* (greenish-gray) uniforms of the Wehrmacht. And it was these German uniforms they wore which, I believe, so infuriated our soldiers against the surrendering Vlasovites. Together with their weapons, which they had left in the woods, the Vlasovites were led under a heavy escort to our divisional HQ but, as I afterward heard on the way, some of those already badly beaten up had been shot.

Let me now return to the "scorched earth" plan. The plan allegedly originated with a special order issued on Hitler's behalf by Goering on 7 September 1943. But even before that most secret order of the *Reich-Marschall,* the chief of the general staff of land forces, General Zeitzler, issued on 30 August 1943 his own secret *Befehl* regarding "the evacuation of the Donets region," in which he gave orders "to organize and carry out the reception of evacuated population groups and economic assets of all kinds arriving in the domestic theater of operations as well as in the occupied eastern territories as a result of the evacuation of the Donets region."

There were two parts in that diabolical plan. First, German Army commanders were to carry off all stocks of foodstuffs and raw materials, all the livestock of collective and state farms, the industrial and agricultural machines of armament works. Grain and oleaginous fruit, horses, cattle, sheep and pigs, threshing machines and tractors, lathes and machine tools, as well as vehicles of every kind were to be taken along to behind the Dnieper. This part of the order had been implemented in a thorough German fashion. According to postwar German sources, the Wehrmacht forces retreating from the Donets region and the eastern Ukraine to the west took with them 200,000 head of cattle, 153,000 horses, 270,000 sheep; some 40,000 peasant carts were jolted toward the Dnieper; 300 trains were carrying grain, oleaginous crops, tractors, threshing machines, machine tools, and damaged tanks—not to mention human beings "evacuated" to Germany.

Second, in order to delay the Soviet advance as much as possible, a zone of twelve to twenty-five miles east of the Dnieper was to be turned into a desert. Whatever could not be removed was to be destroyed—blown up, burnt down, devastated—every house, every bridge, every road, every barn. The Russians were to enter a wilderness, where they would find no place to lie down for a rest, nothing to eat or drink. *Scorched earth.*

Concerning the second part of that plan, there is a tendency in postwar German military history to minimize and even justify destruction (see, for instance, P. Carell, *Scorched Earth*, pp. 327–33). On the one hand, the reader is told that the order to leave behind nothing but scorched earth could be implemented only to a limited extent. On the other hand, he is reminded that war is cruelty, that anyone who ever waged war also practiced scorched earth. In the Second World War—the apologist claims, repeating Manstein's argument (see F. E. von Manstein, *Lost Victories*, p. 470)—it was Stalin who first proclaimed it and made it an essential part of his own operations during retreats. But did Stalin's 3 July 1941 appeal to the population, the troops, and the partisans for a merciless fight against an enemy who invaded Russia really provide the Germans with an alibi?

After the war, German generals and officers of lesser rank received jail and some even death sentences for executing the "scorched earth" plan. To the apologist, however, this is no proof of their guilt. Why not? Because most were sentenced by courts of the Soviet Union. And what about those who, like Marshal Manstein himself, were sentenced by a British military court in Hamburg in 1949? Again, the apologist finds mitigating circumstances; there was a long list of the scorched earth indictments and on seventeen points Manstein was acquitted, because the court acknowledged the military necessity of the measures. There was only one point the British court did not accept as military necessity, the abduction of some of the civilian population. On that account and some others, Manstein was found guilty.

Manstein was probably Hitler's most brilliant field commander, but perhaps also one of the most eager executors of his policy, including the implementation of scorched earth as well as the anti-Jewish measures. Moreover, the marshal—sometimes hailed also as the general-gentleman—was in the field of policy, as in his military field, capable of invention and initiative, as indicated in the following order of his:

> The Jewish-Bolshevist system must be exterminated. . . . The German soldier . . . comes also as the bearer of a racial concept. He must appreciate the necessity for the harsh punishment of Jewry. . . . The food situation at home makes it essential that the troops should be fed off the land, and that the largest possible stock should be placed at the disposal of the homeland. In enemy cities, a large part of the population will have to go hungry. Nothing, out of a misguided sense of humanity, may be given to prisoners or to the population unless they are in the service of the German Wehrmacht. (*Trial of German Major War Criminals Before the International Military Tribunal,* Volume XX, p. 642)

Since the term "scorched earth" cannot be quantitatively defined, it is difficult to assess to what extent the order was implemented. On the basis of what I witnessed myself, however, I would say that the Germans were certainly good at this job and, moreover, it went far beyond those twelve to twenty-five miles east of the Dnieper. As a matter of fact, as soon as we crossed the Donets, I saw railway lines that had been blown up or cut at regular intervals by German engineering crews. They invented a special device, the "trackwolf," to rip up railroad ties. Railroad stations, water towers, and all the requisite paraphernalia of a properly run railroad had been completely destroyed. Since fuel and ammunition for Soviet tank and motorized troops were being supplied mainly by rail, it may perhaps be said that all this was measures hindering their race to the Dnieper. But I also witnessed scorched earth deeds having very little to do with any "military necessities." And it was not just dynamited factories and demolished agricultural machinery repair stations along with small wooden bridges over streams on dirt roads leading to those stations. In numerous villages, barns and storage facilities were burnt down, grain silos blown up, and farmers left without grain to tide them over until the next harvest. In Kramatorsk and Konstantinovka as well as in many other places German soldiers set fire to houses and shot inhabitants who resisted. I saw mile after mile of signs of cruelty, devastation, and misery. The Russians have a special capacity for suffering no other people seem to have, and so the only bitter complaints I heard were mostly about boys that had been "evacuated" and young girls who had been taken away to slave labor in Germany. Could one interpret the latter in terms of "military necessity"?

In spite of the boasting about the Wehrmacht's most brilliant and boldest withdrawal of troops in military history, the Red Army scored a decisive victory in its push to the Dnieper. The Central, Voronezh, Steppe, and Southwestern Army Groups had advanced between 110 and 200 miles. They reached the Dnieper on a 450-mile front, captured many bridgeheads, and laid solid foundations for future offensive operations.

From the first week of October our 78 Division, supported by tanks and heavy corps artillery, was taking part in the battle for Zaporozhye. It was a city of great importance to the Germans and even more so to us, though, of course, not just for its past rich history. This was once the place, in the sixteenth through eighteenth centuries, where the Zaporozhye cossacks had their headquarters on the mid-stream island of Khortitsa. Under the Soviets, Zaporozhye with its gigantic dam—then the biggest in Europe—and its huge power station became a showpiece of the hydro industry, supplying power to the Ukrainian industrial region. For the same reason it was important to the Germans, because the generating capacity, which had been partly damaged in 1941 by the retreating Soviets, was by then restored to about half a million kilowatts, keeping alive the iron mines of Krivoy Rog and the Kirovograd metallurgical plants working for them.

Most significant, however, in the fall of 1943 was the strategic position of Zaporozhye. In order to hold the dam in their hands, the Germans formed a large and well-defended bridgehead, on the eastern side of the Dnieper. The German bridgehead provided a serious obstacle for the entire Soviet offensive, because it was a threat to the forces advancing toward Dniepropetrovsk from the north, while at the same time preventing the thrust of the Southern Army Group to the south between the Dnieper bend and the Sea of Azov toward the approaches to the Crimea. That was why General Malinovsky was attacking Zaporozhye with a force of three armies, a tank corps, and an air fleet. The 78 Division, which included my regiment, was but a tiny fraction of that force. Obviously I can describe only what I witnessed within that relatively small section of the front line.

In the second week of October our regiment took part in repeated attacks against the bridgehead. Its German defenders inflicted on us heavy losses in killed and wounded. Several times our infantrymen had broken into the German lines and each time they were thrown back by enemy counterattacks. In the first day alone, half a dozen T-34 tanks supporting our attacks were left in the field, most burning like torches only two of their crews escaped unhurt from their "matchboxes."

Our *razviedka* was now hunting for "tongues" on an almost daily basis with less than a twenty percent rate of success. The information we got from them and their documents proved to be very important. Around 10 October, I, too, went with Kravchenko and the *razviedka* in search of a "tongue." It was scary; our reconnaissance was detected by the enemy and we came under dense machine-gun fire. Two of our comrades were wounded, one in the head, the other in the arm; I ended up with light scratches on my belly. But it was not in vain. We caught a German infantry grenadier together with his *Panzerfaust*. His interrogation went smoothly, there was no problem in making "his tongue loose." Presenting himself as an antifascist—and he made the impression of telling the truth—he was eager to talk. He told me about preparations to dynamite the dam, but could not or would not provide any specifics; he was sent almost immediately to the HQ of our division. As we learned later, two hundred tons of dynamite had been stacked in the turbine hall of the power station, and forty tons had been placed in the mine chambers of the dam itself, together with a hundred aerial bombs, all of them 1,000-pounders, making another fifty tons.

The battle for Zaporozhye intensified. German positions were bombarded day and night by our heavy guns. But this was nothing in comparison with the massive artillery barrage that came at the end of the second week of October. It was the first time that I witnessed independent artillery divisions concentrated on such a scale to provide rapid and continuous fire at focal points for about an hour. Now it was the real *Bog voiny*—god of war, as the artillery was called—that spoke. The intensity of the bombardment was enormous and it proved to be crucial for the breakthrough. On the night of 14–15 October, our 78 Division entered the city. The horizon was bright red from the fire of thousands of our guns. Around midnight we heard a noise like a crash of thunder nearby. It was the German attempt to demolish the hydropower dam. But in spite of the enormous quantity of dynamite and other high explosives used, only a few gaps were torn in the massive concrete wall of the 800-yard-long structure.

The liberation of Zaporozhye was perhaps, by comparison with others, not a spectacular victory, but it had far-reaching consequences, as was recorded in the Soviet book *The History of the Great Patriotic War of the Soviet Union, 1941–1945:* "With the liberation of Zaporozhye the situation in the southern Ukraine was fundamentally changed." The Soviet High Command recognized the contribution made by our division in the battle for Zaporozhye. It was mentioned

in an order of appreciation and was given the honorary title Zaporozhye Division. From now on it was the 78 Rifle Zaporozhskaya
Division. I do not know if there were any other divisions that received
the same title. For my part in capturing the German grenadier, I got
the *Medal za Otvagu* (medal for bravery).

The Germans had to withdraw from their bridgehead at Zaporozhye on the east bank of the river, but they were still able to hold
for the next couple of months to the inside bend of the Dnieper at
Krivoy Rog and Nikopol, where there were precious manganese ores
and nonferrous metal deposits—copper and nickel—considered vital to their armaments industry. Thus, we in turn were moving to the
northwest with the aim of crossing the Dnieper to a bridgehead on
the west side of the river.

The Dnieper is a mighty river, the third largest in Europe. There
was no bridge at the crossing, and our passage to the bridgehead had
to be accomplished just in a few ferryboats under German long-range
artillery fire. I vividly recall this. It was evening, the skies were dark,
the cold autumn rain had been pouring nonstop for the last couple
of days. An artillery shell hit the water, our barge turned over, and,
together with others from our *razviedka*, I found myself in the cold
water of the Dnieper. I could not swim and would have drowned had
it not been for the helping hands of my comrades. Luckily for all of
us, we were not very far from the western shore of the river.

But when we extricated ourselves from the muddy water, rain was
still pelting down and there was no village in sight. After several miles
of walking, all wet, the commanding officers, having found a single
house for themselves, ordered the soldiers to spend the night nearby.
Shivering, I was looking for a place to rest, and noticed a small dog-
house with man's best friend in it. I am not proud to admit that I
chased the dog out of its own house; there was no room in it for the
two of us.

We had been moving slowly along the east bank of the Dnieper
in a northwest direction. For a couple of weeks we were engaged in
a kind of trench warfare, but just then the war came to a standstill.
It was one of those memorable events. I do not recall the name of
the place, it was somewhere to the northeast of Krivoy Rog, on a small
but widely flooded area full of mosquitoes. For days there was no

shooting whatsoever, as most of our regiment—and the same was probably the case with our enemy on the other side of the swampy river—got sick with malaria. I, too, succumbed to that dreadful disease, and felt extremely fatigued going through recurrent chills and fevers. We were treated with large doses of quinine.

It must have been mid-November—winter was fast approaching—when we were transferred from that malaria-infested region to the reserve and to a resting area. It was a complete rest for the first time since my "real war" had begun. Here our regiment received its military reequipment and was outfitted with winter uniforms. I got a complete warm outfit, including a pair of brand-new light beige and perfectly fitting *valenky*. We all quickly, at least temporarily, recovered from malaria and, not bothered by much military training, were just resting, writing letters, rereading old ones, listening to the by now mostly good news.

Gomel was liberated on 26 November 1943. In July 1941 many Jews succeeded in fleeing from that city into the Soviet interior, as Hanna managed to do. But now I also learned about the fate of some of those who had been unable or did not try to escape before the Germans occupied Gomel on 19 August 1941. The Jews had been herded into a short-lived ghetto and were soon exterminated. In the month of December alone, about twenty-five hundred were shot and buried in military trenches near Retchitsa; another four thousand Jews from Gomel were put to death in antitank ditches on the outskirts of the city. The women and children were gassed.

I recall a conversation I had at that time with Colonel Shevchenko. A group of my countrymen-refugees had formed the ZPP—the Union of Polish Patriots—under the leadership of the writer Wanda Wasilewska, a favorite of Stalin's. There were hundreds of thousands of Poles and Polish Jews scattered over the USSR, including some ex–war prisoners, who for one reason or another had not been incorporated in the Anders army, which left the Soviet Union in 1942. Subsequently, in the spring of 1943, ZPP became the official sponsor of the Kosciuszko Infantry Division, which, at the time the conversation took place, had already been engaged in frontline combat on Soviet soil. The birth of a friendly Polish Army, closely cooperating with the Soviet army, had been given extensive coverage in the press, and this was actually the topic of the conversation when I entered the regiment's HQ. I must have said something that the regiment's commander construed as a hint of my willingness to join the Polish Army. He felt offended. *"Razvye tebye u nas plokho? Razvye my khuzhe Poliakov voyuyem?"* (You have it bad with us? You think we are worse fighters than the Poles?) I could give only the respectful reply in negative to these questions: *"Nykak nyet"* (By no means). And I really meant it.

Somewhat later, the topic of the Polish Army appeared in my correspondence with Hanna. She was considering joining the army, while I strongly urged her not to. I did not want her to join any army, not only because I did firmly believe that front lines were not a place for women. I was afraid of what could possibly happen to her. Hanna was all I had, my only link to the past and my only hope for the future. Whenever I thought of the future, I was thinking of her. I wanted her to be alive, waiting for me, not just on the photo I had with me all the time.

While in the resting area, we tried to amuse ourselves as best we could. I liked most of all to listen to the songs of the local girls, which were often accompanied by Zvyzda, a cheerful guy with an angelic face from the submachine gun company, playing the accordion. The Ukrainian girls, like the Russian ones, have a great natural gift for singing, and are second to none in forming impromptu small, well-integrated choirs. It is perhaps due to that natural flair that they have also those many rich, beautiful folk songs famous all over the world. These choirs had become our favorite pastime. The girls would gather in front of a house, ostensibly to do some work, like spinning wool into yarn. While at this work they would joke and swear, but as soon as enough soldiers came to watch and ask for songs, they would begin the show. I sat on a bench across from them, listening, engrossed in the songs about past triumphs and disasters, but especially those expressing sorrow as well as joy. During intermissions a girl would lay her head in the lap of another and ask: *"Poishchyy menya"* (Look for lice). They would take turns picking lice from each other's hair in the same natural way they sang.

The regions west of the Dnieper had fertile black earth, and the people here were comparatively better off than those on the other side of the river, thanks, perhaps, also, to the proximity to the Donbas and other industrial centers. Still, the villages, like those I saw elsewhere, were by any standards extraordinarily poor. The average peasant house was a large one-room hut made of clay and straw, covered with a thatched roof. The cowshed was sometimes attached to the entrance and thus, before entering the room, one had to remove the dung off one's boots, usually with a multipurpose knife, sometimes the only one in the household. There was, of course, no running water nor indoor plumbing, and often no outdoor facilities either. Because of the latter, it was quite common to see people—men, women, and children—squatting behind a house to relieve themselves and, as paper was in very short supply—newspapers when available were saved for rolling up a smoke—pulling a straw out of the roof to clean themselves up.

Before holidays the earthen floors inside the huts were cleaned and made glossy by rubbing cow manure into them. Afterward they were lightly sprinkled for embellishment with yellow or pink-reddish sand, whatever was locally available. It was called making the *dolivka* (the floor, in Ukrainian), a difficult job because the floor was as hard as concrete, and rubbing in the manure was done by hand. Since it was quite a chore, neighbors often talked about it and invited one another to see their work: "I am already done with my *dolivka*, come and take a look how it came out." It was, of course, best to postpone the visit for a day or two untill the smell evaporated. Inside the hut on the earthen floor stood a few pieces of furniture, hewed out by a local carpenter or anyone handy with an ax: a rough table, several chairs and/or stools, and a large trunk. The trunk was usually most impressive, often an inherited piece of furniture that served both for storage and to sleep on. On the walls hung shelves with earthenware on them, as well as embroidered towels and other handiwork, while in the center one could see an old, usually inherited icon.

On top of centuries of poverty, the average village had been impoverished by collectivization and dekulakization, and made quite miserable by the German scorched earth policy. The past and recent battles led to the complete destruction of many villages, where fire and shells left only the chimneys standing. Still people stayed behind in the ruins of their houses or in dugouts, while those living in bullet-ridden huts were considered to be lucky. The village where I was staying with the *razviedka* had been relatively unscarred. Yet my *khozyaika* was desperately poor, had no flour to bake her own bread, and enjoyed the soldiers' bread that I shared with her. Reciprocating, she would put on the table the few potatoes in her possession. She was a kindly soul. "Let me wash your shirt, or blouse or drawers," she would propose, and when I mentioned that I had no soap, which she had neither, she would still insist, "Let me at least fry them a little in the oven to kill the lice."

The village was lucky also in another respect: it was one of the very few, out of the hundreds of Russian and Ukrainian villages I saw during the war, with a church still standing in it. It was reopened under German occupation, and a priest, who under the Soviets had been hiding, reappeared to provide religious services. Now, however, with the return of the Soviets, the church was closed again and the priest must have, as before, gone into hiding.

I got to know and became very fond of those village people, good-hearted, their hands callused by endless toil, desperately poor and yet ready to share with strangers whatever little food and dreadfully cramped shelter they had. Almost every family had lost someone in the war or, before the war, during the famines associated with the collectivization of agriculture and the deportations of the so-called kulaks in the beginning of the 1930s, or in the purges during the second half of the 1930s. The upheavals of the 1930s took away from them not only many of their loved ones and many of their possessions, but also some basic human freedoms, including religious freedom. These were mostly religious folks, but there were no places of worship for them to pray. The churches in almost all the villages, even in those that escaped the ravages of war, had been destroyed already in the first half of the 1930s by the Soviets themselves; they had been demolished, burnt, or, half in ruin, transformed into warehouses.

16. The Gullies of Korsun-Shevchenkovsky

A renaming of Soviet army groups had taken place on 20 October 1943. The Voronezh Army Group became known as the First Ukrainian Army Group, and the Steppe, Southwestern, and Southern Groups as the Second, Third, and Fourth Ukrainian Army Groups respectively. The latter three army groups, taking advantage of the tremendous victory at Kursk, crossed the middle Dnieper River in October but were unable to achieve a decisive breakthrough before the winter. Now, since mid-December, our 78 Rifle Division, as part of the Third Ukrainian Army Group, had been preparing itself intensively for the forthcoming operations.

Our *razviedka* was required to deliver a "tongue," one a week, which proved to be too difficult for our boys. For encouragement they would get before each action two hundred grams of alcohol, twice the amount that was given to other frontline soldiers to keep them warm during the winter. Fortunately, it was not pure alcohol, because on the way down to the frontline soldiers water had been added to it by all the middlemen trying to get a share of the "firewater." Though mixed with water, it was still strong enough to knock out a guy like myself, who could not get used to drinking the dregs. On the eve of the new year, 1944, I got drunk and *doigralsya do bedy* (got into trouble). Our *razviedka* had just returned from a mission without a "tongue," and having lost two comrades, Trofimov and Zubov, who were killed and left somewhere in no-man's land, I decided to join the others in an attempt to recover the two bodies. Being drunk, however, I did not even duck and went straight ahead almost into German hands. Luckily, the other guys, who were not as drunk as I, caught up with me and pulled me back in time. The bodies of our two dead comrades had not been recovered. As we sat in despair and sorrow, the guys pulled out a couple of bottles of ill-smelling moonshine. It was New Year's Eve. "Let's drink, friends, nothing else left to do." Somebody poured the stuff into my cup. I did not feel like drinking anymore, yet I said to myself, "To hell with it, go ahead." All I remember about what came next was that I was sobbing and crying, drinking in sorrow with the rest of our *razviedka,* and crying more and more. I think I was crying bitter tears not only because I had been plunged in grief over the death of my comrades. Their death brought out of me the deep, hidden feelings of frustration with this terrible just war I was in up to my neck. But to get dead drunk was not the right way to mourn fallen comrades. Next day I made up my mind to rigorously keep myself from drinking too much and to avoid getting drunk the way it happened on the dawn of 1 January 1944.

The winter offensive began to the north of us. In mid-January 1944, the First Ukrainian Army Group, commanded by General Nikolai Vatutin, after an advance of 50 to 125 miles in three weeks, halted its offensive southwest of Kiev. The group's left wing enveloped the German forces that were still entrenched on the western bank of the Dnieper in the vicinity of Kanev. The Second Ukrainian Army Group, headed by General Ivan Konev, which had been on the offensive since 5 January, captured Kirovograd and enveloped the south flank of the same German force, subsequently known as the Korsun-Shevchenkovsky group. This presented an opportunity for encirclement and liquidation of nearly eighty thousand German troops, according to Soviet estimates. Generals Vatutin and Konev were therefore ordered to encircle and destroy that group by advancing in converging directions and to link up at Zvenigorodka. Marshal Georgii Zhukov, Stalin's best general, formally as representative of the GHQ, was charged with coordinating the operations of the two army groups in the field.

According to Zhukov, twenty-seven divisions, four tank and one mechanized corps, comprising 370 tanks and self-propelled guns, were committed to liquidate the Korsun-Shevchenkovsky group. The quantitative superiority over the enemy was 70 percent in infantry, 140 percent in guns and mortars, 160 percent in tanks and self-propelled guns—which was unquestionably sufficient to encircle and rout the enemy (*The Memoirs of Marshal Zhukov,* New York: Delacorte Press, 1971, p. 501). Other independent sources, probably counting also some additional reinforcements—I will return to this—provide estimates of even greater Soviet superiority: the ratio of forces in its favor: 3 to1 in men, 3.2 to 1 in artillery, 1.9 to 1 in tanks and assault guns, the ratio in aircraft 1to 1 (Colonel T. N. Dupuy and Paul Martell, *Great Battles on the Eastern Front: The Soviet-German War, 1941–1945,* Indianapolis/New York: The Bobbs-Merrill Co., 1982, pp. 130–31).

The Korsun-Shevchenkovsky operation lasted from 24 January until 17 February 1944. On 3 February the encirclement of the German forces in the pocket was complete. (Korsun-Shevchenkovsky was located to the west of Cherkassy, hence in German military history it is often termed the "Cherkassy pocket.") The Red Army formed two rings, the inner, made up of infantry, to squeeze the Germans in the pocket, and the outer ring, made up of tank units, ready to repel the anticipated German counterattack, which indeed soon materialized in an effort to relieve the encircled troops. To prevent the rescue, Soviet GHQ committed the Second Tank Army from its reserves. In addition some reinforcements from the Third Ukrainian Army Group, among them our 78 Rifle Division, were rushed toward Korsun-Shevchenkovsky.

It was midwinter, with temperatures about fifteen degrees below freezing, when we were ordered to move north. Thick layers of icy snow were covering the fields and the road conditions were just impossible even for our foot soldiers and the horse-drawn vehicles carrying ammunition, food, fodder, and most of our commanding officers. During that winter march we rarely slept in huts. I vaguely remember the three of us—Kravchenko, Titov, and myself—sharing the floor with some peasant family and a pair of sheep or a goat, taken in because of the cold, all in one room. But ordered to hurry, the regiment walked literally day and night most of the time. Everybody dreamed of sleeping one's fill, but the only sleep available for those on foot was during what we called *perekur s dremotoy* (a break for a smoke with a catnap). At night we had often to move *po*

azimutu (according to the azimuth), and this task of leading our regiment in the right direction with the help of a map, a compass, and
the observation of the starry skies was given by Colonel Shevchenko
to our *razviedka.*

We arrived in the Korsun-Shevchenkovsky area on 16 February, my
twenty-third birthday, during a blizzard followed by a heavy snowstorm. By that time some German troops had been able to break out
of the ring most were already killed or wounded or captured, though
a fierce battle was still raging as Soviet troops were finishing the job
of annihilating those resisting to the very end. Our 78 Infantry Division came too late to directly participate in the Korsun-
Shevchenkovsky operation.

What I saw the next morning, however, looked like something out
of this world. It was a terrain of large valleys and many eroded *balkas*
(gullies), which offered good cover to both attackers and defenders.
Indeed, one could see numerous signs of the ferocious battles that
had taken place here a day or two earlier: shot-up tanks and self-propelled guns, smashed and burned-out trucks, dead horses, even a
couple of shot-down planes. But all this was ordinary stuff on battlefields. I had witnessed such scenes already before. It was something
else and completely different that caught my eye. A large valley amid
the gullies was covered with grayish-white snow and dotted up to the
horizon with hundreds of dead people. That, too, was not altogether
uncommon. It was an unusual and indescribable scene because almost all of the corpses were completely naked; the skin of their
frozen bodies under the rising sun was less gray than pinkish, as if
they just went to sleep after a hot shower. I stood transfixed, watching that unreal, unearthly sight. I could not take my eyes off it.

I had seen people before wearing articles of clothing taken from
the bodies of fallen German soldiers, but I never thought it was done
in such a thorough way and almost directly under fire. Yet another
horrible sight was waiting for me that same early morning. Soon after leaving the valley, I came across a local woman emerging from a
gully and I noticed something bulky under her winter shawl covering her coat. I gave her a curious look and in response, without the
slightest hesitation, matter-of-factly, she lifted her shawl, revealing an
ax and a pair of glossy officer boots with protruding legs cut off above

the knees. She liked the boots, she told me, but could not take them off because they stuck tight to the stiff's frozen legs. At home, as they thawed, the legs could easily be removed without damage to the boots.

On 18 February Moscow saluted the troops that took part in the surrounding and destroying of the enemy group at Korsun-Shevchenkovsky. Estimates of casualties vary depending on the source. Soviet sources reported that the Germans lost 55,000 dead and wounded and 18,000 men captured; no figures were given for our own losses. The Germans claimed much lower casualties. German postwar military historians insist that the Soviets had a totally mistaken idea of their enemy's strength caught in the pocket. They estimate that no more than 56,000 men were surrounded and that out of that total, 2,188 wounded were flown out, while 35,000 men broke out of encirclement and safely arrived at reception points. Hence the casualty balance sheet of Korsun-Shevchenkovsky was 18,000 men (P. Carell, *Scorched Earth*, pp. 432–33).

Still, there is no denying that the Russians scored a major victory in the Korsun-Shevchenkovsky operation. First, even at the much lower figures, it meant the elimination of the fighting power of six and a half German divisions that had lost all their weapons; none of the troops saved from the pocket were fit for action. Second, it had enormous strategic consequences, which were vastly more important than the numbers of casualties in the Korsun-Shevchenkovsky pocket. The Third Ukrainian Army Group, of which we were part, could now push toward the Soviet-Romanian border, because there were no adequate German forces and, in wintertime, no natural barriers left east of the Romanian frontier.

17. On the Road to Romania

We had been moving at first on the left flank of Konev's Army Group, which in the beginning of March stormed the fiercely defended town of Uman, wiped out the enemy force there, crossed the Southern Bug River, and continued to race toward the Dniester River. Uman had a centuries-long history of Jewish pogroms. In 1768 a Zaporozhyan cossack, Maxim Zheleznyak, collected a band of *gaidamaks* (bandit-rebels) and slashed, burned, and terrorized his way up to the gates of Uman, where subsequently hundreds of Jews were massacred. On the eve of World War II, a significant percent of Uman's population was Jewish. I did not know how many were evacuated before the German onslaught and the bloody battle that raged here in the summer of 1941. To annihilate the Germans at Uman was a symbolic revenge for the Red Army soldiers killed, and the almost 100,000 men they captured alive at that town in August 1941. A month later the Jews of the town of Uman and its subdistrict—men, women, and children—were massacred by special units of SS soldiers. Now, two and a half years later, Uman was a destroyed ghost town. If some Jews survived there in hiding, I had not met a single one.

We left that forsaken place for the Vinnitsa district, and there made a sharp turn, heading in a southwestern direction across the Southern Bug and toward the Dniester. Both these rivers run into the Black Sea, west of the Dnieper, which also flows into that sea. We were advancing through the southern Ukraine toward Bessarabia and Bucovina. In the cities and towns between the Dnieper and the Dniester a considerable part of the population was Jewish. While many had been evacuated or escaped in 1941 with the retreating

Soviets, several hundred thousand Jews remained there. Immediately after the invasion the Germans murdered thousands of them and set up ghettos in various places, including those we were now passing or came close to, but as a rule their existence was very short-lived, filled with incessant deportations and extermination. Even in big cities the Germans were in a rush to murder Jews as quickly as possible. I already mentioned the fate of the Jews in Kharkov in December 1941, two months after the Nazis captured that city. They did the same thing earlier in Kiev, the capital of the Ukraine, immediately after taking it in September 1941. Jews were brought to the Babi Yar ravine, outside the city, and 34,000 were machine-gunned to death by the SS. Altogether, more than 100,000 people, mainly Jews, were killed in Babi Yar during the German occupation. One *Einsatzkommando* that had been killing Jews in the Ukraine reported already in April 1942 that the whole of the Crimea was "purged of Jews." The same unit had killed 91,678 Jews in just four and a half months.

Of course, I did not know all these statistics in the first days of March 1944 when we were moving southwest toward Romania. But passing through the many places known to have had large Jewish populations, and where we were presently being welcomed as liberators by the surviving inhabitants, I met not one Jew. By that time, however, I had already a pretty good idea of the calamity that had befallen the Jews under the Germans, and in particular about some of the Nazis' evil deeds in the Ukraine and my native Poland.

AlthoughI could find few details in the available newspapers, I knew about the uprising in the Warsaw ghetto and its quelling in April–May 1943. I read (at the end of 1943 or in the beginning of 1944) excerpts from Vasily Grossman's *The Ukraine Without Jews*; Ilya Ehrenburg's antifascist articles, some with Jewish themes, among them pamphlets on Jews who escaped from ghettos and joined Soviet partisans; dispatches of war correspondents about liberation of death camps; and so on. News about the fate of the Jews in Poland was of particular interest to me. More and more often I had dreams about my mother—all dreadful.

I began to probe lecturers who happened to come to our regiment to give talks on international affairs with questions about the uprising in the Warsaw ghetto, the assistance it received from partisans, and, particularly, from the Polish underground. I could not squeeze out of them any specifics. After the war, I learned that while there were some Poles who had tried to help, by and large, with the exception of those few righteous people, the remnants of the young Jews fighting in the ruins of the Warsaw ghetto were to the very end on their own. Tadeusz Bor-Komorowski, the commander of the *Armia Krajowa* (home army), the main underground army of the Polish government in exile, wrote in his book (*The Secret Army*, Nashville, Tenn.: Battery Press, 1984) of actions he had taken in the face of mass deportations and killings of Jews. But his contentions about assistance given to Jews have no basis in fact (see Israel Gutman, ed., *Encyclopedia of the Holocaust*, Vol. 1, p. 232). The other, much weaker underground organization under PPR (Polish Workers Party) was, after the party gained power in Poland in 1944–45, even more boisterous about its alleged assistance to the Warsaw ghetto fighters. However, under the scrutiny of research, these claims were gradually toned down; it was only "some" or "modest," or just assistance that was "too little too late." The fact is that there was literally none.

An acknowledgment of that fact came finally from such an authority as Wladyslav Gomulka, who at the time of the Warsaw ghetto uprising held the highest post in the PPR, the first secretary of its Central Committee. In his memoirs, published posthumously, in a chapter titled "Uprising in the Warsaw Ghetto," Gomulka describes how he was approached by a representative of the JFO (Jewish Fighting Organization) asking for arms and explosives. "Naturally, from our own resources we could not deliver anything, even one gun," says Gomulka. Then he mentions that his underground people had gotten hold of a box of detonators for hand grenades without the grenades themselves. At the next meeting with the same representative, Gomulka told him that "if the JFO had that kind of grenades without detonators, we could deliver them." The JFO had been eager to get the box of detonators, assuring him that it would make good use of them in its own production of explosives. "I was not sure about that," writes Gomulka. For that reason he had decided on having a new meeting in the same place, "where I would give him the first ten detonators." Still, for conspiracy reasons but mainly because of Gomulka's skepticism about the efficacy of the Jewish fighters, even those ten detonators never reached the JFO (W. Gomulka, *Pamietniki,* Tom II, Warszawa: PGW, 1994, pp. 274–75).

When we crossed the Southern Bug in the beginning of March, there was a sudden change in the weather with early spring floods all over the still-frozen earth. My beautiful *valenki* became completely useless. Supplies were lagging and I could not count on getting army shoes soon. The only solution left was to turn to village people and barter away my winter footwear for regular shoes, which I did, like some other imprudent soldiers who neglected to keep a pair of leather shoes in their knapsacks. Since I did not like heavy packs on my back, I was among those guys who followed the Russian—not always sensible—proverb: *Bog dast den', dast y pishchu* (God gives the day, God will provide).

The winter was definitely over, and it was followed by *rasputitsa,* the muddy season, which in this region of black earth and mostly dirt roads has always been synonymous with *bezdorozhye*—roadlessness. It would be incorrect to describe such a road as a river of mud, because the mud was not moving as water in a river does; it was stationary and sticky, often more than two feet thick. Whom did "General Mud" threaten more, the Soviets or the Germans? The fact is that not even the most up-to-date technology could cope with these road conditions, so one might say that the *rasputitsa* should have immobilized both advancing and retreating troops alike. Two important qualifications must be added. The first is that while it posed grave problems for Soviet motorized units, bringing their advance to a halt, the withdrawing German troops lost a good deal of their equipment in the *rasputitsa,* to a great extent because of lack of motor fuel that could not be delivered under these weather conditions. We were passing hundreds and hundreds of abandoned trucks, numerous pieces of self-propelled artillery, and many tanks concreted into the deep mud. I said, "We were passing," and this brings me to the second point. The muddy roads, which brought the advance of Soviet motorized forces to a standstill, were still not impassable for the *Tsaritsa Poley.* Amazing, but it is a fact to which I can testify because I was there and participated in that incredible endeavor.

How did we move through that sea of mud? There were deep though narrow furrows in the mud made by the retreating German tanks, armored carriers, and the tractors on tracks, not to mention the thousands of wheels under heavy trucks. Caterpillars of Red Army infantrymen were now walking in those narrow furrows, carrying everything on their backs, including machine guns. An attempt was made by Captain Baron's artillerymen to move some of his disassembled 45mm guns this way, but it failed, while infantry was able to move ahead. Walking in those furrows, one had, however, to be very careful not to step into the knee-deep black morass; it pulled the boots off one's feet. In order to progress at all, we had to follow the old proverb: *Tishe yedyesh, dalshe budyesh* (Slow and steady wins the race).

Due to the *rasputitsa*, all delivery of supplies, including foodstuffs, came to a stop. We soon reached a point when not a crumb of food could reach us. And we could not count for much on the local inhabitants. The area was sparsely populated, the few villages we saw on the horizon had for sure also been buried in mud, and we would not dare leave the main road anyway. This was sugar beet country with sugar beet refineries on the state farms. Already in the mid-nineteenth century great landlords of the Ukraine established sugar factories here, based on large-scale cultivation of beets; several great sugar fortunes were also made by Jews. In the Soviet period, the area of sugar beet plantations had been significantly enlarged again and, at the same time, sugar beet refineries had been equipped with new technology. Now, in mid-March 1944, these sugar refineries, more or less evenly scattered among the plantations, their storage facilities usually on the main road, became a major source of our food supplies, providing us with molasses and refined sugar.

I have a vivid recollection of that muddy road, and it is associated in my mind with sugar. One morning, Colonel Shevchenko stopped the long line of his soldiers walking along the furrows in the mud. "Take off the packs and open them," he ordered. Many were full of sugar. "And now," came the next order, "empty them into the mud and fill up your knapsacks with cartridges—you may need them badly soon." The soldiers, willy-nilly, followed the orders; it was a pity to part with the sugar. We left behind us rows of white mounds;

looking back from some distance it was like an icing on a mile-long chocolate cake.

The *Tsaritsa Poley* defeated "General Mud." When about 20 March we arrived at the Prut River bordering Romania, somewhere southwest of Faleshti, the *rasputitsa* was no more, though it rained for days on end. We had also left behind us the entire region of "Transnistria," which, almost without noticing, we passed walking along all those muddy roads.

I put the name Transnistria in quotation marks because it was an artificial geographic term, created in World War II. It was the designation of the part of the Ukraine conquered by German and Romanian forces in the summer of 1941, which Hitler handed to Romania as a reward for its participation in the war against the Soviet Union. Geographically it was the region between the Southern Bug and the Dniester rivers, the Black Sea in the south, and the line beyond the city of Mogilev in the north.

Badly beaten under Stalingrad, Romanian troops had no desire to fight for Transnistria in the early spring of 1944. They had abandoned the region even before the *rasputitsa* arrived. Russian soldiers were now mocking Ion Antonescu, the Romanian dictator, and his exorbitant ambition to create a *Romanya Mare* (great Romania). Our soldiers, mixing Russian and Romanian words, ridiculed the dictator to the tune of a popular Romanian song. They sang: *"Antonescu dal prykaz vsyem Rumynam vzyat' Kavkaz, oy yoy, oy yoy oy, oy yoy, a Rumyny inapoi, na caruta y domoy, oy yoy, oy yoy oy, oy yoy"* (Antonescu had given an order for all Romanians to conquer the Caucasus, but the Romanians got scared, hopped on their carts, and turned back home).

Romanian troops had not accompanied the Germans in their drive to the Caucasus, but they participated in the mass murder of Transnistrian Jews in 1941. In October of that year, on the day the Germans and Romanians captured Odessa after a two-month siege, they burned alive nineteen thousand Jews. The next day they massacred another sixteen thousand Jews from Odessa in the nearby village of Dalnik. However, after the terrible atrocities committed together with the Germans, the Romanians introduced their own ways of dealing with the Jews.

The Jews of Transnistria, from places that had escaped being slaughtered by the *Einsatzgruppe D,* were herded into ghettos. Transnistria was also used for the concentration of Jews from Bessarabia, Bukovina, and northern Moldavia. They were expelled from their homes in the years 1941–1942 on the direct order of Antonescu. After Stalingrad, however, the Romanian dictator began having second thoughts. In February 1943, C. L. Sulzberger reported in *The New York Times* that the Romanian government had offered to move seventy thousand Jews from Transnistria to anyplace of refuge chosen by the Allies. Romania suggested Palestine and offered to provide Romanian ships for the voyage. The United States State Department dismissed the rescue possibility. Whatever reasons, if any, were given by the State Department, the Romanian offer had probably little chance of succeeding, since the Germans were in control of the land route to Istanbul and the Black Sea. Still, in November 1943, Antonescu, fearing retribution from the Allies, had opposed further killings of Jews. He advised his cabinet to resist Nazi plans concerning the Jews who had been deported to Transnistria. As quoted by R. Hilberg (*The Destruction of European Jews,* Vol. II, New York: Holmes and Meier, 1985, p. 792), Antonescu told his cabinet: "Regarding the Jews who are in danger of being murdered by the Germans, you have to take measures and warn the Germans that I don't tolerate this matter, because in the last analysis I will have a bad reputation for these terrible murders." Many Jews had indeed been saved from death as Antonescu moved to win credit with the Western Allies. I believe, however, that the many Jews I saw myself in several shtetls of Romania proper in the summer of 1944 had been rescued mainly because of the speed with which the Red Army moved through that country. I will return to this later.

Crossing Frontiers with the Red Army

18. Over the Prut River

It was the last week of March 1944 on the Soviet-Romanian frontier at the Prut River. Our HQ needed information about the enemy on the other side of the river, and so the *razviedka* got orders to get a "tongue" and, if possible, to peek at the enemy a little closer. Kravchenko had decided to lead the *razviedka* platoon by himself, and this time he wanted to have me by his side. He was perhaps reasoning like Chapayev, the well-known hero of the Civil War. When asked if he could command an entire army, the cocky Red partisan leader without education, but possessing natural military talents, would not hesitate for a moment, *smogu*—I could. What about commanding all the Red Army forces? *Tozhe smogu*—I could likewise. And what about being in command of all the Red Armies on an international scale? *Nyet, nye smogu*—no, this I couldn't. Why? *Yazykov nye znayu*—I don't know foreign languages—was allegedly Chapayev's modest response. My friend Kravchenko, too, knew no foreign languages, but he evidently imagined them to be all alike. Gavryusha speaks German, so he must also know Romanian; besides, it's his problem—after all, he was the *perevodchik* (translator).

Since supplies had in the meantime caught up with frontline troops, we were well equipped for the mission. Together with Kravchenko there were sixteen of us, including the radio operator. We were armed with submachine guns, proto-Kalashnikovs, and we also had one light machine gun, plenty of ammunition and hand grenades, a two-way radio for communication with the regiment's HQ, and signal flares. Kravchenko himself checked if we had taken red flares, just in case they were needed as signals for our artillery and mortars to initiate fire covering our recrossing of the river. All this equipment, in addition to a big demijohn full of wine, not to mention what was already in our stomachs, had been loaded into three small rowboats at our disposal. We had only a vague idea of the significance of our assignment, or of the strength of resistance to be expected, but observing the trenches and the village across the Prut during the day, we spotted no Germans, just Romanian infantrymen armed with rifles and one or two machine guns.

Dusk fell late on the Prut, followed by a dark but warm night. Our three rowboats noiselessly crossed the river, and in no more than half an hour we captured two Romanian soldiers snoring in a foxhole close to their machine gun. There were no other riflemen in the trenches, and we guessed, rightly as it turned out, that they were having a good night's sleep in the village. We could have caught them all by surprise had it not been for the lack of discipline in our *razviedka*, which did happen quite often whenever it acted as a larger group, more than three to five men together. This time it was a pig in the yard of a hut near the trenches. The pig caught not so much the eye as the ear of one of our guys, as it was grunting and snoring even louder than the two Romanian soldiers. That guy wanted to send it together with the two captured prisoners, so that our cook could prepare a roast in time for our return. However, as he was pulling it on a rope to the river crossing, the pig, being obstinate as it should be, protested so loudly that it roused the entire Romanian unit from sleep, not to mention all the village cocks. The soldiers ran out of the huts, shooting in our direction. We then charged ahead, shooting wildly from our submachine guns and throwing hand grenades, aiming at nothing and nobody in particular, just making as much noise as possible. It was a brief engagement, and the Romanian soldiers fled.

In the meantime Colonel Shevchenko, having received the message that we caught not one "tongue" but two, had sent an order for Kravchenko to return immediately to the regiment's HQ. But the initial success was too encouraging for Kravchenko not to pursue the enemy. As he kept the two-way radio with the wireless operator at the river crossing, he pretended not to have gotten Shevchenko's order. Under a convoy of two of our guys, he sent the prisoners with their

4. Crossing Frontiers
With The Red Army (I)

100 km

Soviet Union

Prut R.

Faleshty

Satu Mare

Debrecen

Simleul Silvaniei

Bistrita

Tirgu Neamt

Seret R.

Hungary

Oradea

Cluj

Iasi

Kishinev

Turda

Tirgu Mures

Husi

Szeged

Transylvania

Prut R.

Timisoara

Romania

Brasov

Transylvanian Alps

Carpathian Mts

Ploesti

Bucharest

Danube R.

Black Sea

Bulgaria

rifles, machine gun, and the pig to the other side of the river with an order that as soon as they made the delivery, they should immediately come back in the rowboat, bringing with them as much additional ammunition as possible. Next, taking advantage of the horses left by the Romanian soldiers, Kravchenko decided to get, as he put it, a glance at the nearby villages. He took with him two guys on horseback. The rest of us were to remain "in control of the village already taken." Specifically he left two guys to safeguard the river crossing and the boats, and two others with the machine gun in a place overlooking the road he was embarking on, while myself, five *razviedchik*s, and the radio operator were to find and occupy "a decent place for our HQ" and maintain constant radio contact with the regiment. We found a suitable place in a big house on a hill close to a church. Looking for it, we could not fail to notice that almost every house had on its roof, door, or window some white piece of fabric—the village people were "surrendering." Before dawn Kravchenko returned and told us that the nearby villages had been deserted, not a single soldier in sight. A message to this effect was conveyed to Shevchenko, who again ordered immediate return. "You accomplished what you were supposed to, no point in sitting there, drinking and resting, when there is so much to do"—these were approximately his words. However, Kravchenko had too much imagination and initiative to follow orders obediently. He had other ideas and pretended again not to have received the order. He liked to play his own game, especially since he firmly believed that those SOB Romanian soldiers must be hiding somewhere in the village; they could not have evaporated into the thin air, he insisted. And as it turned out, he was right.

Kravchenko had an uncanny gift for improvising. "From now on I am not your senior lieutenant, forget about this, call me colonel, and don't dare address me otherwise," he ordered. I instantaneously promoted him to Colonel Kravchenko—that much Romanian I knew. He put two *razviedchik*s in front of the office, where "the colonel was resting." Submachine guns in their hands, they were to snap to attention the moment anybody approached. Others ran from house to house, telling the frightened inhabitants that the Russian colonel wished to receive small gifts of good wine from them. It took a very short time and the colonel was graciously acknowledging such gifts. Then came the real catch; seventeen armed Romanian soldiers, holding some white straps in their raised hands, came asking the colonel to take them as prisoners of war. This was the moment Kravchenko had been waiting for all the time, while trying to impress upon the Romanians that a significant force of Russian troops had crossed the Prut River, making any further resistance hopeless. Now it was Kravchenko who got directly in touch with the "boss," reporting what the *razviedka,* "implementing the boss's orders," had accomplished getting not one "tongue" but nineteen. "Return at once, all of you, with all the POWs, or you will be court-martialed," heard Kravchenko, again reduced to the rank of senior lieutenant. And, as it was appropriate for those of much lower rank, he just replied: "Yes, sir!" He was unable, however, to get additional boats from Colonel Shevchenko—nothing was immediately available—therefore we had to go back and forth several times in order to get ourselves and our prisoners across the Prut. Neither we, nor, as it seemed, the Romanians, had incurred any casualties.

On the other side of the Prut, more than the roasted pig was waiting for us. We all, Kravchenko first of all, were received by Shevchenko and others literally with open arms. My own respect for Kravchenko, of whom I was fond from the moment we met almost a year earlier, grew enormously as I watched him in action. A mix of determination and inventiveness with a touch of anarchism, so characteristic for many Russians, brought admirable results in our mission over the Prut River.

I had little time to interrogate the prisoners, among whom were two sergeants with some knowledge of German. Rochlis and his bosses insisted on sending them right away to the divisional HQ. The information I got from them confirmed what we already knew from our reconnaissance. The enemy in front of us was weak, lightly armed; his fighting spirit was low, which was reflected in the very surrender to us of more than half of a Romanian platoon.

The next day we listened to Radio Moscow news. As was customary, important military news was read by Yuri Levitan, whose voice was perfect for announcing victories. He began something like this: "Today, on March 26th, 1944, our valiant troops crossed the state border with Romania on the Prut River, and after heavy fighting captured several localities in Romania itself. Eternal glory . . ." and so on. The same day Moscow hailed the victory with salutes of the so-called first category—twenty-four volleys by 324 guns.

And there was much more, and personal, still to come. Kravchenko had been promoted to the rank of captain. He and all other participants of the above-mentioned mission received high distinction for bravery. For my part in the over-the-Prut mission, I received the Order of Glory, Third Class.

This is perhaps the place to mention something that had become a peculiarity of the new system of titles and rewards during World War II. In the old times, after the Bolshevik Revolution, officers of the Red Army did not wear epaulettes and received no title except the simple "Comrade Commander"—everything was very "democratic." In 1942, shoulder straps—which for more than two decades were a subject of scorn—were reintroduced for everybody in the Red Army, and so were the ranks and insignia. There was no more pretending that a general and a lance corporal were equals. Moreover,

Stalin reintroduced a system of granting military rewards *po tchynu*—according to rank. This meant abolishing a principle that any soldier, no matter a lance corporal or general, could earn any distinction for bravery. Thus, for example, only officers could receive the Orders of Suvorov, or Kutuzov, or Khmelnitsky, and the like; they all came in three classes. We were told that Stalin himself took care to stipulate for what services and by what rank of officer each order and its class could be awarded. For instance, the Order of Suvorov, First Class, could be given to army commanders; second class, to division and brigade commanders; third class, to regimental and battalion commanders. The soldiers' Order of Glory, also with three classes, was introduced in the fall of 1943.

The capture of nineteen Romanian prisoners on the west side of the Prut, in Romania proper, created a cheerful mood in our regiment. Guys were bragging, *"Kak Russkye na-Prut, tak Rumyny na-Serut,"* which is a play on words that's difficult to translate because of the double meanings of the words used. Seret was the river still farther west of the Prut. The sense of the saying was that as the Russians advance to the Prut (*na-prut* means also putting pressure on), they make the Romanians run to the Seret (but *naserut* means they had been scared shitless).

When the supply situation generally improved, our troops in large numbers crossed the Prut River, initially meeting little enemy resistance. But the battle for Romania was far from over. To Germany that country was very important not so much as a military ally, especially after Stalingrad, but for strategic reasons. Romania had oil and was providing Germany with an important part of its mineral oil requirements, even though the oil output of the Ploesti oil fields had been cut by about fifty percent due to air strikes by long-range bombers of the United States. Thus significant German forces had been concentrated on the Romanian-Soviet border, holding the front lines there for more than four months.

Soviet attacks west of the Prut River in the direction of the city of Iasi had been repelled time and again, and our repeated attempts at a breakthrough failed. Moreover, the Germans still had enough strength to inflict heavy casualties on us, and by skillful use of combined tank and air forces in their counterattacks were able to force us to flee in panic more than once, though not back over the Prut. During one such panicky escape, German infantrymen killed many of our wounded soldiers who had not managed to withdraw in time. When we recaptured the terrain, we found them all with bullets fired at close range into their heads or necks.

This period, which lasted several months, could again be called trench warfare, but it was on a much larger scale than that of a year earlier at the Donets bridgehead because of the attacks and counterattacks in which both sides were using tanks, airplanes, and heavy artillery. Many events and scenes from those months of trench warfare north of Iasi have been deeply imprinted in my memory.

The countryside was poor, some huts had no chimneys, others had very small windows, village women often walked barefoot either because they had no shoes or to save them for Sundays to go to church. Our soldiers, who despite—or perhaps because of—what they were told by *politruks* about poverty prevailing in Romania believed in their hearts that life must be better abroad, were now saying: *Vezde kchorosho gde nas nyet* (Life is good everywhere where we are not). They had been especially surprised to see a strange staple diet instead of bread. It was *mamalyga*, a kind of maize porridge; hence Romanians were derisively called *mamalyzhniki*—*mamalyga* eaters. Our soldiers were now expressing contempt for all things Romanian, making up some mocking one-liners, for instance: *Romanya este mare, este apa nui caldare* (Romania is a great country, it has water, but no bucket).

From the beginning of May my regiment was directly involved in combat operations and suffered many losses due mainly to air strikes and artillery bombardment. It was a bloodbath. For the first time in a year we were being hit, and frequently, by German planes, though presently we had solid air defenses provided by our corps' special antiaircraft batteries. It was a surprise to me, because by now I had come to believe that German aircraft ceased to play a significant role in the war on the eastern front. I realized my mistake seeing and smelling the havoc wreaked by the air strikes, one after the other: craters, where moments earlier were trenches packed with soldiers, streams of wounded on stretchers, houses destroyed, in flames and smoke, and the unbearable stench of dead horses. It was frightening.

19. Fear and Cowardice, Comradeship, Courage and Heroism

I have been asked many times, especially since the war, if I was scared during combat. Sure I was, who would not be? *Zhyv chelovek smerti boit-sya* (One who lives fears death). To be honest, I was often profoundly scared. When under direct German attack my anxiety was twofold: Not only was I afraid of being killed, even more fearful was the thought of being captured alive. I was seized with terror whenever the possibility of being taken a POW crossed my mind. It became an obsession with me until the end of the war. Moreover, as in a kalei-doscope, in an endless variety of changing patterns, these fears combined with others haunted me in my nightmares for many years after the war. I would see myself either as a POW in a German camp, or being led by Nazis to gas chambers and even crematoria, or both.

But one cannot permanently be in fear, and I was not either. It is just not possible to participate in a terrible four-year war and always be scared, especially if one is, as I was, a generally healthy young man between the ages of twenty and twenty-four. Besides, there are so many kinds and degrees of fear, so many nuances of it, shades and variations. It was the great collective fear of annihilation, turned into hate, the desire for revenge, and finally into the "cause," which in-spired the Red Army during this war. And there are the individual's "ordinary," everyday fears. For the inexperienced soldier there is above all the fear of the unknown, as was the case with me during the first night at the bridgehead when I felt completely lost amid the sounds and flashes of war. There is fear that some people can keep under control, while others cannot; and there is fear that the same person can sometimes cope with, though at other times is unable to do; even the bravest are frightened by sudden terrors. There is fear that if not overcome turns into cowardice, more or less harmful to others, and there is fear which, having been subdued, does not prevent people from performing acts of bravery or even heroism. I can only try to describe some of my own fears, and perhaps make a few observations on the fear of others insofar as I had witnessed it or had known about acts defying it one way or another.

I already described my dreadful fear as a POW and under German occupation of being identified as a Jew, as well as my fear of losing my real identity. Again there is fear and fear, it is not all alike. I mentioned how much in fear I was during the crossing of the Dnieper under German artillery fire. It was not only the fear of being killed or wounded, it was also the simple fear of water: I could not swim! To this day, though I love traveling by plane, I feel uncomfortable at times flying over the ocean or sea, as I still cannot swim! During the war a similar superstition would make me feel relatively safe as long as I could get into a trench or a foxhole, particularly one dug out by me, with a niche on its bottom—like those I have already mentioned. I remember how during artillery bombardments, under which we found ourselves quite frequently in May 1944, I was listening to the roar of shells in the air and was in splits of seconds counting, *nyedolot* (falling short), *perelot* (passing). I knew, of course, that if it was going to be a direct hit, I might not hear the missile at all, but I just disregarded such a possibility. Although it was irrational, the same belief in my good luck accompanied me under air strikes as long as I could throw myself into a hole, any hole in the ground.

My regiment was often the target of bombing raids north of Iasi. One day, German planes in several waves were cruising over us, bombs were making craters, big splinters together with chunks of earth were flying around, while I, having jumped into one of those fresh craters, was telling myself, now you are safe, a bomb would never hit the same place twice. It was probably so statistically, but it was not statistics that were on my mind. And at that particular time, my trust in the hole as a safe bet got a bad shakeup. A bomb hit very close to the crater where I had been hiding. I was contused by its explosion, and my hearing became temporarily impaired. Still, my superstitious belief that a hole in the ground provided a safe place remained with me throughout the entire war. People sometimes tell me, "You just got used to the war." I never thought so. No one could get used to that war.

Fear can lead to cowardice, which has also more than one meaning. Mild forms of cowardice such as lack of courage are quite a common phenomenon. Moreover, wanting courage sometimes characterizes otherwise brave men. I think that unless the term depicts some base, mean, despicable behavior, it is perhaps by itself not always unethical. As for my own behavior, I hope that if any of my fears had made me a coward, it was not the kind of cowardice that was harmful to others; at least I am not aware of that. I will describe a form of cowardice due to fear, which many would presumably associate with ignoble, contemptible behavior and which was severely punished during the war. What I have in mind was called *samostrely* (self-inflicted wounds). There were soldiers brought to such despair that they would cripple themselves in order to escape frontline duties. Were they arrant cowards at heart? Did not their cowardice require a kind of courage? Would not some others become such cowards if they had dared to?

At times of heavy trench warfare, like that at the Donets River bridgehead in May 1943 and then, a year later, southwest of the Prut River, one could observe in the very early morning long strings of wounded soldiers streaming out of the front lines and walking slowly toward dressing stations. Most had their left hands bandaged. The experienced, cynical cutthroats from the *razviedka* had no doubts that many of those left-hand wounds were *samostrely* cases. "They just got fed up and decided to call it quits" was their brief explanation. "But won't they be punished?" "Only the stupid, who shoot their hand directly or through a piece of wood or anything else at close range. The smart guys do it differently. Before dawn, when Fritz's bullets are buzzing in the air, they stretch their hand out of the trench and wait for the lucky hit." "And why the left hand?" "Well, for work they would still need their right one."

It was not long before it became known in our regiment that a *samostrel* was detected and that preparations for a field court-martial were on the way and would begin as soon as the military court sent by the army's HQ arrived. Delegates from all infantry companies holding the front line as well as all other units in full complement were to witness the fate awaiting the coward. The procedure was long, with the dreadful scene divided into four acts. In the first one, the prosecutor spoke of the crime committed, the *samostrel* pleaded guilty once, and then, in his last word again, and again as he was begging the just court to show mercy for his mother and spare her the shame of which he was guilty. After that the court's sentence was pronounced. *"Razstrelyat"* (To be shot). In the second act we watched the execution and the burial of the *samostrel* from a distance, while in the third one everybody had to come close to the grave and by himself see the description on a piece of plywood stuck into it: "Eternal shame on the coward, who has betrayed his comrades and his motherland, and for that crime was shot and buried here." Finally came the last act, the most horrifying one, which it was meant to be, as a warning to all potential *samostrely*. A *politruk,* stressing every word, read slowly and loudly a letter signed by the commander of the 458 Rifle Regiment to be sent to the collective farm and the people of the *samostrel's* village about the ignoble deed committed by their fellow countryman.

The antonym for "cowardice" is probably "bravery". I had the good fortune to have known and to be together with many brave men. For instance, Kravchenko, who deserved no doubt more than the compliments I paid him describing the mission he led in taking those nineteen Romanian POWs.

I found in my friend Titov, the same Titov who had been sentenced to ten years for homicide, and came to our *razviedka* after fighting in a penal battalion to erase his prison sentence, a rare combination of bravery and comradeship. I owe Ivan Titov very much and I want to mention at least one episode.

In mid-May I got very sick, though I had no idea what was wrong with me. Days went by and there was no improvement whatsoever. I lost my appetite, felt more and more exhausted, and got so weak that I could barely walk. As I stopped eating the rather good food our *razviedka* cook was preparing, my friends began looking for appetite-stimulating food for me, and found something they liked themselves, which they called *kvas*. It was sauerkraut brine, and it became almost my only food for days. I am not sure that it did much good to my liver, which, as I was told later on, was enlarged due to a viral hepatitis that also caused jaundice. My friends noticed that the whites of my eyes got yellow, and then, looking closer at my skin, I saw that it was yellowish too. However, neither my *razviedka* friends nor I considered jaundice serious enough to warrant going to see a doctor. Taking it lightly, they were making a little fun of me: "Gavryusha is turning Chinese." At that time, quite suddenly, German tanks succeeded in breaking through our regiment's front line and, having created a gap in it, attempted a small pincer movement. The regiment, or, rather, part of it, including our HQ, the *avtomatchiki* (submachine gun platoon), and the *razviedka*, hurriedly withdrew four miles to the rear, where a second line of defense supported by heavy artillery finally repelled the enemy attack. But those four miles of "withdrawing" turned into a real panicky retreat that I could hardly ever forget. I was so sick that I could not walk, let alone run. And if it had not been for my buddy Ivan Titov, I would have been lost. He put me on his back as if I were a sack of potatoes, told me to hold on to him, and ran all four miles like hell, chased by artillery fire. Afterward he delivered me to a military hospital, where I was treated with glucose injections for about two weeks.

I must also tell the story of our regiment's hero, a real one and formally recognized as such. It happened during one of the attempts by a German armored unit to penetrate our positions. If it had succeeded, the Germans would have been able to encircle the regiment. One of our infantry companies had abandoned the front lines at the very sight of the oncoming German tanks. Subsequently, seized by tank panic, the entire battalion fled, with the exception of one soldier, who stood up to the German assault. He behaved according to the book. In front of him were the silhouettes of several German tanks. As they came close, he remained, crouched in his trench, waiting until the smoking dragons would rumble over, and at the moment they passed it, he ran in his trench, from one to another, hitting them from behind with heavy antitank grenades. He was calm enough to wait until a tank was revolving its turret in search of a target, and then to aim at its fuel tank.

What was the source of his brave acts? Was he a brave man on instinct, blessed naturally with an unusual degree of courage? Or was it just a spark of inspiration that came to him when the occasion called for it? Well, what was in the head and heart of that fearless (was he fearless?) man is anybody's guess. The fact was that he single-handedly knocked out three enemy tanks; two burst into flames, one turned back damaged. He became the first and only soldier in our division to be awarded the title of Hero of the Soviet Union.

20. "Where Zhukov Is, There Is Victory"

When I returned from the hospital in the beginning of June, I was told of severe blows inflicted on our division by German air strikes. Waves of Stuka divers and other bombers had decimated the 78 Rifle Division. Some infantry companies were reduced to a handful of men and needed reinforcements badly. Kravchenko, too, was busy trying to find the right replacements for losses in our *razviedka*.

There was other personal bad news. The day after I returned, my good friend Grishin, senior lieutenant and commander of the regiment's submachine gun company, was mortally wounded by an artillery shell splinter. I was not far away and saw him crouching and squeezing his bloodied guts as if trying to push them back into his open belly. Pale and sweaty, his lips trembling as bloody foam was coming from his mouth, he was half conscious when I bid him farewell. He died on the shaking horse-drawn cart even before reaching the hospital.

Like bad news, good news sometimes comes in pairs also. The Allies finally opened the second front, of which there was so much talk in previous years and so little—that was how we saw it—action. D day, the Allied assault on Hitler's western Europe, began on 6 June 1944. To me and others, especially in the regiment's HQ, this was all very exciting and promising. A little surprising were the rather subdued reports in our newspapers of the Allied troops' successful landing on the French coast. This was in sharp contrast with what I remembered as a constant clamor in our newspapers in the fall of 1941 and spring of 1942 for a second front. The difference, as I tried to explain it to myself, was probably due to the fact that our military situation had since changed so dramatically. When the advantage in armed strength was clearly the Germans', as it had been until Stalingrad, the establishment of a second front in Western Europe could have changed the imbalance by drawing some of their large forces away from our front. Now we had the upper hand; the Red Army had regained lost territories, already fighting outside the Soviet Union's old borders. Still, it was great that the real thing had finally started there too; unity with our Western Allies spelled the Nazis' doom.

There was also good news from the Belorussian front, where a tremendously successful Soviet offensive ended on 3 July with the liberation of Minsk, the capital of Belorussia. In the process the Red Army encircled large German forces—a total of about 100,000 had been taken prisoner. Two weeks later, 57,600 of them, led by nineteen captured generals, were marched through the streets of Moscow.

The next good news was no less exciting. On 22 July 1944 a provisional Polish government, created by the PCNL (Polish Committee of National Liberation), moved to the just-liberated city of Lublin. The shtetl of Komarov, my grandmother's hometown to where my father had returned in 1940, was in the Lublin district. This gave me a new glimmer of hope about my family's possible survival, illusory as it turned out to be.

As if to dampen my enthusiasm, the news from Poland quickly became a mix of the good and the bad. The Soviet Army Group under Marshal Konstantin Rokossovski, having reached the vicinity of Warsaw, took up defensive positions along the east side of the Vistula and, farther east, along the San River. At that time the Polish government-in-exile and General Bor-Komorowski of the home army decided to raise Warsaw against the Germans.The decision was made without consulting or coordinating the plans with those of the Soviets. The Warsaw uprising, which began on 1 August, ended tragically after several weeks of fighting. It claimed a terrible loss in human lives: 16,000 insurgents and more than 150,000 civilians killed, many thousands wounded. The Germans massacred the Poles inside the city and destroyed the Polish capital.

The Warsaw uprising became another sore point in Polish-Soviet relations. In the London-Pole version of events, the lack of proper Soviet support for the insurrection was deliberate. If the Red Army did not capture Warsaw, so the argument went, it was not because it could not do it, but for purely political reasons: It did not suit the Russians to have the Polish capital liberated by a popular uprising, which was directed by the Polish government in London. As for the Soviet version, it pointed to purely military considerations. Warsaw and the Red Army were separated by a wide river, and it was not possible to cross it and take the city with troops exhausted after a long advance of almost four hundred miles without a break. A large-scale offensive across the Vistula needed months of preparation.

The Soviet claim that the Red Army could not have forced the Vistula and seized Warsaw in August or September tallies with the opinion of General Heinz Guderian, at that time the chief of the German general staff. "We Germans had the impression that it was our defence which halted the enemy rather than a Russian desire to sabotage the Warsaw uprising" (*Panzer Leader,* New York: Dutton, 1952, p. 359).

To this I would add the following: Politics were definitely involved, and both sides had played it. The Polish government in London and the home army in Poland had decided to raise Warsaw against the Germans and preempt the Soviets and the communist PCNL. The latter was a political decision. They must have known Stalin's disinclination to aid them, but had probably been under the wrong impression that the Wehrmacht was already routed. On the other hand, Stalin's decisions on the "Polish question" were this time, as always, purely political. For example, he did not allow planes from the west that had dropped supplies on Warsaw to land on Soviet airfields. This was callousness typical of Stalin. He wanted to install a PCNL government in Poland. For him goals were to be achieved regardless of losses—losses of his own people, let alone Poles.

After the offensive thrust of the Red Army had petered out on the central front, the Soviet High Command had evidently determined not to pursue attempts of breaking through to Germany in the summer of 1944. Instead, the Red Army would strike out in the south. This was our sector of the front, and we were preparing for the big summer offensive in Romania. During the months of June and July our division was reinforced and reequipped. Most important, columns of tanks, self-propelled artillery, and big guns of unseen-before caliber—everything covered with dust—were rumbling into our sector not only by night but also by day, as if the Luftwaffe had ceased to exist; it had indeed disappeared from our skies. The noise of engines was so loud that we had to yell to hear each other. Finally, concealed under tarpaulins on American trucks, the famous rockets—*Katyusha*s, "Little Kates" for the popular Russian love song—came in. It now became clear to us what the Germans were trying to achieve in their May attacks—forestall our forthcoming great offensive.

With the mountains of equipment pouring in, rumors spread: "Zhukov is coming!" Beginning with the Moscow counteroffensive in the winter of 1941–42, Zhukov had been impressing his personality on all major battles. Like his boss, Stalin, Zhukov had a heavy hand and did not count losses. But soldiers were very fond of him, and this was not the prevailing attitude toward his boss despite everything that was said and written about the people's love for Stalin. True, he was feared by everybody—his comrades, generals, soldiers, civilians—in this there were few exceptions. Stalin's deeds were terrifying, though many believed that without his iron will and heavy hand the Soviet Union could not have survived the German onslaught. He was the supreme commander in chief, but his troops never saw him. Stalin always stayed busy in his Kremlin office. Marshal Zhukov, on the other hand, had been personally in touch with soldiers in combat, and was sincerely hailed by them as a heroic military leader. *Gdye Zhukov, tam pobyeda* (Where Zhukov is, there is victory)—our soldiers believed.

The offensive into Romania by the Second and Third Ukrainian Army Groups had been planned, in its first stage, as the Iasi-Kishinev operation. A couple of months before the offensive, perhaps in May, transfers of armies had taken place with new assignments. General Malinovsky's, by then the Second Ukrainian Army Group, positioned north of Iasi on the west side of the Prut, was to move southeastward, while General Tolbukhin's, still on the Dniester River, was to attack northwestward, the ring to be closed at the town of Husi. According to Soviet sources, the total strength of the two army groups was ninety rifle divisions, six tank and mechanized corps, fourteen hundred tanks and self-propelled assault guns, seventeen hundred aircraft, and 900,000 men. The total strength of the enemy group had been estimated as the equivalent of forty-seven divisions, including three panzer divisions and five infantry brigades, numbering over 800,000 men, of which 360,000 were Germans and the rest Romanians; it had 7,600 artillery pieces and mortars, 400 tanks and assault guns, and 800 aircraft. According to reliable estimates (Dupuy and Martell, *Great Battles on the Eastern Front*, p. 184), the ratio was in Soviet favor—1.5 to 1 in men, 2.1 to 1 in artillery, 4.7 to 1 in armor, and 2.7 to 1 in aircraft.

The German command had focused its attention on the Kishinev sector, where it was expecting our main thrust, and thus had concentrated the bulk of its best forces there. But the Soviet High Command had decided instead to achieve a breakthrough in the Iasi sector, where it created a marked superiority of forces. Our 78 Rifle Division, by then part of the 27 Army in the Malinovsky group, became directly involved in the main thrust operation.

The offensive in our sector, north of Iasi, began in the early morning of 20 August with a devastating air and artillery preparation. Wave after wave of low-flying, mostly Il-2 Shturmovik (assault) fighter-bombers were heading toward enemy positions. It was a massive Soviet air onslaught the like of which I had never witnessed before. On the ground, it was artillery, the embodiment of the Soviet army's power; 240 guns of a caliber no less than 76mm were for more than an hour pounding each square kilometer on a front of fifteen kilometers in length, where the enemy's defense lines were to be breached. It was to soften up the enemy's strong points in depth. Having the *Katyusha*s around, hearing and seeing them in action, was by itself something unforgettable. These multiple rockets blasting off from the truck-mounted rails delivered their explosives in salvos, each *Katyusha* distributing 4.35 tons of ordnance over an area of ten acres for a span of between seven and ten seconds.

Altogether the air and artillery fire proved to be a most powerful blow. The shells fired by thousands of guns smashed into the concrete bunkers and literally lifted the enemy defense positions into the air. By the afternoon of the first day of the offensive our division had advanced about eight miles. Moving southwestward, we found in concrete bunkers of the fortified zone many corpses with no traces of wounds; they must have been killed by impact forces due to the artillery pounding. The next day the German-Romanian defense disintegrated. The encirclement was closed as planned at Husi on 24 August.

On 23 August, three days after the offensive began, the young Romanian king, Michael, announced the formation of a new government, and informed the Germans that he had to conclude an armistice and that they had a few days to remove their army from the country. Soviet-Romanian peace talks had already begun in April, when many influential Romanians became determined to get out of the war in the face of an impending Russian invasion of their country. Those peace talks were kept secret from the Germans. Now, furious at what had happened, Hitler wanted to have the king arrested and to impose a suitable Romanian general as head of the Romanian state. But it was too late for all that. On 25 August, immediately following a 150-sortie bombing attack on Bucharest by the Luftwaffe, the new Romanian government declared war on Germany.

With Romanians turned from friends to enemies, it became even more difficult for the Germans to extricate their troops from the pocket. Very few escaped; others continued to fight until 29 August. The Soviets claimed 106,000 prisoners and 150,000 German dead. According to German-based sources, the actual German losses, unlikely ever to be known, were no less than 180,000 (see Albert Seaton, *The Russo-German War 1941–45*, Novato, Cal.: Presidio Press, 1971, p. 483). What were Red Army losses? Judging by the number of casualties in our 78 Division, they were probably slight. Of course, this was just a guess. The Soviets were not in the habit of reporting their own losses.

Our soldiers were right; where Zhukov was, there was victory. They were mistaken only about one little thing. It was Timoshenko, not Zhukov, who had the difficult task of coordinating the Malinovsky and Tolbukhin army groups. Marshal Timoshenko could finally claim having supervised a highly successful offensive—the Iasi-Kishinev operation.

21. "Making Near What Was Far"

After the Romanian turnabout we were moving completely unopposed. There were no German troops in sight. The Wehrmacht would have to assemble and regroup transferred troops before being able to take a stand against the Red Army. The only natural obstacle hindering our advance west of the Prut River was by now the southern part of the Carpathian Mountains. Starting in Poland, the Carpathians run southeastward almost to the valley of the Seret River. There—on the southern edge between the Carpathians and the Transylvanian Alps running from east to west—we could have entered central Romania. Indeed, that was the route chosen by Soviet tank and motorized units. Our 78 Division, however, and some other *Tsaritsa Poley* divisions, got orders to move from Iasi straight westward and cross the Carpathians through one of its passes. As it turned out, these passes—or maybe just the pass we had been using—were not only unsuitable for tank formations, they were good enough perhaps only for mountain troops. "Why not skirt the mountains and move along their southern edge?" I asked myself, and I could see that others, too, including Colonel Shevchenko, thought it was a crazy idea. But our superior generals had an obsession: They wanted the heavily wooded mountains to be thoroughly swept in order to catch German soldiers who might have chosen that inconspicuous route for their desperate escape. Not a single German soldier, however, fell into our regiment's "net," and the effect of the Carpathian Mountain crossing was a significant delay in our advance, not to mention the efforts of both human and horse. The *Tsaritsa Poley* had spent much time, and quite unnecessarily, in the mountain passes, while tank and mechanized troops were thrusting ahead to Ploesti and Bucharest, then farther south and westward. Tolbukhin's forces overran Bulgaria and established contact with the Yugoslavs. In the meantime, the mobile troops of our Second Army Group had reached the Hungarian border, where infantry support was badly needed.

On the west side of the Carpathians was northern Transylvania, which Romania, compelled by Germany, had had to cede to Hungary in August 1940. It was a high plateau (one thousand to sixteen hundred feet), with vineyards, orchards, and pastures, and a mixed population of Magyars, Romanians, and Saxons (German-speaking colonists who settled there in the Middle Ages). We were now in open country with no fortified enemy positions before the old Hungarian border. It could have been an easy conquest and the entire operation would have taken not much longer than the time required for the army to cover the distance between the mountains and the Romanian-Hungarian frontier. But that was the crux of the problem: time was extremely short.

If the *Tsaritsa Poley* were to proceed at its "normal" pace of advance, the Germans would have enough time not only for regrouping but perhaps also for mounting a significant counterattack on the Romanian high plateau. The maxim "Slow and steady wins the race" was now good for nothing. What, then, was the solution? What was found was a crude one, but quite ingenious. Our commanding officers never spelled it out; it was left to the *smekalka* (natural wit) of the Russian soldier to be deciphered. The regiment had just gotten orders regarding the distances to be covered daily: the first day— twenty miles, the second—thirty miles, the third—forty miles, and the latter was to become the "normal" pace of advance. The result was what had no doubt been expected; the *Tsaritsa Poley* climbed into horse-drawn wagons taken from Romanian soldiers—our enemies yesterday and allies today—but mostly requisitioned from local peasants; all kinds of farm carts, even panje carts (basketlike wagons), as long as they had strong wheels. The horses foundering after a long day of hard work would be replaced by a fresh pair, and the next day's ordered distance would again be covered in time.

On the first day of this gallopade, Colonel Shevchenko told our *razviedka: Z sevodnyashnevo dnya vy budete konnaya razviedka* (Beginning today you will be a mounted *razviedka*). As our *razviedka* was composed of guys with a highly developed sense of that native wit—*smekalka*—they got horses for themselves from the royal stud belonging to King Michael. These were, of course, quickly taken away from them and turned over to the division and then corps, but our *razviedchiki* developed a taste for thoroughbred horses. At any rate, while on the road they were never again on foot; until the end of the war it was either on horseback or in horse-drawn carts.

The two highest officers in our 458 Rifle Regiment, Colonel Shevchenko and his chief of staff, Major Buldyshkin, got themselves motor vehicles—jeeps—by just taking them away from Romanian officers, who though by now formally allies, were mistrusted anyway. I was told that a supply unit of our 78 Rifle Division acquired its trucks in a similar manner. General Mikhaylov, the divisional commander, appeared one day in front of the soldiers of that supply unit and ordered: *"Shofera wystupit'"* (Drivers come forward). When more than ten of them presented themselves as drivers of motor vehicles, the general declared, "What kind of drivers are you without trucks, a driver can be called a driver only when he has a truck, understood?" The reply was equally clear. *"Tak, tochno"*—Yes, Comrade General.

We had to fend for ourselves, but plundering was formally forbidden, and we were given Romanian currency—occupational *lei*—to pay for the goods taken from stores or local inhabitants. Our money, however, was not much appreciated by the Romanians. The guys in our *razviedka* would steal a pair of geese in one village, and bring the birds to a hostess in another village asking her politely to prepare a good meal. The hostess would oblige smiling, glad that Russian soldiers carried their own food with them.

People in towns would stop us to ask how soon they could expect the Russian army to arrive. They took us for partisans, and no wonder; they saw hordes of armed men riding in a mishmash of peasant carts; the only thing they seemed to be surprised about were the great numbers of "partisans." Regular Romanian troops, our former enemies and present allies, were nowhere to be seen. But the local inhabitants would soon be able to enjoy the sight of real Romanian soldiers in brand-new Romanian uniforms, armed with new Russian submachine guns, in brand-new American trucks. These were former

Romanian POWs, mostly captured under Stalingrad and subsequently reeducated by Soviet/Romanian Communists. Now soldiers of the First Romanian Tudor Vladimirescu Division, they were traveling from one city to another, paraded for everybody to see that their country was not just being occupied by the Russians, but liberated by their own Romanian troops.

After crossing the Carpathians, we had turned south at Bistrita to Tirgu-Mures and toward the Transylvanian Alps. Our superior generals, however, perhaps to spare us an encounter with the bloodthirsty Count Dracula, soon ordered us away from those mountains back to the high plateau, where moving northwest we quickly passed Cluj, Simleul-Silvanie, and finally, Oradea.

Miles-long caterpillars of horse-drawn carts carrying armed Russian soldiers and their supplies were moving at top speed on all main Transylvania-Romanian roads. The only troops getting ahead of us were Red Army cavalry divisions, most of them cossacks. They disappeared in front of us as quickly as they suddenly appeared, squadron after squadron galloping through the dust on their splendid horses. Scenes like these had probably not been seen here since the times the Huns, Magyars, and later the Mongols overran Europe. And like the invasion of the Mongolian hordes, ours, too, was an impressive military operation resulting in the quickest possible arrival at the Romanian/Hungarian borders. As Mangku Khan said in a letter to King Louis IX of France written in 1254, we, too, almost seven hundred years later, "made near what was far."

We were forbidden to stay overnight or even stop for longer breaks in cities or towns. In two such small towns south of Cluj and close to Turda, I was astonished to see Jews, and in large numbers. These were the kind of small towns called in Yiddish shtetls (hamlets) because they were mostly populated by Jews. In the first one I stayed somewhat longer. I saw an open, small synagogue and, as I entered, I could not believe my eyes—it was a closely packed place of familiar-looking people, some praying, others talking. There was a cantor and a *shammes* (sexton), as well as the traditional chants. Soon I was recognized as a Jew and surrounded by people surprised to see a Red Army soldier in their *shtible* (house of prayer). At first they cautiously offered me a *siddur* (prayer book), inviting me to *daven* (pray), and then began bombarding me with questions in a mixture of Yiddish, Russian, Romanian, and Hungarian. It was not a smooth conversation, mainly because I, being in a hurry, was interrupting them with my own questions. Despite the language barrier, it soon became typical Jewish chatting, where a question is answered with a question. What I learned from them about the fate of the Jews of Romania was quite confusing. I was told about a pogrom in Bucharest in the beginning of 1941, the murders of thousands of Iasi Jews by Romanian and German soldiers at the end of June 1941, and the killings carried out by members of the Romanian Iron Guard in many other cities and towns, where they plundered, raped, and destroyed houses and shops in Jewish quarters. But here I myself was in a synagogue of a quiet shtetl, undamaged by the war, and full of Jews. One thing was certain to me as well as to them. It had been the speed with which the Red Army was moving through Romania that saved their lives. *Multumesc* (thank you very much), I heard when I finally said *la revedere* (good-bye). The *multumesc* was not addressed to me personally, it was to a soldier of the liberation army. Not for the first time was I proud to be part and parcel of this just war. Of the large Jewish community in Romania, about half, 400,000, survived the Holocaust.

The sight of the Romanian Jews ignited in me a spark of hope about my own family. After all, the Soviet army had already reached the Vistula River and was in Praga—the eastern part of Warsaw. I did not know at that time that only a month earlier, my mother and two of my younger brothers were among the sixty-seven thousand Jews of the Lodz ghetto deported to Auschwitz, where more than sixty thousand of them had been exterminated.

22. Entering Hungary: Debrecen

Having swept through Romania, our troops needed some time for rest, to replace losses in men, and to bring up supplies. There was also another good reason for a respite. Our men were hoping that the Hungarians would extricate their country from the war, as the Romanians had just done.

Indeed, the stunning defeat of German forces in the Iasi-Kishinev operation, and the surrender of Romania to Russia that followed it, shook Hungary. As in Romania, influential circles in Hungary had tried to disentangle their country from the war. Miklos Horty himself, the regent of Hungary, attempted to reach an armistice with Russia just after Romania changed sides. Unlike its neighbor, however, Hungary could not slip away from its Axis alliance, and was to stick with Germany to the very end and thus also to share its fate. This was mainly due to the fact that again, unlike in Romania, German troops were in a position to quickly occupy the country. In the beginning of October, the Nazis seized all Hungarian communication centers. On 15 October Horty broadcast to the Hungarian people that Germany was on its way to defeat, and that for Hungary the war was at an end. But the next day his son was kidnapped by the SS, and he was forced to resign. The Germans set up a puppet government under Szalasi, the chieftain of the Arrow Cross, the most pro-German and extremely anti-Semitic party. For Hitler, Hungary was Austria's last bulwark.

Among us, however, there was great disappointment and anger when we realized that the Hungarians decided—that is how Red Army soldiers saw it—to stick with their German allies. *Voron voronu glaz nye vykluet* (Crow will not pick out crow's eyes). Since it became clear that Hungary would not sign an armistice agreement, let alone change sides like Romania, hasty preparations for the forthcoming offensive began on our side, including political indoctrination on a scale and of a kind I had never witnessed before. The *Frontovaya Gazeta* (front newspaper) and *politruks*, some dispatched from our corps or the army's HQ, were coming one after the other to lecture about Hungary, Hitler's last satellite in Europe, and the most stubborn of all. The Hungarian troops, we were reminded, had together with their Nazi allies behaved abominably at Voronezh, on the Don, at Chernigov, and at Kiev. "We are entering the enemy's den, we will avenge!"

In the first half of October 1944 our division, reinforced and re-supplied, was getting ready in the vicinity of Oradea for the forthcoming action. A strong army group composed of a tank army, cavalry units, and the 33 Rifle Corps, of which our 78 Division was then a part, had been poised to take Debrecen. Our regiment was in the front lines, and since Kravchenko and his *razviedka* had successfully been hunting for "tongues," we got valuable information on the enemy's regroupings and concentration of forces in the Debrecen sector. The Germans intended to hold the city as long as possible in order to safeguard the withdrawal of troops to the Tisza River. Nevertheless, their resistance, though fierce, did not last long. And because our attack seemed to have been a tactical surprise to the enemy, we captured many artillery pieces and motor vehicles intact. We were also able to render helpless their counterattacks, during which they incurred heavy losses in killed and wounded. The city was captured on 20 October. Our regiment had been only one of many army units that took part in the battle for Debrecen. Still, it was our 458 Rifle Regiment—I do not know if it was the only one—that was mentioned in an order of appreciation, and as a title of honor it had gotten the name *Debrecenski.*

During the battle I was with Kravchenko and his men on reconnaissance, ahead of our infantry. Our task was to find the shortest and safest way into the city, which we did. It was here that for the first time I was directly involved in street fighting while we were chasing Fritzes and *honveds* out of houses which they had turned into bunkers on the outskirts of Debrecen. We cleared the way for our

5. Crossing Frontiers
With The Red Army (II)

100 km

Slovakia

Austria

Vienna

Rimavska
Sobota

Tokaj

Nyiregyhaza

Miskolc

Graz   Furstenfeld   Szekesfehervar   Budapest   Debrecen

Zalaegerszeg   L. Val.   Danube   Tisza R.   Oradea

Nagykanizsa   Lake
Balaton   Hungary

Baja

Szeged   Romania

Yugoslavia

infantry, and in the process managed to capture four German and seven Hungarian soldiers. But we had some casualties ourselves—two of our comrades had been lightly wounded. For our part in taking Debrecen, we were all awarded medals. I received the Order of Krasnaya Zviezda (red star), and my name was mentioned in the *Frontovaya Gazeta.*

Debrecen was Hungary's third largest city. Founded in the fourteenth century, it was an attractive place, and, since it had been captured almost undamaged, it was soon to become the administrative center of a provisional government.

More than ten thousand Jews lived there before World War II, and I was looking for Jewish survivors. But all I could find in Debrecen was a part of a high wall built around the ghetto where Jews had been assembled by the Hungarian gendarmes in the spring of 1944. I was told by some local inhabitants that after a short while all the Jews from the ghetto, several thousands of them, were deported either to Austria or to Germany.

Entering Hungary, I asked myself more than once what it would be like coming to that country. After all, I had vivid and unpleasant, to say the least, memories of the Hungarian soldiers. I had not forgotten the *honved*s hunting for *Zsido* in our prisoner-of-war camp, the sadistic games they played on us there, the execution of the POW who attempted an escape, the poking of the rifle butt in the ribs I received during the forced "evacuation" from Olkhov Log to the west, and the horrible treatment of their own Jews drafted into what, as in a mockery, they termed "labor service." I thought of all this in terms of revenge, "I will pay them back." But who were "they"? There were, of course, still *honved*s; more than 200,000 fighting on the side of the Nazis. In the towns and villages, however, I saw people like ourselves, tired of war and having more than enough of their German masters. Some were sympathetic toward us, many were hostile, but most were in great fear, especially after all they heard about rape, which many women no doubt experienced themselves. I saw all this, and particularly children, those most innocent victims of war, and my desire for revenge evaporated.

I will not pass in silence over the problem of rape, but I firmly believe that what has been written regarding ill treatment of children by Red Army soldiers was just not true. Whatever their behavior toward adults might have been, on the basis of what I myself witnessed I would claim that Russian soldiers had generally too many tender, gentle, soft feelings for children to hurt them deliberately.

From Debrecen we moved north, but encountered fierce resistance in the vicinity of Nyiregyhaza. Moreover, German tank and motorized troops recaptured that city and, having inflicted severe losses also on our division, forced us to a retreat of about fifteen to twenty miles, a retreat that at one point became panicky. In the middle of the night my friend Urazmukhambetov kicked open the door to the room where some others and I were sleeping. He was all excited and shouting: *"Udirayem!"* (We are fleeing!) In no time I got into his cart and off we went at top speed in the direction of Debrecen. German and Hungarian troops had been extremely brutal when they retook Nyiregyhaza. They slaughtered many of our wounded who had not been evacuated in time and were left in the city in homes of local residents. It was a carnage. Afterward, as the savagely killed victims had been collected and buried with due honors in a common grave, revenge was in the hearts of their comrades.

That was also when Kravchenko was killed. He had taken two mounted *razviedchiks* with him and they went to the *puszta*, the grazing lands on the Hungarian plain, to examine the territory and to estimate the strength of the enemy in front of us. The two guys returned and told how he was killed by an artillery shell; he died instantly, they said. His body could not be recovered, they reported, because they came under heavy tank fire and were forced to flee by enemy infantry. And so Andrey Kravchenko was gone without even a decent burial, a sign on his grave. Our regiment lost a brave, intelligent, quick-witted P.N.Sh.—and the *razviedka*, a commander very hard to replace. I lost a dear friend.

It took some time before we could advance again. Having learned from recent losses, our tank and infantry units were now moving forward in well-coordinated all-arm groupings. We crossed the Tisza River in the northeast corner of Hungary, and at the confluence of the Bodrog and Tisza rivers we found ourselves at Tokay—the region famous for its rare, fine sweet wine. Nagy (big) Tokay and Kis (small) Tokay, the two places where we had been resting for a while, had much too much golden wine for the ill-disciplined *Tsaritsa Poley*. When I entered a huge wine cellar with rows of tall, black oak barrels, I saw an incredible scene. The floor was knee-deep in wine and floating in it lay three drowned soldiers. They had used their submachine guns to make holes in the barrels as "the easiest way" to fill up their mess tins with wine, and then, having tasted it, evidently could not stop drinking and became so intoxicated that they had drowned in it. I had been hardened to such an extent that all that came to my mind at the sight of this trio was the popular wartime song about three *vesolych druga* (merry friends). These three friends' lives ended in a drinking bout on the delicious Tokay wine. Maybe this was not such a bad end for a soldier of this hellish war.

To the west of Tokay was Miskolc, Hungary's second-largest city and its main heavy-industry center. Here at the Szinva River we were involved in fierce fighting at the end of November. German and Hungarian troops, trying to hold the city and prevent our access to the Miskolc-Budapest railroad, were frequently counterattacking. But they lost many tanks, self-propelled guns, and other military equipment. Miskolc was finally taken but not before our artillery smashed the enemy's defense positions in the Bukk hills, and our infantry engaged in street fighting in the city itself. We captured many prisoners, mostly Hungarians. Some of them were deserters, who hated the Germans and expressed a desire to fight them from our side.

In Miskolc, which used to have a large Jewish community, I met several Jews. One of them was drafted into the *Munkaszolgalat* in the spring of 1944. He believed that being in a labor service unit had saved his life, because otherwise he would have been forced into the ghetto and afterward deported, like most of his family. The others had been sent in the summer to brickyards outside Miskolc, where they were liberated by the Red Army. They all had horrible stories to tell about the crimes committed by the Hungarian gendarmerie and the Arrow Cross—killings, rapes, deportations, and what they called "death marches." In a mixture of German, Hungarian, and Russian, they spoke feverishly, in despair over the fate of their relatives.

23. Spoils of War

To the victors belong the spoils. Poor victors, poor spoils! What could a soldier on the march grab as his personal loot? A watch, of course. As we crossed state frontiers, especially after entering Hungary, wristwatches attracted attention more than anything else and indeed became the most "valuable," and certainly the most visible, booty of the victorious soldiers.

In Hungary, the victorious Soviet soldiers had seen a country undamaged by the ravages of war, and also with a much higher standard of living than their own. I recall exclamations I heard as we were passing through towns and, particularly, the flat and fertile Hungarian countryside with villages showing signs of prosperity: *"Nu i Kulachzye!"*—What loaded folks!—an expression of envy and resentment. It enhanced the hatred of the enemy. And it made the taking of spoils, mostly those wristwatches, morally painless, justified, almost an act of social justice.

I would add that the gist of that expression was anything but peculiar to Russian soldiers. It is to be found almost everywhere and also in peacetime. Somebody coined a phrase, "anticapitalist nostalgia of the masses." This vague longing, the source of which is envy, a nostalgia by far not only "of the masses," is also quite common among people living in affluent societies, and even among those made personally prosperous by capitalism; jealous of those richer than themselves, they are also those who most often express contempt for "materialistic desires." A good deal of the idea of equality, catching up with those "more equal than others," is based on that anticapitalist, antimaterialistic nostalgia.

Goods other than watches began attracting the attention of our soldiers—not on their initiative—only in the last several months of the war. As 1944 was coming to an end, we were told that the Soviet High Command, Stalin himself, had decided that soldiers should let their families know, by sending parcels back home, how victorious the Red Army became. It was not just a message conveyed to all soldiers. We were reminded about our duty to help our families, who were working hard to supply the front with all it needed for final victory.

One day our regiment was visited by the divisional commander himself, who wanted to have a personal chat with his soldiers. The infantry battalions had been ordered to form, and the general, going from one soldier to another, asked while they were saluting: *"Kak dela, soldat?"* (How are you getting on, soldier?) *"Nichevo, Tovarishch General"* (All right, Comrade General). Almost everybody's reply to the next question was also similar. *"Posylku domoy poslal?"* (Sent a parcel home?) *"Tak tochzno, Tovarishch General"* (Exactly, Comrade General). But then came a negative reply. *"Nikak nyet, Tovarishch General."* The general wanted to know why. *"Nye uspel nakhvatat', Tovarishch General"* (Haven't managed to grab anything) was the soldier's answer. The general's order in response to this was short: *"Nado lutshe khvatat'"* (Try to grab better). It was amazing that during the last months of the war such parcels sent home were being delivered, and quickly, by military mail. I had never heard a complaint about any parcel or anything in it missing. Stalin must have warned Beria that if any of these spoils of war were stolen, it would cost him his head.

There was still a peculiar kind of spoil of war exacted by more than a few victorious soldiers, which brought upon the Red Army a bad reputation—rape. In Hungary and later in Austria incidents of violating women ceased to be a sporadic phenomenon. And the higher-ups' attitude toward rape was running in circles, from one extreme to another.

Soldiers were ill disciplined and morale was dropping as the war progressed, and especially after we entered Hungary. The soldiers' conduct in this enemy country was influenced by the press and the *politruks'* talks invoking hatred and calling for revenge and retribution for the evil crimes the Hungarians, along with the Germans, had committed in the occupied parts of Russia and the Ukraine. The sto-

ries of shooting, hanging, torturing, raping, looting, and burning
could have hardly been exaggerated. Every soldier could have told
similar stories from his own experience, or from what he had heard
from eyewitnesses from the Volga westward. The desire to avenge,
to "get back" for all this, did not need to be instilled by propaganda,
which found only receptive ears. And the "simplest" way to avenge
was to prevail over the enemy's women, to satisfy a sexual need while
simultaneously retaliating for factual or perceived wrongs.

Add to this tolerance of rape and, at times, even encouragement
on the part of some of our higher-ups. I recall a send-off Red Army
troops had once received from a commanding officer. Wanting to
save them the stale propaganda of the *politruks* just before the attack
on Miskolc, he decided that it would be best if he himself warmed
them up with a brief talk of substance. It was indeed brief. Not a word
of the great and wise Stalin, or the idyllic life they could expect under full communism, not even a whisper about sacred motherland.
Instead, he offered his soldiers a little solace. *"Rebyata! Vperedi gorod,
a tam vina, bab skolko khosh."* Men! Ahead of you is a city, and there
are wine and women there, as much as you desire. Of course, to give
a city up for spoils was to permit rapes, even though only for a while.

From time to time the higher-ups would try to eradicate rape by
means of ruthless punishment. One day our entire regiment was
made to witness a rapist's court-martial, which was afterward reported
in frontline newspapers and made known to the local Hungarian
population. Like the *samostrel* court-martial, this one, too, was
presided over by a prosecutor from the army HQ, though in some
important respects it ran differently. The prosecutor's speech was
very short, and the rapist was executed by a firing squad. But we were
spared the sight of his burial and grave, and there was no mention
of any letter to be sent to his family and native village. After the execution the prosecutor wept openly; all in tears he was bitterly addressing the other members of the court: *"Y za chto my yevo rasstrelyali,
za etu neprilichnuju blad'?"* And why have we sentenced him to be shot,
all for that indecent whore?

Why wouldn't the soldier make use of a "decent" prostitute instead
of raping and being executed for that? The prosecutor could not
have asked or mentioned this simply because he knew well that

unlike in all other armies in wartime, there was no such thing as brothels organized for Red Army soldiers in the rear. Our regiment had once received, as "spoils of war," a large number of condoms captured from the Wehrmacht. These "spoils of war" were distributed equally, as befitting a Red Army, and the soldiers blew up the condoms and played with them like children play with balloons.

I have already written about furloughs, or, rather, their almost complete nonexistence. Unless heavily wounded and afterward released from hospitals, soldiers could not normally go home for any period of time, even if they had been on the front for many months or years.

There were, of course, women in the army, though not in active infantry combat. I often felt pity for the young girls in forward front lines who served bravely as medical orderlies, nurses, and telephone or radio operators. "War and women in trenches do not mix well," I heard many times, and I shared this view.

In a regiment like ours the ratio of women to men was approximately one hundred to one. A young, healthy woman, for months or even a couple of years without a furlough, always surrounded by so many equally young, healthy men, did not have to be harassed or abused to become a willing sex partner. Sooner or later she would be in some relationship with a man (or men), either because she fell in love, or just to satisfy sexual desires, or to improve her lot, or because she expected to find a husband, or she wanted to get pregnant and as such be released and go home. Some became what was called derisively PPZh (*Pokhodno-Polevye Zheny*), "marching field wives." These were willing partners almost exclusively of male officers, usually of higher ranks.

A few words about their partners. A man like Colonel Kamkov, our former regiment commander, could pick among several prospective PPZh. I remember one such girl, she was a telephone operator, skinny, looking unhappy, and sloppily dressed. As the colonel's PPZh, she blossomed, had a smile on her face, and in a very short time became pregnant and was sent home. P.N.Sh. 4 (in charge of the personnel section) and his companion, a wireless operator, had a love affair; she left the regiment when she got pregnant, and was expecting him to marry her after the war. Most "field wives" were in the supply units. But some could also be found in bunkers of infantry battalions and company commanders in frontline positions—that is where, in my opinion, PPZh relations have often caused harm. I knew of damage not only to discipline but to life caused by the absence of battalion and company commanders, sleeping with PPZh in the bunkers while their leadership was badly needed. The PPZh arrangements added much to resentment, often unjustly hurting the reputation and feelings of innocent women soldiers. It made many men soldiers suspicious of women wearing well-earned medals. Thus, for instance, the medal *Za Boyevye Zaslugi* (for military services) when worn by women was often derisively called *Za Polovye Zaslugi* (for sex services).

24. At the Danube in Pest

The northwest advance had led us to the old Hungarian-Czecho-slovakian border, which we crossed in the second half of December, and before the end of 1944 we were engaged in a dogged battle in the vicinity of Rimavska Sobota in Slovakia. There I learned about an anti-German anti-Tiso uprising by Slovakian partisans, who managed to grow in numbers in the forests of their country. Two or three days later, however, we were suddenly ordered to make a 180-degree turn and march at top speed toward Budapest, about 150 miles away. Malinovsky's 27 Army, including the 33 Rifle Corps of which our division was a component part, had gotten that order and was going south to the capital of Hungary.

Since the *Tsaritsa Poley* was by now moving in horse-drawn carts and through territory already under Red Army control, our voyage by itself was rather uneventful. But I wondered about the reason for that unexpected change of direction. For a full answer to that question I had to wait until after the war, when I found firsthand information in the *Historical Memoir*, edited by Marshal Malinovsky himself (*Budapest-Vienna-Praga*, Moscow: Publishing House "Science," 1965, pp. 81–83). It contains Malinovsky's recorded conversation with Stalin, which took place by telephone in the evening of 28 October 1944. Stalin conveyed to him the urgency of capturing the Hungarian capital as soon as possible, literally within the next few days. "It must be done at any cost. Can you do this?" asked Stalin. Malinovsky responded that "the mission can be carried out five days from today after the 4th Mechanized Guards Corps links up with the 46th Army." He added that the arrival of that corps was expected by 1

November, and that the 46th Army, reinforced by two mechanized guards corps (the 2d and 4th), "can inflict a powerful, entirely unexpected blow and take Budapest in two or three days." But Stalin would not have any delay.

"We cannot give you five days," he said. "Try to understand that for political reasons we must take Budapest as soon as possible." Malinovsky still tried to convince his boss about the military necessity of postponing the attack for a few days. "If you give me five days now, then in another few days, five at most, Budapest will be taken. But if we attack at once, the 46th Army will not be able to make rapid progress owing to insufficient forces. It will be dragged inevitably into long, drawn-out battles at the very approaches to the Hungarian capital. In short, we will not be able to take Budapest from the march." At this point Stalin accused Malinovsky of "being needlessly stubborn." He cut him off, making it plain that the subject was closed. A few minutes later, the phone rang again. General of the Army Alexey Antonov, the chief of the general staff, asked Malinovsky for the precise time when the 46th Army would attack, in order to report it to Stalin. And right then and there Marshal Malinovsky ordered the commander of the 46th Army to strike against Budapest on the morning of 29 October.

Whatever "political necessity" Stalin had in mind, his orders followed by those of Malinovsky's did not produce miracles. The 46th Army was repulsed in the southern outskirts of the capital. Protracted battles lasting more than three months had to be fought before twenty-four volleys from 324 guns could be fired in Moscow saluting the capture of Budapest. It was only on 20 December that the Second and Third Ukrainian Army Groups could jointly resume the offensive to encircle the capital. Four German divisions and one Hungarian were trapped inside Budapest. Pest, its larger part on the left bank of the Danube, was taken on 18 January, while Buda, on its right bank, was captured on 13 February 1945.

It was during preparations for the offensive north of Budapest that the 27 Army was hurriedly moved south. The mechanized units of the 27 Army joined in time to participate directly in the battle for Pest. The *Tsaritsa Poley* of the 33 Rifle Corps, including ourselves, arrived a few days later when the enemy's main resistance in Pest had already been broken, and so we were involved only in mopping-up operations on the left side of the Danube.

Hitler demanded that Budapest be defended house by house. Fortunately, it was not, otherwise its inhabitants would have been exposed to even greater sufferings. There was visible and in some places heavy damage to the buildings in Pest. All bridges over the Danube had been blasted by the Germans as they retreated to Buda, the hilly part of the city on the west side of the river, where they became encircled. Buda was presently being flattened by Soviet artillery fire.

Our regiment's frontline position for the next two weeks was along the east bank of the Danube close to the Parliament buildings, where fierce street fighting had been going on for days and had just ended. The regimental HQ were housed in a sound, large residential building a few blocks behind, while our *razviedka* made itself comfortable in one of the Parliament houses until it was chased out of it by officers of a rival army unit.

Before the regiment's HQ were to settle in the apartment building, it had to be cleared of all residents. They could take with them only those belongings they could carry on their backs, with some help from the platoon of submachine gunners, responsible for the HQ security and thus also for clearing the building. I was given the unpleasant task of telling the residents—in German and in the few Hungarian words I had picked up—about the eviction order and, much to my chagrin, I had to face a dilemma. As I entered a corner apartment on the uppermost floor in the building, a Hungarian man in his thirties began begging me to let him stay with his wife in his home. His wife was in the last days of pregnancy, and to turn her out of doors in midwinter would endanger her life and that of the unborn baby. Feeling like I was between the hammer and the anvil, I finally gave in to his pleas. "To hell with it!" I thought of Shevchenko and Buldyshkin. "At most they will give me a good dressing-down." The Hungarian got my okay, but I warned him not to open the door to anybody but me and, in case of forced entry, give the intruder(s) my name. Fortunately, there were no intruders. Several times, while visiting them in the evening, I brought some dry peas, though they had enough stored food of their own and even shared it with me as we

were conversing in German about many things, mostly the war coming to an end soon. These sometimes quite long chats brought us together, and a warm relationship developed between Ferenc and me.
The guys guarding the HQ may have had an inkling about my little
secret, but they could not have cared less what Gavryusha was sometimes doing on the upper floor. When the war ended, on the way
back to Russia I visited my Hungarian friend in Budapest. He greeted
me with a *köszünom* (thank you), and before we said *viszontlatasra*
(good-bye) to each other, gave me a photo of his baby daughter. I
still keep it in one of my family photo albums.

As soon as the HQ moved in, I went for a visit to the *razviedka*. I
found the guys in a basement of one of the Parliament buildings in
a merry mood, drinking fine French cognac. They were not drunk,
just having a good time, a little break in the hellish war. Playing host
and imitating true Russian hospitality, *Mylosti proshu k nashemu sha-
lashu* (Welcome to our tent), Lieutenant Timoshkin, the platoon
commander, invited me over to a long table on which there was white
and dark bread, Hungarian salami, ham, sardines, anchovies, pickles, and some other things none of us had seen before. "Help yourself; the main course, *pyrozhki* (little meat pies), made by our cook
will soon be ready." The Parliament buildings overlooking the west
bank of the Danube served our *razviedka* as excellent observation
points and, at the same time, as a rich source of spirits, food, and
other supplies. Indeed, some of the basements in the Parliament
houses had been packed with all kinds of goods, which now became
spoils of war. I noticed a pile of beautiful down comforters, which
like other things were stored there perhaps for emergency situations
or for some other reasons, and I did not think twice before taking
one of those comforters with the idea of sending it to Hanna in
Leningrad.

Hanna had a new address; she was by then a student in the Department of Philosophy at the University of Leningrad. In 1941,
nearly three million people were trapped in that city. It was not until January 1944 that the Leningrad blockade was finally broken. By
that time its population had been enormously reduced by constant
bombing, shelling, and famine. Some 200,000 civilians had been
killed by German bombardments and about 700,000 had died of star-

vation. There were only 600,000 people who, having gone through incredible human suffering, were still alive after the fearful thirty-month siege. However, when the ordeal of Leningrad was over, some of the factories, which in 1941 had been moved to the east, began slowly returning to that city. In January 1945, it was also Leningrad University, temporarily in Saratov, which had returned home with some of its laboratories, libraries, faculty, and students; Hanna was among them. Life in the city was still very hard; there was an acute shortage of heating fuel, and the Hungarian comforter kept her warm for the rest of the harsh Leningrad winter. And it saved us both during the 1945–46 winter, when we were living in an unheated room in a half-demolished building that used to be a student dormitory before the war.

A few days after the regiment's HQ had been established in Pest, I went to Colonel Shevchenko to ask him to do me a favor, something I had never done. It had something to do with news from Poland, where the Red Army's winter offensive had just began. Warsaw had been liberated by the Red Army on 17 January and, among reports of war correspondents, Lodz was also mentioned as having been freed the same or next day.

I wanted my regiment's commander to write an official letter to Soviet authorities in Lodz asking them to inquire about the fate of his soldier's family, the Temkins—Chaim-Mayer, Baila-Hinda (née Bialogorska), Rubin-Moses, and Icchok. Colonel Shevchenko approved the idea and immediately sent the requisite letter. Less than two months later he handed me the official reply he received from Lodz. A certificate in Polish with a letterhead "Office of the Population Registry" informed me that the above persons were not listed among the names of inhabitants of the city of Lodz. I should have expected that, but I could not accept the unacceptable. In Budapest, in January–February 1945, it was still hope against hope. I wanted to believe in miracles despite all the hell that war and the Nazis made me witness. More than 230,000 Jews lived in Lodz at the outbreak of World War II. When Lodz was liberated by the Red Army in January 1945, there were fewer than 900 Jewish survivors in that city.

Where were the Jews of Budapest? I wondered. More than 200,000 Jews lived in the city before the war. As I learned afterward, Adolf

Eichmann operated with his commandos in the capital of Hungary until it was almost completely encircled by Soviet troops. He managed to send tens of thousands of Jews from there to Auschwitz, while Raoul Wallenberg and some others, mostly diplomats also, tried to frustrate Eichmann's deportation plans, and rescued several thousand. The Szalasi government established in mid-October collaborated actively with the Nazis. In the beginning of December the Jews of Budapest were driven into two ghettos: the general ghetto and the international ghetto for Jews under some kind of diplomatic protection. Members of the Arrow Cross became increasingly violent; they would enter Jewish houses, looting, shooting at random, and raping. During December 1944 and January 1945, between 10 and 20,000 Jews were killed by them. Many Jews were horribly tortured before being dragged to the Danube and shot so that their bodies would be carried away by the river. The favorite method of the Arrow Cross was to handcuff the Jews together in threes, strip them naked, line them up facing the river, then shoot the middle of the three in the back of the head, so that the victim would drag the other two with him when he fell into the Danube. Still, on 18 January 1945, when Pest was taken and Soviet troops entered the general ghetto, they found about 70,000 Jews alive there, while in the international ghetto there were 25,000 survivors. Later on, when Buda was captured, another 25,000 hidden Jews, often with "Aryan" papers, were rescued. In all, some 120,000 Jews of Budapest were saved by the Red Army.

At the time I was in Pest, I had not even heard the name Eichmann, though I already knew from newspapers as well as from what I had seen in Debrecen and had been told by survivors in Miskolc about the fate of Hungarian Jews under German occupation and the Szalasi puppet government. My regiment entered Pest in the last week of January. The two former ghettos were located in Pest, and I should perhaps have met some of its by then liberated Jews. Unfortunately, I did not. During our regiment's more than two-week stay in Pest, I could not and did not leave the vicinity of the Parliament, which as a front area was in turn off-limits to any civilians. That was probably why I had not met a single Jew in Budapest. Less strange, of course, was that I had also not heard the name Wallenberg or about the fate of that noble man, who single-handedly had done so much trying to rescue Hungarian Jews and who, arrested in Pest by the NKVD, was killed or died in one of their infamous camps.

Buda was captured on 13 February 1945; some 110,000 enemy soldiers, Germans and Hungarians, were marched into captivity. Like all the others who took part in the battle for the Hungarian capital, I, too, got the "Medal for Taking Budapest." On 16 February, the day I turned twenty-four, our regiment crossed the Danube on a hastily constructed pontoon bridge.

At that time, in preparation for a new offensive, some reshuffling of Soviet armies took place. It involved the 27 Army and thus also our 78 Rifle Division. The 27 Army was transferred from the Second to the Third Ukrainian Army Group commanded by Marshal Tolbukhin.

25. The Battle at Lake Balaton

With the 27 Army, on the flanks of the two army groups, our division and regiment were advancing along the west bank of the Danube in a southwest direction. Everything was more or less smooth until we passed the small Lake Velencei and in the beginning of March arrived at the northern tip of Hungary's biggest mass of water, Lake Balaton.

It was a pretty place. We all sensed that our hellish, just war would soon come to an end, and that happy feeling made us also increasingly tired of war. Lake Balaton, with its gorgeous, quiet summer houses surrounded by trees, could have been a perfect place for the exhausted, victorious soldiers to have a rest before going home. But that was not to be. We still were to pay a heavy toll in killed and wounded before we would leave Lake Balaton and the war would be over.

While several Soviet army groups much farther to the north were preparing their final offensive, this time toward Berlin itself, Hitler attempted to hang on at any price to western Hungary in order to safeguard a vital oil supply and, above all, to prevent the fall of Vienna. Thus, he ordered a major counterstrike in Hungary. Army Group South was to strike through a gap between the Balaton and Velencei lakes with the aim of cutting off the part of the Third Ukrainian Army Group between the rivers Danube and Drawa, destroying it, and then swinging north to retake Budapest, cross the Danube River, and recapture eastern Hungary. The time was over for German pincer movements, and what the plan envisaged was too big a chunk for the by now shrunken Wehrmacht to snap off, but the 27 Army, and with it our 78 Division, was caught exactly in that gap between those two lakes.

The German counteroffensive at Lake Balaton was launched on 6 March. General Woehler, commander of Army Group South, in his plan code-named *Frühlingserwachen* ("spring awakening"), envisaged an operation by a strike force totaling ten panzer and twelve infantry divisions. The force included troops from the 6th SS Panzer Army, known as the best shock army the Nazis had; its commander was Sepp Dietrich, a favorite of Hitler's. Both General Woehler's plan and the strength of his troops were known in general outlines in all the divisional HQ of our 27 Army. Since our *razviedka* captured several German prisoners, I also knew directly from interrogating them about significant regroupings and reinforcements they had recently received from Germany, and in particular about newly arrived SS divisions in front of us.

While the information from captured "tongues" indicated that the real strength of the Germans was less than on paper, we had in front of us very formidable forces. We were under frenzy attacks by motorized infantry, numerous tanks, and self-propelled guns. The enemy's strong striking force was poised for a breakthrough against positions defended essentially by an artillery-supported *Tsaritsa Poley*. But the latter was not the same as in the past, when it would often run in panic at the very sight of tanks. Now our infantry was retreating slowly, while our artillery—and it was plentiful—was knocking out German tanks and Panthers with the most accurate hits I ever saw. True, the terrain was also good for defense. The ground, covered by marshes, ditches, and canals, was an obstacle to the attacking forces, slowing down their advance and thus turning their tanks into good targets for our gunners. They lost many of them and paid a heavy price in killed and wounded, but our own casualties in men were grisly. After putting up the toughest possible resistance, the 78 Rifle Division was at the end of its tether. Our regimental *razviedka* incurred losses too, and among them were two comrades of the "May 1943 class," Pyrla, who was killed on 14 March and Lisevich, wounded the next day, both in bloody combat south of Lake Velencei. I was with Pyrla and the others on reconnaissance, and I saw how he was killed—a splinter of an artillery shell hit his head, cutting it like a knife across his forehead over the eyebrows. Some of my comrades insisted they had had a foreboding of him being killed like that when they saw a photo of our *razviedka* made a couple of months earlier in which the top of Pyrla's head was cut off.

Woehler's offensive, following Hitler's directives, aimed at the destruction of the Red Army in Hungary. The Soviet High Command had significantly different ideas. A major offensive that would lead the Red Army to the "beast's lair" was in the final stages of preparation to the north of us. In the meantime, we at Lake Balaton were to wear out and bleed the enemy white, to do everything possible and impossible in order to thwart its attempts to reach the Danube. That was what everybody knew about. What was known only to HQ of our division and regiment, and thus also to me, was the answer to requests for reinforcements. I myself heard our corps commanders repeating messages from Army HQ: "You won't get a single soldier, there is nobody to spare, we know it's asking for sacrifice, but it can't be helped." Our 78 Rifle Division, and probably others too, had been sacrificed so that all available reserves could be used in the main thrust toward Vienna.

The sacrifice made of our men had not been in vain as far as the outcome of the Lake Balaton battle was concerned. Indeed, German attacks were halted on 17 March, a day after the expected large-scale Soviet offensive was finally launched from positions northwest of Lake Velencei. In twenty-four hours we recaptured all the ground the Germans had gained before.

Woehler's army group had been defeated. After the failure of his offensive, the general himself was dismissed by Hitler. The Führer also could not forgive Sepp Dietrich's "treacherous" behavior. His favorite *SS-Oberstgruppenführer* had hoodwinked him. He left major units of his 6th Army in the Reich in order to have them available for his next operation on the Oder River front, and so went into action in Hungary with forty thousand men instead of seventy thousand. The Führer dispatched Himmler to Hungary to punish SS formations for retreating without orders; their armbands were taken away, which by itself had, according to Goebbels, a devastating effect on their morale.

Our 78 Rifle Division, like others in the entire 27 Army, was worn down in the defensive battles at Lake Balaton. The division had been reduced to less than three thousand men, much below the average range of five thousand to six thousand it used to have on the eve of major offensives. Since we would receive no reinforcements until the end of the war, our battered division would never come close to full strength, established at about twelve thousand men, a figure which during World War II no division had probably reached. All our soldiers were utterly exhausted.

26. The Final Days of War

In the last days of the war, everybody, much more than ever before, was thinking about life and death—his own. It was a distressing thought, difficult to drive away. And it also became a topic of conversation. "We survived the hell for so long and now, when the war is coming to an end, are we to be killed? It would, indeed, be highly unfair!" Some were commenting seriously, others mockingly. Most of the time, however, my friends were pretending to be taking it easy or to be reconciled with whatever fate had in store for them. *Chemu byt', tomu nye mynovat'* (What will be will be).

I remember well those take-it-easy talks about life and death. That is perhaps why, as my thoughts go back to those final days of the war, I see before my eyes mainly those killed and wounded at a time when this seemed to make even less sense than ever.

It was 23 March, the day our troops captured Szekesfehervar, northeast of Lake Balaton, after bloody fighting. The town, having changed hands several times, was in ruins. I walked with our *razviedka* through this old town's narrow streets littered with debris and, on its southwestern outskirts, somebody decided to take a shortcut. We were looking for the road running southwest between Lake Balaton and the hills of the Bakony Forest. It was a stupid idea. Soon we found ourselves in the midst of a mine field, but we realized this when it was too late. My friend Efremov, who had been walking not far behind me, stepped on a mine and was mortally wounded. Why him, not me? I was not even scratched by the small splinters flying over my head. He died in our arms as we were carrying him out of the mine field. We buried him on the outskirts of that faraway Hungarian town with a name so difficult to pronounce. A star made of a piece of plywood with a few Russian words written on it with an ink pen was put on the grave of Efremov, a profound man of few words, a good friend, and reliable comrade.

Now, half a century later, as I walk the beautiful beach on Siesta Key in Sarasota, Florida, a scene one can see almost daily brings Efremov back to my mind. It is the sight of people with metal detectors in their hands searching for coins in the sand. Had we had similar gadgets, the simplest mine detectors, Efremov, and thousands like him, could have survived the war.

Moving between two tank and armored groups, one advancing northwest toward Vienna, the other toward central Austria, we stopped and stayed overnight at Badacsony, another well-known wine-producing area close to the northwestern shores of Lake Balaton. It was a relaxing spring evening. I was afraid to see somebody drown again, and it was not, of course, the Balaton waters, but the Badacsony wine that I feared. Our ancestors had it right about Bacchus having drowned more men than Neptune.

At the end of March, ferocious fighting was still going on at Nagykanizsa, the region of oil fields and the center of the oil industry in southwest Hungary near the border with Yugoslavia. Somewhat to the north, our regiment got involved in that battle, close to the town of Zalaegerszeg. It was here that my buddy Balychev was hit in the leg by a submachine-gun bullet. He was one of the better-educated guys in the *razviedka*. For hours he would recite poems by heart. Since he had a high school diploma, and literary inclinations, he was telling me just a few days before about his desire to go to college to study Russian and foreign literature. Now, not too heavily wounded, already on a horse-drawn cart, he was smiling at his comrades seeing him off to the hospital. "Tell us a poem, and I'll give you five thousand pengo," said Volgin, the supply sergeant, carefully putting a bag under his pillow. It was a large amount of money in those days. From where did it come? The guys of our *razviedka* had recently broken into the HQ of a Hungarian Army corps and took a huge safe full of documents and money. Once captured, the money was treated as spoils of war and used to pay for what they were taking from pubs, stores, and the local population. Now playing the wit, Volgin declared aloud: "We are not robbers, we generously pay for whatever we take." As it was 1 April, he was presently teasing Balychev on the occasion of April Fools' Day: "You are the luckiest of us, you must always be the first, also to go home." There was a lot of laughter on that day of fool's paradise as we were waving farewell to Balychev. After the war I got a letter from him. His leg had been amputated above the knee. I hope he realized his dream of going to college to study literature.

Two days later Major Buldyshkin, the chief of staff as he liked to be addressed, was wounded by a stray bullet, or perhaps by a German marksman, in his version of events. He seemed to be glad to be relieved finally of his no doubt difficult duties. Pompous as always, he summoned all his subordinates, including his regimental translator, to HQ to bid farewell and express hope that everybody would continue fighting as well as before.

Not long afterward, it must have been in early April, the HQ of our regiment was shaken by what happened at our division on the Raab River, on the Hungarian-Austrian border. It was an event and story involving General Mikhaylov personally as well as his entire 78 Rifle Division.

He was a general highly respected by officers and soldiers alike, and was said to have more than once pulled out his division from difficult situations, including encirclements. The event and the story I am referring to were told and retold in our regiment's HQ.

The general, who was in his mid-forties, had a much younger wife, whom he had not seen for a long time and who was living in Moscow in the general's apartment and on his pension. As the war was coming to an end, General Mikhaylov sent a colonel, his artillery assistant, on a matter of official or perhaps not entirely official business to Moscow. While in Moscow he was to surprise the general's wife with a visit and a gift from her husband. The artilleryman did exactly what was expected of him. He came unannounced, and then and there, in the open door of the Moscow apartment stood the general's wife at the side of a young captain, a newborn baby in her arms. The bad news struck our general like a bolt from the blue. He sat for hours depressed—it was said—drinking and grumbling: *"O blad', generala na kapitana zamyenila!"* (What a whore, a captain for a general!) Then he drove to the nearest front lines on the Raab River, where he was informed by a battalion commander about the enemy's stubborn resistance. The general just ignored the commander, got out of the trench, and addressing the soldiers who had gathered around him, yelled with all his might: *"Za mnoy, rebyata, vperiod!"* (Follow me, men, forward!) Many did indeed follow, but the general, running far ahead, was soon wounded and fell. Now it was the Germans' turn. Having noticed a general's uniform, they wanted to take him alive and were thus shooting wildly at the soldiers behind him until they forced them back into the trenches. With the general lying in no-man's land, wounded and in imminent danger of being captured alive, hell was raised in the HQ of the division. At stake was not only the general himself, but the honor of his division as well; had he been taken prisoner, the division would have been stripped of its banner and disbanded. And so, all able-bodied men in and around the nearby trenches were rushed to the rescue of the general. They got him back, he soon recovered, and his wounded leg was patched up. The general refused, however, to be taken out of the front line, and was instructing the battalion commander where and how to continue the attack. He let himself be driven to the hospital only after the Germans fled and our troops crossed into Austria. The honor of the 78 Rifle Division had been saved, and its commander, General Mikhaylov, was awarded the well-deserved title of Hero of the Soviet Union.

During the last weeks of the war, I became very close to a soldier more than twice my age. I called him Dyadya (uncle) Vanya. Being almost fifty but not eligible yet for discharge from the wartime army, he was transferred to a supply unit, delivering ammunition, food, and fodder to the front lines, a dangerous job but still considered manageable for a man his age. And so he served in the army as a driver of a horse-drawn wagon.

Uncle Vanya, a half-literate Russian peasant, was bright and full of folk wisdom. In one respect he was the opposite of my friend Titov. Unlike him, Uncle Vanya would often try to reassure me: *"Synok, sviet nye bez khoroshykh ludey"* (Son, the world is not without good people). He himself was a good-hearted man, but was rather cautious with people, rarely saying anything openly and directly, preferring instead hints contained in numerous Russian proverbs and sayings of which he knew so many. Still, I did learn a lot from him. Not about war—I already had my "scientific degree" in this business. From Uncle Vanya one could learn about life, and even more, ideas about life. "Tell me," I once asked him, "what was the life of a peasant in the old times compared with that under the Soviets?" He gave me the shortest possible and fullest answer: *"Khren ryedki nye slashche"* (Horseradish isn't sweeter than radish). At one time I squeezed out of him a direct statement on communism. "It is not possible," he told me, repeating the words as if to himself. "Why not?" I insisted. He just raised his two beefy peasant fists and said: "Look, *synok*, how do our hands bend? Toward ourselves, not away from ourselves. That's why communism is not possible." I did not know if in his figurative speech he meant to say that communism was "too good" for real-life people, or, on the contrary, not good for them at all.

Uncle Vanya did not survive the war. A shell hit his horse-drawn cart and killed him instantly in the vicinity of Fürstenfeld, Austria, not long before the war ended.

We had been in pursuit of the retreating Germans in the hilly countryside west of Fürstenfeld on a main road to Graz, when in the evening of 7 May, I was summoned to the regiment's HQ. Inside, there was a small crowd of officers with a German soldier brought to us from army HQ. He was my age, in a regular German uniform of a private, spoke no Russian, and his German had a heavy Bavarian accent. In the High German dialect, he was telling and retelling his story, how he became a POW, was well treated by the Russians, and why he got associated with the "Free German" movement. Now his patriotic mission, as my bosses put it, was to try to save as many lives as possible of his still-fighting German comrades. Specifically, he was to go over to them with a simple message: Surrender! I was given the task of leading him to them as close as possible. While my task was clear-cut, his mission—if indeed this was his mission—seemed strange to me. Surrender to the Russians was not a very attractive proposition for German soldiers free to run westward. But an order was an order. After midnight I led the messenger through our observation posts to a small mountain stream; the other side was in German hands. Unlike at our HQ, he was mute with me the entire way, no doubt worrying how, coming out of the Russian side, he would be received by his compatriots. At the stream we shook hands and I wished him good luck. I have no idea what happened to him. As for the message, if it was conveyed, I can only say that it produced no defectors; not a single German deserter came over to us at that place.

Having performed my task, I took a long rest at the stream. Like two years earlier, on 5 May 1943, on the bridgehead where my "real war" began, it was a dark night with no moon. But everything else was different. The remnants of the once-mighty Wehrmacht were in a panicky flight. My real, just war was coming to a victorious end here in Austria. There was little, only sporadic rifle and machine-gun shooting, mostly by our infantrymen trying to keep themselves awake. And so, waiting for dawn, I could hear the birds—their chirping, hissing, humming, their calls and songs of love getting louder and louder. At daybreak I fell asleep.

It was 9 May 1945. At long last came the day of victory over Nazi Germany. The war was over! We were embracing, touching each other as if to make sure that we were not daydreaming, that we had indeed survived! We were firing salvos, having a jolly good time, drinking wine, and celebrating victory.

The war was over, but for the next couple of days we were still under orders to pursue and catch the dispersed German soldiers fleeing toward the city of Graz to the Americans. The Germans were not easily surrendering to the Russians, and no wonder. But what sense did it make for us to chase after them? While the war was over, Red Army soldiers were still being killed and wounded for no good reason at all. Some of our high-up bosses, too often during the war and even now when it was over, were displaying total disregard for casualties. Luckily, many officers in our regiment, especially those close to the frontline soldier, were now as a rule sabotaging those crazy orders.

The war was over and we were preparing to go home. Trains to the east were running but were not for us. The few passenger trains were not available, as they had generally been turned during the war into hospitals; they were still going east full of wounded. Freight trains were reserved for first priority loads, tanks, heavy artillery, and the spoils of war. The *Tsaritsa Poley*, as befitting its name, was to go home on foot. On the roads to the east we were being passed by many long freight trains loaded with machinery and factory equipment, and above all with thousands of head of cattle.

Discipline was being reintroduced. We were made to march in step again, and sing *kak polozheno* (as it should be). Before entering a town, we were being ordered to *opravitsya* (to relieve nature, to dust off uniforms, to wash faces, and to put clean white strips on the inside of collars so that their white edges would protrude a little, lighting up the faces of the victorious infantrymen). In one Austrian town I saw a young Red Army soldier marching in an orderly column with a big chamber pot tied to his knapsack. *"Znaesh,"* I told him, *"Fritz scal v etot gorshok"* (You know, Fritz did piss into this pot). He looked at me in disbelief. *"Da bros' ty! Dazhe Fritz by nye posmel—takaya khoroshaya, belenkaya posudina"* (Come on! Even Fritz wouldn't dare—such a good white pot). This was his spoils of war and he would not throw it away.

The 78 Rifle Division had its own brass band which, moving on a truck ahead of us, was already waiting every time on the main street of an Austrian, Hungarian, or Romanian town as we entered it. There the band would greet us with lively marches, mostly a tune to which the victorious soldiers composed their own words, singing: *"Ii mamki nyet, ii papki nyet, ii nyechevo boyatsya, prykhodi ko mnye domoy budem tselovatsya"*—Mother is not home, father is not home, there is nothing to be afraid of, come to me and we'll be kissing.

Epilogue

I had not seen Hanna for more than four years. In August 1945 I got my first furlough—a whole month. After several days of travel on freight trains, I finally arrived in Leningrad, of which I had had heard so much. The beautiful city that withstood a more-than-two-year German siege, during which it suffered staggering losses in human lives, was hiding its terrible scars in the shining sun.

Like four years before, when I left Hanna in Gomel, it was again a warm summer day. I was all excited when I crossed the bridge into Vasilevsky Ostrov—the large island where Leningrad State University was located on Nabieryezhnaya Street, running parallel and close to the Neva River. Hanna lived in a student dormitory just across the entrance to the university on the small Mendelyeva Street. As soon as I entered it, I noticed her walking toward me. She was on her way to the railroad station, just in case, having no idea when I would arrive. We were both in shock, meeting like that. I was speechless. We just looked at each other. She was the same pretty, sweet girl I had left ages ago to go fight what I call my "just war." It was all real and unreal, as in a dream with a happy ending.

The next day Hanna told me that she had enrolled me as a prospective student at Leningrad State University. All I had to do to be admitted was a mere "trifle"—pass the entrance exams. It left me little choice, and so I spent a good deal of my furlough preparing for the tests. I did quite well on all written exams, but not so well on the oral test on Russian literature. The two lady professors asked me about some hero of a novel by, I think, Turgenyev, and hearing me say that I did not know, with a kind of a motherly smile exclaimed: *"Malchik vsye zabyl"* (The boy has forgotten it all). They would not believe that I had never known it. Still, I got a passing grade and was admitted to the Economics Department as a correspondence student.

A demobilization decree was announced just after I had returned to my 458 Rifle Regiment stationed in southern Ukraine. Those born in 1921, like myself, were still too young to be eligible for discharge, but all college students regardless of age were, and I was discharged from my 458 Rifle Regiment on 18 October 1945. It was a nice coincidence that I just fell into the last category, the more so because Marshal Malinovsky's army, of which my 78 Rifle Division was again a part, had received marching orders to the Far East to fight the Japanese in Manchuria. And so, thanks to Hanna, I was spared participating in yet another war. She always has been my good angel, guiding me in crucial moments of my life.

In Leningrad, on 14 July 1946, I went with Hanna to a registry office to get our marriage license. The ceremony was short, fifteen minutes altogether, and cost only fifteen rubles. The clerk was friendly; she smiled and wished us luck.

It was good to be students at the university, though life in Leningrad during the first postwar year was difficult. We did not mind the hardships of everyday life. It was terribly depressing, however, to watch a growing wave of anti-Semitism, especially the one from "above," and the reappearence of repression and spymania. In spite of my war record, I was still an alien, and I realized that I would never feel truly at home there. And so, when Hanna became pregnant with our first child, overtaken by nostalgia, we decided to return to Poland. In July 1946, as the academic year came to an end, Hanna's second, my first, we left the USSR. Soon afterward most of my professors and many of my fellow students at Leningrad State University ran into deep trouble.

Ugly campaigns against "cosmopolitanism" and an alleged "pro-American Jewish conspiracy" started as early as 1946. Then, in 1949, came the so-called "Leningrad affair." Numerous political leaders, factory managers, scientific personnel, and people in higher education were arrested and many of them lost their lives. The campaign began with the "disappearance" of Nikolai Voznesensky, a Politburo member who headed the Gosplan for eleven years and was in charge of the Soviet war economy. His brother, Alexander Voznesensky, the rector of Leningrad State University, was likewise executed. Professor V. V. Reikhardt, a distinguished economist and dean at L.S.U., was arrested and shot, and the entire faculty of the Department of Economics was decimated.

We went back to Lodz, but there was no one there to greet us. Among the records of the Lodz ghetto registry, which I got much later from Yad Vashem, I found an entry stating that the Temkins— Baila-Hinda, Rubin-Moses, and Icchok—had been "deregistered," all on the same day, 10 July 1944. In the *Chronicle of the Lodz Ghetto* (op. cit., p. 523) under the date Monday, 10 July 1944, there is a note: "Today, Transport VIII, under the leadership of the physician Dr. Felix Proscauer (Berlin), left the ghetto with 700 people. The dispatch took place as usual, without incident. Today's transport was composed of 202 men and 498 women, a very small percentage of them resettled from Western Europe." I have found no trace of the fate of my father, Chaim-Mayer, or my sister, Pola (Perla) Hostik. Hanna's father, Moshe-Chaim Rabinowicz, and her mother, Eidel (Ajgel), died in the Lodz ghetto. Hanna's older sister's name, Sara Sztrubel, appears only once in the registry of the Lodz ghetto with no date given; the younger sister, Hinda (Helena), was deported from the Lodz ghetto in the summer of 1944 and perished in Studthoff. Those immediate relatives who did not perish in the Holocaust had survived outside Poland: Hanna's sister, Rachel Sztrubel, and her family, in Belgium; her older brother, Mayer, with his wife, Dora, her brother, Abram, my brother, Jakub—all four in the Soviet Union.

We had come back to Lodz. The place where the ghetto had been located was in ruins, houses completely or in part demolished by Poles who, after the Germans had left, went on a rampage of looting the empty place, taking whatever was there and searching for treasures believed to be hidden in those mostly poor Jewish homes. All this was followed by pogroms, of which the most gruesome was one in Kielce, where, in the spring of 1946, local inhabitants killed and wounded many Jews, survivors of German death camps or returnees from the Soviet Union. It was horrifying and it did not augur well for the future of the few Jews in Poland. Still, we not abandon the forsaken place at that time.

I remember standing with a friend at a border street that used to separate the "Aryan" side from the Lodz ghetto. "One should not begin a new life on a cemetery," he told me, and he was perhaps right.

Yet, we evidently could and did. Hanna was carrying our boy, whom we expected to be born soon. We both wanted to continue our university studies. Here, in Lodz, a dormitory was provided for young Jewish people like ourselves, supported by a newly created Jewish Committee and the American JOINT. So we had a place to live and the company of about a hundred young people, survivors of concentration camps and returnees from Russia. All were trying to begin a new life; many had enrolled in high schools or universities. As education in the new Poland was free, and the Jewish dormitory provided shelter and basic food, the initial period was relatively easy, and so began a second chapter of our lives, which lasted till 1968.

Our son, Henryk, was born in Lodz, on 15 February 1947. Our daughter, Helena, was born in Warsaw on 8 July 1951. We moved to Warsaw in 1949 and made our home there for the next twenty years.

We got our academic degrees. Both Hanna and I became university professors: she taught history of philosophy, I economics. We published articles and books in our respective fields. During the last decade in Poland, 1958–1968, I was economic adviser to the deputy prime minister of Poland. We were settled and did not expect that fate would turn us into refugees once more.

With the Six Day Arab-Israeli War in June 1967 came a thunderstorm for us too. The Polish government unleashed an ugly campaign against the Jews in Poland. Jews were being deprived of jobs and harassed in many ways with the intention of forcing them out of the country.

There were two stages in the "anti-Zionist" campaign, June 1967 and March 1968, a campaign which at the same time aimed at suppressing the unruliness of the Polish intelligentsia and, above all, played a significant role in the power struggle within the leadership of the PZPR (Polish Communist Party). The party leaders feuding with each other were using anti-Semitism as a weapon to discredit political opponents. To finish off a rival—they believed—it was best to suggest or only to pass along a story that he was a Jew or his wife was Jewish. We became a card in the political game.

The anti-Semitic wave of June 1967 had passed me by, for on 5 June I left Warsaw for Moscow and Leningrad, where I was to spend six weeks collecting data for an anthology on Soviet economic and planning debates in the years 1917–1930.

In March 1968 there were demonstrations at the University of Warsaw, where my son, Henryk, was a student in the Physics Department. Then, on 17 March, he was called up for active duty in the army, though as a student he was doing his military service within the framework of military training at the university. Forty students from various universities, mostly of Jewish origin, were sent to a field camp near Zagan, where they were in many ways harassed. For example, my son, who in his personal questionnaire answered "Polish" under the question about nationality, was badgered about hiding his origin, while another boy who "admitted" his Jewishness was reproached for living in Poland without feeling he was Polish.

In the meantime the press, radio, and TV constantly berated the "Zionists" in gutter language and at the same time demanded from them "national affirmation" and a "choice of fatherland." It became increasingly clear that the initiators of the campaign were determined to make life so difficult and unpleasant for "persons of Jewish origin" that they would leave Poland "voluntarily." I came to believe this firmly as I watched Gomulka's speech to the party activists at the Palace of Culture and Science in Warsaw on TV on 19 March. When the first secretary of the party's Central Committee arrived at a point in his speech that said that sooner or later many of the Jews would leave Poland, the congress hall burst into cries: "Sooner! Sooner! Sooner!" Then Gomulka stopped reading his prepared text, spread his arms in a theatrical gesture, and all excited, exclaimed: "But they are not volunteering yet!" An anti-Semitic hysteria engulfed the Communist Party.

After Gomulka's speech I renounced party membership and things began to move swiftly. The minister of higher education fired me from my tenured professor position in the Economics Department at the School of Social Sciences. My wife, Hanna, a tenured professor in the Department of Philosophy at Warsaw University, was likewise dismissed.

At the Council of Ministers, where I had a full-time position as economic adviser to the deputy prime minister, Eugeniusz Szyr, party activists concocted a list of Jews to be fired. I was among those on the list, which was signed by Prime Minister Josef Cyrankiewicz; the same Cyrankiewicz who half a year earlier had personally decorated me with the *Krzyz Oficerski Odrodzenia Polski* (the Offcer's Crest of the Revival of Poland) and handed me the relevant certificate dated 2 August 1967. The chief of the Office of the Council of Ministers, Janusz Wieczorek, informed me in a letter dated 19 April 1968 that I had been relieved of my duties. He found no time to hand in the letter personally, though this was customary practice. But I must add that 19 April was a busy day for him. After all, being also the chairman of the Commission for the Protection of Monuments of Martyrdom, he was in a hurry to attend the celebration commemorating the twenty-fifth anniversary of the Warsaw ghetto uprising; he was the keynote speaker at that solemn occasion.

I described the above events in some detail in an article, "Flight from Poland—1968," *Midstream*, April 1969, pp. 3–12; also in a more elaborate form in "Exodus 1968," *Lewy Nurt*, London: Summer 1970, pp. 33–59—in Polish.

Hanna and I, with our daughter, Helena, left Poland on 25 November 1968; our son, Henryk, a little earlier, on 25 June. We had been deprived of Polish citizenship and had no passports of any kind; instead, we received travel documents from the Polish authorities, thin folders, blue and white in color (new Jewish-Israeli colors?), where across the first page was written in large letters: "The holder of this document is not a citizen of Poland." For the second time in our lives Hanna and I, and our children for the first, hopefully the only one in theirs, became refugees. But relatively soon we were admitted to the United States. The American Consulate in Rome stamped the entry visas into our Italian travel documents for refugees, and we arrived in New York on 18 March 1969.

In the United States Hanna was awarded a research fellowship from Harvard University, and spent the 1970–71 academic year there. I worked initially with the Economics Department of the State University of New York at Stony Brook. Soon I received a tenured full professorship position with the Department of Economics at Brock University in Ontario, Canada. Hanna joined me, and we both became citizens of Canada, and lived more than twenty years in that hospitable country.

In the meantime, our children, Henryk and Helena, became naturalized Americans, continuing their education in their new country. They got their Ph.D. degrees and started successful careers in the United States—Henryk as a physicist, Helena as an anthropologist. And here our four grandchildren were born: Sarah, Eva, Avital, and Daniel.

After my retirement from Brock University as professor emeritus in 1993, Hanna and I became permanent residents of sunny Florida.

I have tried to be as concise as possible and not elaborate too much on the fifty years of my life that have passed since World War II and my days in the Red Army. These are two quite different life stories of the same person, though, as far as the latter is concerned, I am sometimes not quite sure about it.

A final word on my first incarnation. In 1996, while I was writing these memoirs, the Russian Federation, the heir to the Soviet Union, awarded me the Zhukov Medal, issued in commemoration of the one-hundredth anniversary of the marshal's birthday. Georgii Zhukov had been a great military leader, perhaps the greatest Soviet military figure in World War II, and the Red Army soldiers' genuine hero. I must admit that though a half century had passed since my own World War II service with the Red Army, I was gratified to receive the Zhukov Medal.

When I was a small child, my mother used to sing lullabies in Yiddish to me, and in one of them the last words were about kaddish:

Zug my kynd, my lybes kynd, ey kaddish fir dejn mame (Say my child, my dear child, a kaddish for your mother). For many years after the war I had dreams about my mother. She was alive, but I could not find her or, for some mysterious reasons, which I could not understand in my dreams, she was hiding from me. The child within me refused to let go of my mother. In those dreams, she never reproached me for not having ever said the Jewish prayer for her. Let these memoirs be my kaddish for my mother and my father, my older sister, and my two younger brothers, who all perished in the Holocaust.

Appendix

A brief note of explanation why the following documents are significant: When I left the Soviet Union in the summer of 1946, I could, and did, carry with me certificates of medals I was awarded while in the army, but I had to give up the official document of my service with the Red Army. Among the anomalies of the Soviet bureaucracy was that it was intensely averse to answering inquiries by foreigners, and especially on matters having to do with the military. It took numerous letters before I received these documents from the heir of the Soviet Union—the Russian Federation—in the beginning of 1997.

But these documents are even more important for another reason. Coming to the Soviet Union in the fall of 1939 as a refugee for the city of Lodz, Poland, occupied by the Germans, I belonged to the kind of people the Soviets did not trust enough to send to the front when Hitler invaded Russia. Thus, though drafted into the Red Army in July 1941, I was soon transferred, like thousands of refugees and other not "trustworthy" Soviet citizens, to labor battalions. I have described in detail the circumstances under which in May 1943, more by chance than design, I rejoined the Red Army to serve in the 458 Rifle Regiment, 78 Rifle Division, until the end of the war. The documents corroborate my account.

The documents contain: (1) excerpts from the record books of the 458 Rifle Regiment, 78 Rifle Division, obtained by the North American Department of the Russian Ministry of Foreign Relations and sent to the Embassy of the Russian Federation in Washington, D.C.; (2) a certificate from the archives of the Ministry of Defense of the Russian Federation forwarded to the Defense Attaché office of the Embassy of the United States of America in Moscow, Russia. In no essential detail do the two documents differ. The certificate sent to the U.S. Embassy in Moscow is curiously less specific; omitted in particular are the numbers of the rifle regiment and rifle division in which I served from May 1943 to May 1945.

V. I. Chkhikvishvili
Minister-Counselor
Embassy of the Russian Federation in the USA

Dear Vladimir Iraklyevich:

The Main Personnel Directorate of the Ministry of Defense of the Russian Federation has, in accordance with your inquiry, examined the records regarding G. M. Temkin's service with the Soviet Army in the Great Patriotic War, and provided the following information.

In the registry book of officers of the 458 Rifle Regiment, 78 Rifle Division appears:

"Temkin Gavryil Mikhailovich, senior sergeant, translator, born in Lodz, 1921, called up by the military registration and enlistment office in the city of Gomel (GVK) 12 July 1941, arrived in the regiment from 196 reserve regiment on 5 May 1943 (private), decorated with the medal "For Bravery," order number 04/n of 02.22.44 of 458 RR, the Order "Glory III class" order 78 RD number 020/n of 06.14.44."

In the registry book of privates and sergeants of the 458 Rifle Regiment, 78 Rifle Division appears:

"Temkin Gavryil Mikhailovich, sergeant-major, translator, 2 class, born in 1921, called up by GVK in the city of Gomel 12 July 1941, arrived in the regiment from 196 reserve regiment on 5 May 1943 (private), decorated with the Orders "Red Star" and "Glory III class" and the medal "For Bravery," demobilized 10.18.45.

The 458 Rifle Regiment of the 78 Rifle Division had been part of the active army from 19 July 1942 to 9 May 1945.

Sincerely,

V. Istratov

Deputy Director
North America Department
Russian Ministry of Foreign Relations

СОВЕТНИКУ-ПОСЛАННИКУ ПОСОЛЬСТВА РОССИИ В США В.И.ЧХИКВИШВИЛИ

Уважаемый Владимир Ираклиевич,

В соответствии с Вашим запросом сообщаем, что Главное управление кадров Министерства обороны Российской Федерации рассмотрело вопрос о проверке сведений о службе в рядах Советской Армии в период Великой Отечественной войны, сообщаемых гражданином США Г.М.Темкиным, и информировало нас о следующем.

В Центральном архиве МО РФ проведена работа по выявлению документов о прохождении им службы в Советской Армии в период Великой Отечественной войны.

В алфавитной книге учета офицерского состава 458 стрелкового полка 78 стрелковой дивизии за 1943-1946 гг. значится:

"ст.серж., переводчик Темкин Гаврил (имя так в документе) Михайлович, 1921 г.р., ур.г.Лодзь, призван 12.7.41 г. Гомельским ГВК г.Гомель, прибыл в полк из 196 аэсп 8.5.43 г. (рядовой), награжден медалью "За отвагу" пр.N 04/н от 22.02.44 г. по 458 сп, орденом "Слава Ш ст." пр.78 сд N 020/н от 14.06.44 г." (дата выбытия из полка не указана).

В книге учета рядового и сержантского состава 458 сп 78 сд за 1944-46 гг. значится:

"старшина, переводчик 2 разряда Темкин Гавриил Михайлович, 1921 г.р., призван 12.7.41 г. Гомельским ГВК г.Гомель, прибыл в полк из 196 азсп 5.5.43 г. (так в документе), награжден орд. "Красная звезда", орд. "Слава Ш ст.", медалью "За отвагу", 18.10.45 г. демобилизован".

458 стрелковый полк 78 стрелковой дивизии с 19 июля 1942 г. по 9 мая 1945 г. входил в состав действующей армии.

ЗАМЕСТИТЕЛЬ ДИРЕКТОРА   **В.ИСТРАТОВ**

I certify that the above is a true excerpt
from the records of Gabriel Temkin's
service in the Soviet Army during WW II.

Yuri V. Menshikov
Attache

Embassy of the Russian Federation to the USA

March 14, 1997

ARCHIVES CERTIFICATE

In the Russian State Military Archives there is available information that TEMKIN Gavryil Mikhailovich, born 1921, served in an infantry regiment of an infantry division from 8 May 1943 to 19 May 1945 in the position of translator, and the ranks of "senior sergeant" and "sergeant-major."

Decorations: medal "For Bravery," 1030518, 3 March 1944, by order of the rifle regiment; Order "Glory 3 class" number 139464, 14 June 1944, by order of the rifle division; Order "Red Star" number 1218185, 29 March 1945, by order of the rifle division.

The infantry regiment of the infantry division had been part of the active army from 19 July 1942 to 9 May 1945.

L. V. Dvoynykh

Director
Russian State Military Archives

30 January 1997

АРХИВНАЯ СПРАВКА

В Российском государственном военном архиве имеются сведения о том, что ТЕМКИН Гаврил (в других документах Гавриил) Михайлович, 1921 года рождения, проходил службу в стрелковом полку стрелковой дивизии с 8 мая 1943 г. по 19 мая 1945 г. в должности переводчика в воинском звании "старший сержант" и "старшина".

Награды: медаль "За отвагу" № 1030518, 3 марта 1944 г., приказ по стрелковому полку; орден "Славы 3 степени" № 139464, 14 июня 1944 г., приказ по стрелковой дивизии; орден "Красная Звезда" № 1218185, 29 марта 1945 г., приказ по стрелковой дивизи

Стрелковый полк стрелковой дивизии с 19 июля 1942 г. по 9 мая 1945 г. входил в состав действующей армии.

Директор
Российского государственного
военного архива   Л.В.Двойных

"__" января 1997 г.

№ 835

**ГОСУДАРСТВЕННАЯ
АРХИВНАЯ СЛУЖБА РОССИИ**

· (РОСАРХИВ)

103132, Москва, ул. Ильинка, 12
Телефон 206-35-11. Телефакс 200-42-05
Телетайп 111134 "Исток"
Рас. счет № 69124542 ОПЕ. У Центробанка
России МФО 191073 г. Москва.

┌ Управление внешних сношений
Министерства обороны РФ.

11. 03. 97 № 2/Т-2353

На № 1567 от 10.09.96

~~1637 4~~
~~28.03.97~~

Направляем архивную справку на гр. ___Темкина Г.М.___

Приложение: анкета на __2-х л.__,
архивная справка на __I__ л.

Начальник управления ~~информационного~~
~~обеспечения, использования и публикации~~ *Pal f* Т.Ф.Павлова

Certificate from State Archives Services of Russia regarding "citizen Temkin."